World Out of Balance

World Out of Balance

INTERNATIONAL RELATIONS
AND THE CHALLENGE
OF AMERICAN PRIMACY

Stephen G. Brooks
and William C. Wohlforth

PRINCETON UNIVERSITY PRESS

PRINCETON AND OXFORD

Library of Congress Cataloging-in-Publication Data

Brooks, Stephen G., 1971–
World out of balance : international relations and the
challenge of American primacy / Stephen G. Brooks and
William C. Wohlforth.
p. cm.
Includes index.
ISBN 978-0-691-12699-9 (hardcover : alk. paper) —
ISBN 978-0-691-13784-1 (pbk. : alk. paper)
1. United States—Foreign relations—2001– 2. Balance of power.
3. International relations. 4. World politics—21st century.
5. Globalization—Economic aspects. I. Wohlforth, William Curti, 1959– II. Title.
JZ1480.A5B76 2008
327.73—dc22
2007048773

British Library Cataloging-in-Publication Data is available

This book has been composed in Palatino

Printed on acid-free paper. ∞

press.princeton.edu

Printed in the United States of America

10 9 8 7 6 5 4 3 2 1

To our parents:

Deborah and Thomas Brooks

M. Felicitas Curti, O.S.B., and Timothy A. Wohlforth

CONTENTS

List of Illustrations   ix

Preface   xi

Acknowledgments   xiii

CHAPTER ONE
Introduction   1

CHAPTER TWO
Realism, Balance-of-Power Theory,
and the Counterbalancing Constraint   22

CHAPTER THREE
Realism, Balance-of-Threat Theory,
and the "Soft Balancing" Constraint   60

CHAPTER FOUR
Liberalism, Globalization, and Constraints Derived
from Economic Interdependence   98

CHAPTER FIVE
Institutionalism and the Constraint of Reputation   148

CHAPTER SIX
Constructivism and the Constraint of Legitimacy   171

CHAPTER SEVEN
A New Agenda   208

Index   219

ILLUSTRATIONS

Figures

2.1 The distribution of capabilities,
    seventeenth–twenty-first centuries   30
2.2 Military expenditures and GDP in China as a percentage
    of U.S. figures, 2006   41
4.1 Foreign direct investment position in the United States
    by historical cost basis, 2005   113
4.2 Foreign direct investment position in the United States
    in the computer and electronics product sectors
    on a historical cost basis, 2005   114

Tables

2.1 Defense Expenditures by the Major Powers, 2006   29
2.2 Economic Indicators for the Major Powers, 2006   32
2.3 Science and Technology Indicators for the Major
    Powers, 2003–6   33
2.4 Approaches to Unipolarity   48
4.1 Top 20 Export Markets for the United States, 2005   107
4.2 U.S. Foreign Direct Investment Inward Stock, 1980–2005   112
4.3 Purchases of U.S. Defense-Industrial Companies
    by Country, 1990–2005   115
4.4 Top 25 Locations for U.S. Foreign Direct Investment, 2005   119
4.5 Value of Foreign-Owned U.S. Long-Term Securities
    and Share of Total Outstanding, by Asset Class   121
4.6 Value of Foreign Holdings of U.S. Securities,
    by Major Investing Country and Type of Security   122
4.7 Total Arms Transfers, 1990–2005 (Trend Indicator Values)   134

PREFACE

AT AN ACADEMIC conference one of us attended recently, a distinguished senior professor of international relations observed that scholars' assessments of constraints on the use of America's power were strongly conditioned by their appraisal of the George W. Bush administration's approach to foreign policy. Only those who approved of this approach would dismiss the salience of international constraints on the exercise of U.S. power, he contended. When the author in attendance protested that, even though his research put in doubt the strength of those constraints, he nonetheless disapproved of the administration's course in world affairs, the senior scholar replied, "But, of course, your coauthor is a supporter." A protest that the coauthor was an uncompromising critic of the Bush approach was met with a quizzical look that suggested profound skepticism.

In fact, the origins of this book lie in our conviction that foreign policy under Bush took a wrong turn precisely because it chafed at the external constraints on American power, many of them identified by the major theoretical schools in international relations. To be sure, prior to embarking upon this book we had concluded that the classic counterbalancing constraint identified in realist theory was no longer operative. The challenge of American primacy, we argued in a 2002 article in *Foreign Affairs*, was to resist the temptation created by the absence of this constraint and follow a policy of "restraint and magnanimity."

"Why?" critics wanted to know. Our answer was that restraint and magnanimity were necessary to avoid the international constraints identified in international relations theories other than realism. When questioned, we had to acknowledge that this was assumption. It had been implicit in the *Foreign Affairs* article, but not directly analyzed and demonstrated. To answer the critics, in 2003 we began to write a paper entitled "A Nearly Unanimous Verdict against the New Unilateralism." We expected to show how liberal, institutional, and constructivist theories identify potent external constraints on U.S. security policy, thus explaining the scholarly near-consensus against the Bush administration's swaggering style and penchant for going it alone. Our punchline was going to be that while realism had the best theory of constraints for bi-and multipolar systems, it had none for unipolarity.

The most power-centric international relations theory was least useful for explaining constraints on an unusually powerful state.

We never completed that paper. Our efforts to show how the major theoretical schools yield arguments for strong external constraints on American power kept encountering insurmountable challenges. The theories simply did not have the implications scholars attributed to them, or, if they did, there was little evidence for their salience regarding the United States today. To be sure of this finding, to test it empirically and, most important, to explain it, would require more than a paper. The result is this book.

ACKNOWLEDGMENTS

THIS BOOK WOULD NOT HAVE BEEN possible had we not had the good fortune to be at an institution strongly committed to the study of international relations. We are indebted to the John Sloan Dickey Center for International Understanding at Dartmouth College for financial support and for organizing and hosting a daylong seminar to dissect a draft of the manuscript. Charlie Glaser and Steve Miller traveled to Hanover to provide critical intellectual guidance at the seminar. Both at that event and through the years of working on this book, our Dartmouth colleagues Dave Kang, Ned Lebow, Jennifer Lind, Mike Mastanduno, Daryl Press, Al Stam, Ben Valentino, Chris Wohlforth, and Ken Yalowitz were sources of moral and intellectual support, which often came in the form of penetrating criticism. Summer support from Dartmouth's Rockefeller Center and, most importantly, faculty fellowships from the College were critical in gaining us the time to complete the research. We are grateful to the Dartmouth undergraduates who helped us: Matt Ailey, Pooneet Kant, Josh Kernoff, Cameron Kistler, Dan Mahoney, Israel Marques, Brian Smith, and David Wolff. Rick Barton from Dartmouth's research computing group provided invaluable assistance on some of our tables and figures.

We also benefited immensely from numerous opportunities to vet our research at institutions beyond Dartmouth. We thank Mike Desch and Eugene Gholz for selecting our book to be discussed in the first meeting of the Lone Star National Security Forum—an annual conference jointly hosted by the Bush School at Texas A&M University and the LBJ School at the University of Texas. Gideon Rose kindly arranged a seminar at the Council on Foreign Relations to discuss a presentation on the book. Richard Betts invited us to present several chapters in his seminar series at the School of International and Public Affairs at Columbia University. In addition, we individually or jointly presented portions of the research presented herein at Cambridge University, London School of Economics, Norwegian Institute of International Relations, Ohio State University, University of Wales at Aberystwyth, University of Nottingham, University of Southern California, College of William and Mary, Harvard University, and University of Virginia. These gatherings involved too many scholars to list here, yet none occurred without our receiving helpful comments. Finally, we benefited from the feedback of

Bruce Russett and the students in his graduate seminar at Yale, who read an early draft of the book.

We would also like to highlight a number of individuals who were kind enough to share their expertise on particular chapters at our request. Chapter 2 went through several extra drafts in response to a set of lengthy comments from Charlie Glaser. Feedback from David Baldwin, Charlie Kupchan, and Steve Van Evera was very useful for developing the argument in chapter 3. Comments from David Baldwin, Eugene Gholz, Doug Irwin, Nina Pavcnik, and Jay Shambaugh were extremely helpful in revising chapter 4. Chapter 5 benefited greatly from the insights of Duncan Snidal and Erik Voeten. And Ian Hurd, Jeff Legro, and Alexander Wendt gave us invaluable critical feedback on chapter 6.

We thank all these scholars for helping us work through the numerous literatures addressed herein, but, of course, we, not they, bear the responsibility for the argument and analysis we present.

World Out of Balance

Introduction

THE DISSOLUTION OF THE SOVIET UNION marked the emergence of historically unprecedented U.S. advantages in the scales of world power. No system of sovereign states has ever contained one state with comparable material preponderance.[1] Following its invasion of Afghanistan in 2001, the United States loomed so large on the world stage that many scholars called it an empire,[2] but the costly turmoil that engulfed Iraq following the toppling of Saddam Hussein in 2003 quieted such talk. Suddenly, the limits of U.S. power became the new preoccupation. Many analysts began to compare the United States to Britain at the beginning of the twentieth century—an overstretched, declining, "weary Titan" that "staggers under the too vast orb of his fate."[3]

---

[1] This point has been stressed by political scientists, historians, and policymakers. Political scientist G. John Ikenberry observes that "since the end of the Cold War, the United States has emerged as an unrivaled and unprecedented global superpower. At no other time in modern history has a single state loomed so large over the rest of the world." "Is American Multilateralism in Decline?" *Perspectives on Politics* 3 (2003): 533. Historian Paul Kennedy stresses: "A statistician could have a wild time compiling lists of the fields in which the US leads. . . . It seems to me there is no point in the Europeans or Chinese wringing their hands about US predominance, and wishing it would go away. It is as if, among the various inhabitants of the apes and monkeys cage at the London Zoo, one creature had grown bigger and bigger—and bigger—until it became a 500lb gorilla." "The Eagle Has Landed: The New U.S. Global Military Position," *Financial Times*, February 1, 2002. And former secretary of state Henry Kissinger maintains, "The U.S. is enjoying a preeminence unrivaled by even the greatest empires of the past. From weaponry to entrepreneurship, from science to technology, from higher education to popular culture, America exercises an unparalleled ascendancy around the globe." *Does America Need a Foreign Policy? Toward a Diplomacy for the 21st Century* (New York: Simon and Schuster, 2001), 17.

[2] See, for example, Michael Cox, "Empire, Imperialism and the Bush Doctrine," *Review of International Studies* 30 (2004); Niall Ferguson, *Colossus: The Price of America's Empire* (New York: Penguin, 2004); and Stephen Rosen, "An Empire, If You Can Keep It," *National Interest* 72 (2003). Ivo Daalder and James Lindsay report that in the six-month period leading up to May 2003, the phrase "American empire" appeared more than 1,000 times in news stories; see "American Empire, Not 'If' but 'What Kind," *New York Times*, May 10, 2003.

[3] The weary Titan metaphor was advanced by Joseph Chamberlain, Britain's colonial secretary, to describe Britain's strategic situation in 1902; Timothy Garton Ash uses this

What accounts for this sudden shift in assessments of American power? For most observers, it was not new information about material capabilities. As Robert Jervis observes, "Measured in any conceivable way, the United States has a greater share of world power than any other country in history."[4] That statement was as accurate when it was written in 2006 as it would have been at any time after 1991, and the primacy it describes will long persist, even if the most pessimistic prognostications about U.S. economic, military, and technological competitiveness come true. For most scholars of international relations, what really changed after 2003 were estimates of the political utility of America's primacy. Suddenly, scholars were impressed by the fact that material preponderance does not always translate into desired outcomes. For many, theories of international relations (IR) that explain constraints on the use of power were vindicated by American setbacks in Iraq and elsewhere.

For more than three decades, much IR scholarship has been devoted to theories about how the international environment shapes states' behavior.[5] Applying them to the case at hand, scholars have drawn on each of the main IR theories—realism, institutionalism, constructivism, and liberalism—to identify external (or "systemic") constraints that undermine the value of the United States' primacy, greatly restricting the range of security policies it can pursue. Scholars emphasize a variety of elements in the international system that constrain U.S. security policy: international institutions, balancing dynamics, global economic interdependence, and legitimacy. The upshot is simple but portentous for the contours of international politics in the decades to come: the political utility of U.S. material primacy is attenuated or even negated by enduring properties of the international system.

Chamberlain quote as the starting point for his argument that "[t]he United States is now that weary Titan." "Stagger On, Weary Titan: The US Is Reeling, Like Imperial Britain after the Boer War—but Don't Gloat," *The Guardian*, August 25, 2005.

[4] Robert Jervis, "The Remaking of a Unipolar World," *Washington Quarterly* 29 (2006): 7.

[5] As Ned Lebow stresses, a core assumption of most international relations theory is that "actors respond primarily to external stimuli. . . . They reward certain kinds of behavior and punish others, and shape actors indirectly through a process of natural selection, or directly by influencing their cost calculus." Lebow notes that "[r]ealist, liberal, and institutional approaches all focus on the constraints and opportunities created by the environment" and that this emphasis also extends to what he calls "thin constructivist" accounts, such as those forwarded by "Alexander Wendt, for whom behavior is

The purpose of this book is to undertake a systematic evaluation of the external constraints that scholars have highlighted and thereby gain a better understanding of the United States' global role. This entails answering four questions: Does the United States face the imminent prospect of having its power checked by a balancing coalition of other great powers? As it has become increasingly exposed to the international economy, has the United States become more vulnerable to other actors' attempts to influence its security policies? Is the United States tightly bound by the need to maintain a good general reputation for cooperation in international institutions? Does the United States need to adhere to existing rules to sustain legitimacy and thus maintain today's international institutional order?

Our answer to each of these questions is no—a finding that overturns the scholarly conventional wisdom, according to which these factors strongly constrain U.S. security policy. On the contrary, the unprecedented concentration of power resources in the United States generally renders inoperative the constraining effects of the systemic properties long central to research in international relations.

Given the likely longevity of American primacy, this general finding has important repercussions for thinking about international relations scholarship and U.S. foreign policy. In the concluding chapter, we outline a new research agenda to address the analytical challenge of American primacy, and identify an important and heretofore neglected grand strategic alternative for the United States.

The Argument

Our purpose is to analyze propositions drawn from all the theoretical schools that deal with the systemic constraints on U.S. security policy. Following many other scholars, we treat security policy as not simply the use and threat of military force, but also the use of nonmilitary tools to advance security interests. By systemic constraints, we mean constraints that are external to the United States itself, and that operate in the international system generally rather than within one set of actors or in response to a particular issue. More specifically, a systemic

---

shaped by external incentives and constraints." Richard Ned Lebow, "Reason, Emotion, and Cooperation," *International Politics* 42 (2005): 42.

constraint is a property of the international system that restricts freedom of action by forbidding, or raising the costs of, certain kinds of actions, or compelling other kinds of actions.

Scholars stress that the shift from the bipolarity of the Cold War to the current unipolarity is not an unalloyed benefit for the United States because it comes with the prospect of counterbalancing, increased dependence on the international economy, a greater need to maintain a favorable reputation to sustain cooperation within international institutions, and greater challenges to American legitimacy. The conventional wisdom is that these systemic constraints impede the translation of U.S. power capabilities into influence over security outcomes, rendering the United States much less capable than its material capabilities imply. Put more generally, existing theoretical arguments sum up to the contention that once a state is at or near the top of the international heap, it confronts more and stronger properties of the international system that greatly diminish the marginal utility of additional capabilities for pursuing its security objectives.[6]

The validity of this view depends on whether systemic constraints function in a unipolar system as they did in the bi- and multipolar systems on which most IR research is based. Yet answering that critical question has not been the explicit object of study. As a result, the research underlying the conventional wisdom suffers from one or more of the following problems: it uncritically applies theories developed to explain past international systems; it does not subject arguments to systematic theoretical or empirical analysis; it considers only a single theoretical perspective; and it is not specifically focused upon the constraints on U.S. security policy. To assess the conventional wisdom, it is necessary to examine the key systemic constraints to determine whether and to what degree their operation is transformed in a unipolar system. Ours is the first book to do this, and it does so for all the systemic constraints highlighted by IR theory.

This study turns the conventional wisdom on its head: our assessment is that as the concentration of power in a state increases beyond a certain threshold, systemic constraints on its security policy become generally inoperative. Scholars are right to hold that systemic

---

[6] Although we call this summation of current scholarship the conventional wisdom, scholars thus far have only focused on the individual arguments that comprise it and not on how they all fit together to produce a general proposition that increased capabilities for the leading state do not lead to a commensurate increase in sway or influence.

constraints are potentially important, but wrong to assume that theories developed to explain previous international systems apply to unipolarity.

Behind the Conventional Wisdom

Two sets of constraints on U.S. security policy are featured in the scholarly literature: systemic constraints and those that emanate from the United States' domestic politics and institutions. The core domestic question is whether the public acts as a constraint on American security policy.[7] Most of the scholarship focuses on how the public reacts to the use of force, and finds that the effect of public opinion varies according to case-specific factors, including the perceived likelihood of battlefield success,[8] the number of actual or expected casualties,[9] the nature of discourse among policymakers and political elites,[10]

[7] This specific literature is, in turn, situated within a broader literature that examines how political institutions can affect the relationship between public opinion and foreign policy; for a useful overview of this literature, see Dan Reiter and Allan Stam, "Democracy, Peace, and War," in *Oxford Handbook of Political Economy*, ed. Barry Weingast and Donald Wittman (New York: Oxford University Press, New York, 2006).

[8] See, for example, Peter D. Feaver and Christopher Gelpi, *Choosing Your Battles: American Civil-Military Relations and the Use of Force* (Princeton: Princeton University Press, 2004); and Steven Kull and Ramsey Clay, "The Myth of the Reactive Public: American Public Attitudes on Military Fatalities in the Post–Cold War Period," in *Public Opinion and the International Use of Force*, ed. Phillip Everts and Pierangelo Isneria (London: Routledge, 2001), who note that "the critical determinant of the public's response is not whether US vital interests are involved, but whether the operation is perceived as likely to succeed" (205).

[9] The dominant view among academics is that U.S. public support for a given military deployment will be lower if large casualties are expected and also that the level of public support will decline if U.S. casualties increase after a deployment occurs. See the overview of the literature on this point in Adam Berinsky, "Assuming the Costs of War: Events, Elites, and American Public Support for Military Conflict," MIT Working Paper, April 2005, available at http://web.mit.edu/berinsky/www/war.pdf (consulted September 19, 2007), 2–3. For a contrasting view, see Christopher Gelpi, Peter Feaver, and Jason Reifler, "Casualty Sensitivity in the War in Iraq," paper presented at the Wielding American Power Working Conference, Duke University, February 7, 2004, who conclude that "under the right conditions, the public will continue to support military operations even when they come with a relatively high human cost. . . . The public has the stomach for costly military action provided the action is successful. The image of the American public as a paper tiger—a mirage of strength that collapses in the face of casualties—is as incorrect as it is popular" (3–4).

[10] The best analysis of this question is by Berinsky, "Costs of War," who concludes that "patterns of elite discourse determine the nature of opinion toward war. When political elites disagree as to the wisdom of intervention, the public divides as well. But

the objectives in a given case,[11] whether the mission is backed by multi-lateral institutions,[12] and the nature of media coverage.[13] The significance of public support or opposition also depends on the normative and political beliefs of the particular president who is fashioning policy.[14]

In contrast to these complex influences is scholars' stark portrait of the systemic constraints facing the United States: rising power meets rising constraints. Perhaps because of the appeal of this relative clarity, scholars who evaluate U.S. policy generally focus on systemic constraints.[15] Their conclusions, however, are not backed up by research that is as careful as that which addresses domestic constraints. Instead, their stark perspective on systemic constraints is initially plausible because it resonates with decades of theorizing on international relations.

Since World War II scholars have pursued general, systematic knowledge about international relations. Starting in the 1950s, this led to a preoccupation with systemic theory. A hallmark of the approach is its commitment to general explanations of patterns over long spans of time, as opposed to details of specific interstate interactions. Scholars developed and tested general propositions about the social system

when—for whatever reason—elites come to a common interpretation of a political reality, the public gives them great latitude to wage war" (1–2).

[11] See, for example, Bruce Jentleson and Rebecca L. Britton, "Still Pretty Prudent: Post–Cold War American Public Opinion on the Use of Military Force," *Journal of Conflict Resolution* 42 (1998); and Eric Larson, "Putting Theory to Work: Diagnosing Public Opinion on the U.S. Intervention in Bosnia," in *Being Useful: Policy Relevance and International Relations Theory*, ed. Miroslav Nincic and Joseph Lepgold (Ann Arbor: University of Michigan Press, 2000).

[12] See I. M. Destler and Steven Kull, *Misreading the Public: The Myth of a New Isolationism* (Washington, D.C.: Brookings, 1999).

[13] See, for example, Richard Brody, *Assessing the President: The Media, Elite Opinion, and Public Support* (Stanford, Calif.: Stanford University Press, 1991); Richard Brody, "Crisis, War, and Public Opinion: The Media and Public Support for the President," in *Taken by Storm: The Media, Public Opinion, and U.S. Foreign Policy in the Gulf War*, ed. Lance Bennett and David Paletz (Chicago: University of Chicago Press, 1994).

[14] Douglas Foyle, *Counting the Public In: Presidents, Public Opinion, and Foreign Policy* (New York: Columbia University Press, 1999).

[15] This is true across the various theoretical schools; see, for example, Robert Pape, "Soft Balancing against the United States," *International Security* 30 (2005); Richard Ned Lebow, *The Tragic Vision of Politics: Ethics, Interests, and Order* (Cambridge: Cambridge University Press, 2003); Christian Reus-Smit, *American Power and World Order* (Cambridge, Mass.: Polity Press, 2004); Kenneth N. Waltz, "Structural Realism after the Cold War," *International Security* 25 (2000); and Lisa Martin, "Multilateral Organizations after the U.S.-Iraq War," in *The Iraq War and Its Consequences: Thoughts of Nobel Peace Laureates and Eminent Scholars*, ed. Irwin Abrams and Wang Gungwu (Singapore: World Scientific Publishing, 2003).

of states with little reference to their internal properties.[16] Even though the influence of systemic theory declined in the late 1980s, most research in the field still either reacts to or develops this approach.[17] Today's scholarship concerning constraints on the United States is the product of this intellectual history.

The provenance of the conventional wisdom on systemic constraints is clearest for realism. Indelibly associated with realism is balance-of-power theory, a quintessential theory of systemic constraints. It stipulates that the absence of a central authority that can enforce agreements (i.e., the condition of anarchy) puts a premium on states' long-term survival (security), which leads them to counter potentially dangerous concentrations of power (which balance-of-power theorists frequently call *hegemony*) through alliances (external balancing) or military build-ups (internal balancing). According to the theory, the stronger a state gets, the more powerful become the incentives for other states to balance it. "Hegemony leads to balance," Kenneth N. Waltz observes, "through all of the centuries we can contemplate."[18]

It is little wonder that scholars reached for this theory to analyze systemic constraints on the United States after the Cold War. No other single proposition about international politics has attracted more scholarly effort than the balance of power. It is perhaps as central in today's thinking as it has been at any time since the Enlightenment, when Rousseau and Hume transformed familiar lore about balancing diplomacy into coherent theoretical arguments.[19] Waltz, who turned those arguments into a structural systemic theory in the 1970s, has been one of the most influential scholars of international relations over the last three decades. The theory's basic proposition, the self-negating nature of power, seemed tailor-made for the post–Cold War era, when

---

[16] See Torbjørn L. Knutsen, *History of International Relations Theory* (Manchester: Manchester University Press, 1997).

[17] See, for example, the discussion in Helen Milner, "Rationalizing Politics: The Emerging Synthesis of International, American, and Comparative Politics," *International Organization* 52 (1998); Alexander Wendt, *Social Theory of International Politics* (Cambridge: Cambridge University Press, 1999); and Michael Horowitz, Rose McDermott, and Allan Stam, "Leader Age, Regime Type, and Violent International Relations," *Journal of Conflict Resolution* 49 (2005).

[18] Kenneth N. Waltz, "The Emerging Structure of International Politics," *International Security* 18 (1993): 77.

[19] Between 1991 and 2001, for example, citations of the chief contributions to the balance-of-power literature dwarfed those concerning all the other major propositions in conflict studies, including the democratic peace. D. Scott Bennett and Allan C. Stam, *The Behavioral Origins of War* (Ann Arbor: University of Michigan Press, 2004).

the United States assumed unprecedented material preponderance in the international system.

Remarkably, scholars from normally competing theoretical traditions have reached similar conclusions about the self-negating nature of contemporary American power. Institutionalist, constructivist, and modern liberal theories all developed in part as critical reactions to realism. All reject simple power-centric models like the balance of power; all feature causal mechanisms that are downplayed or ignored in realist writings. Yet these theoretical schools reach the same general conclusion about the constraints facing the United States today: as its share of power in the international system increases, the systemic constraints on U.S. security policy also increase (though the link between them is not a matter of balancing—the causal pathways are less direct and linear than realism's notion of power begetting countervailing power).

Institutionalist theory shows how states gain from cooperating within international institutions and, conversely, how much they can lose if they fail to cooperate in a world with high levels of interdependence. To avoid these losses, institutionalists stress, states must bind themselves to institutional rules. While these constraints apply to all states that want to benefit from institutionalized cooperation, they are, according to recent analyses, especially salient for the leading state. As it becomes more powerful—as when the relative power of the United States increased with the Soviet Union's fall—it has a greater ability to exempt itself from inconvenient institutional rules of the game without being punished in the short term.[20] Therefore, "the more that a powerful state is capable of dominating or abandoning weaker states, the more the weaker states will care about constraints on the leading state's policy autonomy."[21]

The basic proposition emerging from institutionalist scholarship is that the United States faces a critical need to maintain a favorable reputation for international cooperation; any effort to revise or insulate itself from the current institutional order is dangerous, institutionalists maintain, because it will undermine America's "multilateral reputation," reducing other states' cooperation in areas where Washington

[20] Martin, "Multilateral Organizations," 365, 369.

[21] Ikenberry, "American Multilateralism in Decline?" 535. In this regard, David A. Lake maintains, "In bipolarity, the competition with the Soviet Union constrained American capriciousness. Today, the United States binds itself through institutions that limit its ability to exploit others." "Beyond Anarchy: The Importance of Security Institutions," *International Security* 26 (2001): 159.

strongly values it, such as trade. If true, this argument has major implications for U.S. security policy: to sustain institutionalized cooperation from weaker countries, the United States more than other nations needs to accept the constraints associated with multilateral agreements and rules.

Constructivist scholarship makes a similar argument regarding the constraining force of the international order, in which the concept of legitimacy plays the key role. Constructivists emphasize that America's material resources can translate into political influence only when they are bound by the rules of the institutional order. Christian Reus-Smit summarizes the core claims, namely "that all political power is deeply embedded in webs of social exchange and mutual constitution; that stable political power . . . ultimately rests on legitimacy; and that institutions play a crucial role in sustaining such power."[22] It follows that the more powerful a state is, the more it has to gain by legitimizing its power, and the more it has to lose if others question that legitimacy. The shift from bi- to unipolarity has magnified the salience of this basic proposition. Constructivist scholarship thus generates an argument with profound implications for the United States: failure to hew to the accepted rules in the security realm will degrade American legitimacy and thereby complicate and weaken American hegemony.[23] However inconvenient accepted practices may be, departing from them will erode the foundations of American hegemony.

Thus, both constructivist and institutionalist analyses emphasize the institutional constraints on U.S. security policy. Liberalism, meanwhile, points to another aspect of the international environment: global economic interdependence, which has accelerated dramatically in recent decades. The liberal proposition is that economic interdependence can constrain the security policies of states, including those at the top of the power hierarchy.[24] This effect is particularly significant today because the opportunity cost of reduced access to the world economy is

[22] Reus-Smit, *American Power*, 41.

[23] See especially Bruce Cronin, "The Paradox of Hegemony: America's Ambiguous Relationship with the United Nations," *European Journal of International Relations* 7 (2001); Reus-Smit, *American Power*; and Lebow, *Tragic Vision of Politics*.

[24] See, for example, Richard Rosecrance, *The Rise of the Trading State: Commerce and Conquest in the Modern World* (New York: Basic Books, 1986); John R. Oneal and Bruce M. Russett, "The Classical Liberals Were Right: Democracy, Independence and Conflict, 1950–1985," *International Studies Quarterly* 41 (1997); and Robert Keohane and Joseph S. Nye, *Power and Interdependence*, 2nd ed. (Glenview, Ill.: Scott, Foresman, 1989).

now so high. By embracing globalization to an ever greater extent, the United States has enhanced its economic capacity and hence its overall power. However, this is a Faustian bargain, according to many analysts, because U.S. security policy is more exposed to potential constraints associated with economic interdependence.[25]

The convergence of all of the major schools in international relations on the same basic argument regarding systemic constraints is grounded in scholarship: in each case, the proposition that rising power generates rising constraints is a reasonable first-cut inference from existing theoretical and empirical analyses. It is hardly surprising that when confronted with the novel condition of unipolarity, scholars plumbed existing theories and research for inferences regarding constraints on the United States. After all, scholars are only human. They are cognitive misers. When the world changes, they do not abandon all their theories and start afresh. "Instead of radical change," Jack Snyder notes, "academia has adjusted existing theories to meet new realities."[26]

While this reaction is understandable, it is not optimal in the long run. The degree of U.S. dominance is unprecedented, and this alone is enough to place a question mark after inferences derived from research on previous systems. Unfortunately, the incentive to subject conventional wisdom to theoretical and empirical scrutiny is reduced when normally competitive theoretical schools converge on a proposition— one that initially seems compelling and also aligns with the prescription for foreign policy the overwhelming majority of IR scholars would endorse: restraint in the face of the temptations of power.

However, given the importance of systemic constraints on power for evaluating both U.S. foreign policy and international security more generally, scholarly assessments should rest on firm foundations. Our book provides a thorough analysis of the five key theoretical arguments concerning the systemic constraints facing the United States today.

---

[25] See, for example, Jonathan Kirshner, "Processes of Globalization and Challenges to National Security," paper prepared for the conference "Globalization and National Security," Harvard University, November 14–15, 2003; Stanley Hoffmann, "Clash of Globalizations," *Foreign Affairs* 81 (2002); Theodore Moran, "Defense Economics and Security," in *Grave New World: Security Challenges in the 21st Century*, ed. Michael Brown (Washington, D.C.: Georgetown University Press, 2003); and Audrey Kurth Cronin, "Behind the Curve: Globalization and International Terrorism," *International Security* 27 (2002–3).

[26] Jack Snyder, "One World: Rival Theories," *Foreign Policy* 145 (2004): 53.

Terms of Reference

The question for us is this: how do systemic constraints featured in IR scholarship operate on the United States, given its weight in the interstate scales of power? To address this question, we need to be clear about what we mean by power and the strength of various constraints.

Power and Polarity

In the wake of a Cold War that had been shaped by two leading states, analysts recognized that a world without a nation capable of rivaling the United States would be different in important ways. Observers grappling with the post-bipolar international system have characterized it in such terms as empire, unipolarity, imperium, and uni-multipolarity.[27] These terms reflect a search for theoretical constructions to place in historical and comparative perspective the distinctive political formation that has taken shape around American power. But our analysis concerns constraints on the conversion of material resources into desired outcomes. That topic requires a basic distinction between power as material resources and power as the ability to realize ends.[28] Following the practice of many scholars, we use the term power in the former sense to denote the resources a government can draw upon. The global system today—seen in comparative historical perspective— has very concentrated means of power. Using the term power to denote these material capabilities does not prejudge the character of influence or the logic of political relationships within the global system.[29]

[27] As indicated in note 2, a huge literature has emerged depicting America as an empire. On imperium, see Katzenstein, *A World of Regions*. On uni-multipolarity, see Samuel P. Huntington, "The Lonely Superpower," *Foreign Affairs* 78 (1999).

[28] In this way, we are following a basic distinction that is made in the power theory literature; see, in particular, David A. Baldwin, *Paradoxes of Power* (New York: Basil Blackwell, 1989).

[29] In using this terminology, we nonetheless agree with Steven Lukes that "having the means to power is not the same as being powerful," as he defines that term; see "Power and the Battle for Hearts and Minds," *Millennium* 33 (2005): 478. In addition, by juxtaposing power as resources with power as the ability to attain desired ends, we are aware that there are a great many other ways to conceptualize power, many of which (especially those associated with the works of Lukes and Michel Foucault) have gained currency in international relations scholarship. For an illuminating treatment and guide to this literature, see Stefano Guzzini, "The Concept of Power: A Constructivist Analysis," *Millennium* 33 (2005).

Our analysis does not hinge on the particular term used to describe the current system; our analytical starting point—that the United States has a greater share of power than any single state has ever had in 300 years—is uncontested among IR scholars. Of all the shorthand terms to describe the current system, unipolarity is the most accurate and presents the smallest risk of conflating power as resources with power as political relations of influence and control. Some discussion of the applicability of this term helps to put the unique nature of today's system in sharper relief.

Scholars use the term unipolarity to distinguish a system with one extremely capable state from systems with two or more such states (bi-, tri-, and multipolarity), and from empire, which generally refers to relations of political influence and control rather than distributions of capability. The adjective unipolar describes something that has a single pole. To occupy a pole in the international system, a state must (*a*) command an especially large share of the resources states can use to achieve their ends; and (*b*) excel in all the component elements of state capability (conventionally defined as size of population and territory, resource endowment, economic capacity, military might, and organizational-institutional "competence").[30] By definition, in a unipolar system only one state meets these criteria.

The concept of polarity has deep roots in scholarship on international relations. The core contention is that polarity structures states' probable actions, providing incentives and disincentives for different types of behavior. However, the concept yields few important insights into patterns in international politics over the long term. Even those scholars most persuaded of its analytical utility see polarity as a necessary component of, rather than a complete, explanation of behavior.[31] In part because it suggests a dependence on Kenneth Waltz's writings on polarity, the term is not ideal for our purposes. As we make clear in the chapters that follow, our analysis is not based on the neorealist system of explanation; because we seek to evaluate each school of thought on its own terms, our approach is theoretically agnostic. That said, the concept of polarity is an efficient way to keep clear the vital

[30] Waltz, *Theory of International Politics* (Reading, Mass.: Addison-Wesley, 1979), 131.

[31] For a comprehensive critical review of the polarity literature, see Barry Buzan, *The United States and the Great Powers: World Politics in the Twenty-first Century* (New York: Polity Press, 2004).

distinction between power as resources and power as the ability to attain desired ends.

Polarity is a theoretical construct; real international systems only approximate ideal types. The concept of unipolarity implies a threshold value in the distribution of capabilities among states. How do we know whether a system has passed the threshold, becoming unipolar? According to the definition of a pole presented earlier, an international system is unipolar if it contains one state whose share of capabilities places it in a class by itself compared to all other states. This definition reflects the fact that a state's capabilities are measured not on an absolute scale but relative to those of other states. In keeping with this definition, a unipolar state is preponderant in all relevant categories of capability.[32] According to a narrower, but also frequently used, criterion, a system is unipolar if it has only one state capable of organizing major politico-military action anywhere in the system.[33]

There are periods of history about which scholars disagree over polarity, but ours is not one of them. By consensus, four or more states qualified as poles before 1945; by 1950 or so, only two measured up; and now one of these poles is gone. Since the dissolution of the Soviet Union, no other power—not Japan, China, India, or Russia, nor any European country, nor the European Union—has increased its capabilities sufficiently to transform itself into a pole. The United States alone retains the wherewithal to organize major politico-military action anywhere in the system. The more definite is American material preeminence, the more apt is the term unipolarity. As the empirical analysis in chapter 2 shows, in today's system the term is very apt indeed.

The Power of Constraints

Clarity about our definition of power must be accompanied by clarity about constraints. Each of the theoretical arguments we shall assess is complex, often subsuming numerous propositions, and each has been

---

[32] Wohlforth, "The Stability of a Unipolar World," *International Security* 21 (1999); and Wohlforth, "U.S. Strategy in a Unipolar World," in *America Unrivaled: The Future of the Balance of Power*, ed. G. John Ikenberry (Ithaca, N.Y.: Cornell University Press, 2002).

[33] David Wilkinson, "Unipolarity without Hegemon," *International Studies Review* 1, no. 2 (1999): 141–72; Birthe Hansen, *Unipolarity and the Middle East* (New York: St. Martin's, 2000); and Stuart Kaufman, Richard Little, and William C. Wohlforth, eds., *The Balance of Power in World History* (New York: Palgrave Macmillan, 2007).

articulated in subtle ways by different scholars. Although these theories sum up to what we have called a conventional wisdom on systemic constraints, scholars make distinct claims about the strength of the constraints their theories identify.[34]

Constraints vary along two key dimensions. The first is *conditionality*. The key issue is whether the constraint is triggered by a state's policies: as we move along this continuum from the less to the more conditional, a constraint may be inescapable, avoidable if a state pursues appropriate policies, or inapplicable no matter what it does. The second dimension is *strength*. A strong constraint is one that significantly reduces the practical utility of a state's power resources, whereas a weak constraint has a less consequential effect. The strength of a constraint is a function of both its scope—that is, how large a range of policies it applies to—and how malleable and reversible it is.

These considerations produce a continuum of constraints on U.S. security policy as follows:

1. A *structural* constraint exists as a result of the United States' position in the international system; it will affect any effort to use power in the pursuit of security, no matter what policies the United States follows. Theoretically, a structural constraint may be weak—that is, it only marginally affects the utility of resources—but in practice, scholars almost always contend that structural constraints are strong. As a result, it is not necessary to distinguish between weak and strong structural constraints, since the former do not exist within IR scholarship.

2. A *strong conditional* constraint powerfully affects the ability to use resources in pursuit of security interests, but is triggered only if the United States adopts certain policies.

3. A *weak conditional* constraint imposes relatively minor impediments on the use of power to advance security interests, and then only if the United States adopts certain policies.

4. A constraint is *inoperative* if it is extremely unlikely to apply to the United States under unipolarity, or its scope and significance is so restricted as to render it essentially inconsequential.

The conventional wisdom in IR scholarship is that the international environment tightly constrains U.S. security policy: most systemic constraints that scholars highlight are strongly conditional, and some are

[34] IR scholarship lacks a general theory of constraints. The theoretical understanding of constraints we develop here is consistent with—and allows us to evaluate—the range of propositions we examine from each of the major theoretical schools.

structural. Our conclusion, in contrast, is that the international environment does not tightly constrain U.S. security policy; systemic constraints are generally inoperative.

THE STAKES FOR POLICY

The core of this book is a thorough evaluation of theoretical arguments, but the results of this assessment directly bear on three overarching questions of policy: Can the United States sustain an expansive range of security commitments around the globe? Is the United States well positioned to reshape the international system to better advance its security interests? What are the general costs of unilateralism?

A contentious debate is under way over how large a security "footprint" the United States should have. Three positions dominate this debate: "offshore balancing" (the United States should sharply reduce its security commitments and military deployments overseas, pulling back toward its own borders);[35] "engagement" (the United States should maintain the security role and military profile it had overseas prior to 9/11, wary of any significant expansion);[36] and "primacy" (the United States should augment the footprint it had overseas before 9/11).[37]

Our general conclusion, that the United States does not face strong systemic constraints, has great relevance for this debate. Specifically, if current IR scholarship is right, then, because of external constraints, the United States will have difficulty maintaining its current security profile (engagement) let alone enhancing its military footprint (primacy).

[35] See, for example, Pape, "Soft Balancing against the United States"; Christopher Layne, "The Unipolar Illusion Revisited: The Coming End of the United States' Unipolar Moment," *International Security* 31 (2006); and John Mearsheimer, "The Future of the American Pacifier," *Foreign Affairs* 80 (2001). The extreme version of this perspective is that the United States should pull back from *all* of its foreign security commitments; see Eugene Gholz, Daryl Press, and Harvey Sapolsky, "Come Home America: The Strategy of Restraint in the Face of Temptation," *International Security* 21 (1997).

[36] See, for example, Robert Art, *A Grand Strategy for America* (Ithaca, N.Y.: Cornell University Press, 2003); Joseph S. Nye, *The Paradox of American Power: Why the World's Only Superpower Can't Go It Alone* (New York: Oxford University Press, 2002); and Stephen Walt, "Keeping the World Off-Balance: Self-Restraint and U.S. Foreign Policy," in Ikenberry, *America Unrivaled.*

[37] See, for example, Bradley Thayer's contribution in Christopher Layne and Bradley Thayer, *American Empire: A Debate* (New York: Taylor and Francis, 2007); Michael Mandelbaum, *The Case for Goliath: How America Acts as the World's Government in the 21st Century* (New York: Public Affairs, 2005); and Rosen, "An Empire."

It is perhaps not a coincidence that many who advocate the remaining option (offshore balancing) have also argued that the United States now faces very strong systemic constraints on its security policy.[38]

Our analysis, by contrast, shows that the systemic environment does not undermine, let alone rule out, any of the three options. But it does not show what choice the United States *should* make. It is important to distinguish dispassionate analysis of the underlying structure of international politics from advocacy for one strategic choice.[39] We argue from theory and evidence that the current unipolar system is durable and that the systemic constraints on U.S. security policy are generally inoperative. One can agree with our assessment of the systemic environment while promoting any of the three grand strategies reviewed above, including offshore balancing.

The debate about the long-term direction of U.S. security policy is often restricted to how and where the United States deploys its military resources. Largely unaddressed is a second issue, one for which our analysis has important implications: whether the United States should consider changing the international system. In his groundbreaking book *War and Change in World Politics*, Robert Gilpin argued that leading states "will attempt to change the international system if the expected benefits exceed the expected costs."[40] In the quarter century since that book's publication, scholars have never seriously debated whether the "expected net gain" of such change might be positive for the United States. It is hardly surprising that scholars set aside the question of large-scale revisions of the territorial status quo—plausible arguments for the utility of widespread conquest in an age of nuclear weapons and low economic benefits of holding territory are hard to imagine. But Gilpin emphasizes that revising the territorial status quo is only one of three objectives that powerful states might pursue; the other two are nonterritorial: gaining influence over the global economy, and "creating an international political environment and rules of the system that will be conducive to their political, economic, and ideological interests."[41] Why is there no sustained scholarly

[38] See, for example, Pape, "Soft Balancing against the United States"; and Layne, "The Unipolar Illusion Revisited."

[39] An example of such a mistaken conflation of our work is Layne, "The Unipolar Illusion Revisited," 37.

[40] Robert Gilpin, *War and Change in World Politics* (New York: Cambridge University Press, 1981), chap. 2.

[41] Ibid., 24.

debate on the costs and benefits of system change in pursuit of these nonterritorial objectives?

The answer is in assessments of the distribution of power. In the 1980s, scholars believed that the United States was in relative decline. The costs of changing the system would thus be too high, and conservatism was the order of the day. With the collapse of Soviet power in 1989–91 came a dramatic shift of power in favor of the United States, presumably increasing the attractiveness of system change. Yet most observers assumed that unipolarity was but a "moment," and so long-range projects of systemic activism did not appear germane.

By the end of the millennium, however, most scholars accepted that unipolarity was not about to erode any time soon, and still the question of U.S. systemic activism was neglected. This inattention can be traced to two prevalent assumptions. The first is that any effort to revise the system would be fruitless, costly, or both, in large part because of systemic constraints on the exercise of power. John Ikenberry, for example, stresses the need for the United States "to operate through mutually agreed rules"[42] and emphasizes that "the more willing the U.S. is to act within institutional constraints and tie itself to others . . . the less likely it is that states will seek to balance against it or seek to establish a rival international order."[43] The second assumption is that, in the words of Robert Jervis, "[t]he current international system, although not necessarily perfect, is certainly satisfactory."[44] These assumptions yield a negative cost-benefit ratio for U.S. efforts to revise the system even if unipolarity will long endure. And if activism makes no sense, then conservatism is the only practical route. This perhaps explains why IR scholars have been so reluctant to address the question of system change, and why they instead counsel the United States to be a "very conservative state" and to "seek to maintain the prevailing international system."[45]

This book reveals that the first assumption underlying conservatism has no basis. As we show, systemic constraints on U.S. security policy do not rise with American power; there is no reason to expect that for the next two decades external constraints will meaningfully impede

[42] G. John Ikenberry, "Strategic Reactions to American Preeminence: Great Power Politics in the Age of Unipolarity," manuscript, Princeton University, July 2003, 4.

[43] G. John Ikenberry, "The Rise of China, Power Transitions, and the Western Order," manuscript, Princeton University, December 2005, 33–34.

[44] Jervis, "Remaking of Unipolar World," 7.

[45] Ibid.

U.S. efforts to revise the international system. It then becomes clear that the second assumption at the root of conservatism is debatable, and ought to be debated. Our concluding chapter addresses the pressing need to begin a serious discussion of the potential security benefits of revising the system. That debate would both provide helpful guidance to policymakers and lead to a better understanding of the true security environment in today's unipolar system and how U.S. policymakers are likely to respond to it.

The final long-term policy issue our analysis bears upon is the costs of unilateralism.[46] IR scholars invariably see going it alone as costly, particularly for the United States today. Stanley Hoffman's warning, that "nothing is more dangerous for a 'hyperpower' than the temptation of unilateralism," is typical of scholarly assessments.[47] The general argument is that unilateralism is prohibitively costly because it augments systemic constraints: enhanced efforts to balance U.S. power, reduced legitimacy of the U.S.-led international order, and a damaged American reputation that will curtail prospects for cooperation in international institutions. Our finding, that for the United States systemic constraints are generally inoperative, thus undermines the scholarly consensus on the high costs of unilateral policies.

This does not mean that unilateralism is wise. Any policy may be wise or unwise, and many unilateral policies pursued by the United States undoubtedly fall into the latter category. The core question is whether punishing general costs arise from unilateral policies regardless of their substance. The findings in this book provide no evidence for such costs, although scholars habitually write about them as if there were such evidence. Again, this result does not mean that the United States should be more or less unilateral, or more or less multilateral. What our findings reveal is that the benefit of acting multilaterally rests on the substance of a given policy, not on the purported general costs of unilateralism. Analysts must distinguish procedural criticisms of unilateral policies from criticisms based on substance. The benefits of acting unilaterally in particular circumstances need to be considered,

---

[46] A complete version of the argument in the paragraphs that follow on the costs of unilateralism is advanced in Stephen Brooks and William Wohlforth, "International Relations Theory and the Case against Unilateralism," *Perspectives on Politics* 3 (2005).

[47] Hoffmann, "Clash of Globalizations," 3. For a representative general treatment, see John Ruggie, ed., *Multilateralism Matters: The Theory and Praxis of an Institutional Form* (New York: Columbia University Press, 1993).

not neglected because of the general presumption that systemic incentives ineluctably make such action costly and impractical.

A single point lies at the root of all three of these implications for policy: inoperative systemic constraints mean that, much more than scholars generally believe, U.S. foreign policy is a realm of choice, rather than necessity. IR scholars, now noticeably silent on what choices the United States should make on all three issues, must be heard. As we stress in our final chapter, the fact that IR scholarship currently cannot provide much guidance on optimal choices does not mean that it will never do so; rather, much more research on these issues is needed.

PLAN OF THE BOOK

Our study is as wide-ranging as the theories we consider. It contains purely theoretical critiques, contemporary and historical case studies, and careful analysis of numerical data. Along the way, we develop and evaluate our own theoretical arguments about how balancing, globalization, legitimacy, and institutionalized cooperation operate in a unipolar world.

In chapters 2 and 3, we address balancing—the most prominent proposition within realism and, arguably, IR theory generally. The balancing proposition has two branches, balance-of-power theory and balance-of-threat theory. Chapter 2 addresses the former, which predicts that states will try to prevent the rise of a hegemon. While scholars debate the empirical veracity of this proposition historically, they have not registered a more important point concerning its implications for constraints on U.S. power today: Even if a potential hegemon needs to be concerned about a counterbalancing constraint, as the theory predicts, the theory does not yield this implication for a hegemon that is already firmly established. Indeed, we argue that once a country passes that threshold, the theory's causal arrows are reversed.

Chapter 3 evaluates the argument on constraints that has been derived from balance-of-threat theory. Scholars who have applied the theory argue that balancing dynamics under unipolarity will, at least initially, operate more subtly than the counterbalancing predicted by balance-of-threat theory. Arguably the most frequently cited systemic constraint in discussions of American foreign policy, this argument has never been tested empirically against alternative explanations.

19

We present such a test, and find that the actions analysts regard as balancing are, in fact, better explained by factors that fall outside balance-of-threat theory.

The key liberal argument that enhanced economic interdependence leads to increased exposure to constraints on the security policy of the United States is the subject of chapter 4. The argument comes in many forms, but we show that most founder on the problem of "asymmetric interdependence": the immense presence of the United States within the global economy makes other states more economically dependent on it than it is dependent on them. Precisely because it occupies such a dominant position, the United States is able to grow economically via globalization without the prospect that other countries will use economic statecraft to constrain its security policy. Thus, a systemic constraint widely thought to be strongly conditional—to use one of the terms we have defined above—is largely inoperative. Chapter 4 also evaluates more general, indirect mechanisms by which economic interdependence might constrain U.S. security policy. We find that rising economic interdependence is likely neither to change other countries' ability or preference to constrain U.S. policies, nor lead to constraining actions by nonstate actors.

Chapter 5 addresses the institutionalist argument that the institutional order is imperiled if the United States does not strongly invest in maintaining a reputation for multilateralism. This core argument, we show, depends upon an assumption about the way reputations work that is theoretically implausible and empirically unsubstantiated. There is an alternative conception of reputations that rests on firmer theoretical foundations and is consistent with the empirical record. We thus find that the reputational constraint is inoperative, not strongly conditional as now posited by institutionalist scholarship.

Chapter 6 analyzes the key argument on constraints derived from constructivism, which concerns legitimacy. We establish several considerations that undermine the constructivists' argument. Reviewing key episodes alleged to have imposed legitimacy costs on the United States, we demonstrate the contingent and malleable nature of the supposed constraint. Legitimacy both limits and enables power, and power can fuel legitimacy. The United States needs legitimacy, but the constraint this need imposes on U.S. security policy is conditional and weak, rather than conditional and strong or even structural, as constructivist treatments contend.

The concluding chapter discusses two chief implications. Rather than vindicating existing theories, the reversals and challenges U.S. foreign policy encountered after 2003 underscore the need for a new research agenda for IR scholars. To explain the nature of the constraints on U.S. security policy, scholars must shift away from the standard focus on the external environment and examine other kinds of factors. Analysts also need to examine how the United States can best take advantage of its unprecedented opportunity to change the international system in its long-term security interests. The debate about U.S. grand strategy needs to consider a new alternative: using American leverage to reshape international institutions, standards of legitimacy and economic globalization.

Realism, Balance-of-Power Theory, and the Counterbalancing Constraint

WHEN THE LEADING STATES in the international system use their resources to pursue security objectives, what stands in their way? Realism highlights one answer: other major powers. For realists, "[P]ower is checked most effectively by counterbalancing power."[1] The core axiom of balance-of-power theory—the most influential theory in the realist canon—is that great powers will develop and mobilize military capabilities sufficient to constrain the most powerful among them. Though the theory has been formulated in many ways over the centuries, the "central proposition" of nearly all versions "is that states tend to balance against threats of hegemony over the system."[2] Following the standard practice among the theorists they discuss, Jack Levy and William Thompson use the term *hegemony* to mean both a concentration of material capabilities in one state—akin to the standard definition of unipolarity—and the political dominance that this material strength may enable.[3] Thus, the theory posits that once a state is at or near the top of the international heap in resources of power, increases in its relative capabilities invite more and more counterbalancing.

In this chapter, we show that the theory does not predict and historical experience does not imply that there will be efforts to counterbalance the United States today. Balance-of-power theory predicts that states try to prevent rise of a hegemon. While scholars debate the historical evidence for this proposition, they fail to register a point

[1] Robert Jervis, "The Compulsive Empire," *Foreign Policy* 137 (2003): 84.

[2] Jack S. Levy and William R. Thompson, "Hegemonic Threats and Great-Power Balancing in Europe, 1495–1999," *Security Studies* 14 (2005).

[3] This confusing use of the term *hegemony* reflects the fact that realist balance-of-power theorists generally assume that concentrated power resources are necessary for and prior to hegemony in the political sense. The usage of the term *hegemony* is so deeply entrenched in this literature that it is hard to avoid without amending the theory. We thus employ this usage here, though we maintain the distinction between power as resources and power as political influence. Thus the terms *hegemonic threat* and *potential hegemon* refer to a state that is perceived to have a sufficient share of material power resources to establish hegemony, while a *hegemon* has sufficient power resources to sustain hegemony.

important for constraints on U.S. power today: Even if a potential hegemon must be concerned about counterbalancing, the theory yields no such implication for one that has already established its material primacy. We argue that once a country achieves such a position, it has passed a threshold, and the effect of increasing power is reversed: the stronger the leading state and the more entrenched its dominance, the more unlikely and thus less constraining are counterbalancing dynamics.

Our explanation for the absence of counterbalancing against the United States emphasizes a simple point: counterbalancing is and will long remain prohibitively costly for the other major powers. Because no country comes close to matching the comprehensive nature of U.S. power, an attempt to counterbalance would be far more expensive than a similar effort in any previous international system. Matching U.S. capabilities could become even more formidably costly, moreover, if the United States decided to increase its defense expenditures (currently around 4 percent of GDP) to Cold War levels (which averaged 7.5 percent of GDP).[4]

General patterns of evidence since the advent of unipolarity are consistent with our argument and inexplicable in traditional balance-of-power terms. The principal change in alliances since the demise of the Soviet Union has been the expansion of NATO, and the biggest increases in defense spending have been on behalf of the Pentagon. The other great powers have not attempted to constrain the United States by allying together: No counterhegemonic coalition has taken shape, and none is on the horizon. Nor have they balanced increases in U.S. military power through internal spending. Notwithstanding increased expenditures by a few great powers (notably China), in aggregate their commitments to defense have declined compared to the United States: the U.S. share of total defense spending by the major powers grew from 47 percent in 1991 to 66 percent in 2006.[5] No major power has exhibited any propensity to use military capabilities directly to contain U.S. power. This is not the pattern of evidence balance-of-power theory

[4] Calculated from *Budget of the United States Government Fiscal Year 2005: Historical Tables* (Washington, D.C.: United States Government Printing Office, 2005), table 3.1, pp. 45–52.

[5] Calculated from Stockholm Peace Research Institute, Military Expenditures Database (www.sipri.org); with "great power" defined as in the Correlates of War Project, www.correlatesofwar.org.

23

predicts. Were the theory not already popular with scholars and pundits, nothing about the behavior of the major powers since 1991 would have called it to mind.

What is at stake in our debate with balance-of-power theory? Relatively little, if concentrations of power only matter when great powers expect to go to war with each other. Many factors currently militate against such a war, and some observers might claim that the absence of counterbalancing is both overdetermined and unimportant. We demonstrate that this objection is reasonable but wrong. Much realist theory is uncertain whether counterbalancing occurs only when power concentrations elsewhere threaten a state's own territory, or can arise from other security and nonsecurity interests. Those analysts who take the former view would argue that in our present system, where no great power threatens another's survival, we should not expect counterbalancing. But history is rich with evidence that counterbalancing is a response to hegemonic threats to interests less basic than survival of a state. As the compact case studies presented in this chapter will show, in a counterfactual world where states such as China or Russia had the same power potential as the United States, they would likely engage in counterbalancing even if they were confident the United States did not threaten their survival. And that would be a very different world.

We begin the chapter with the theoretical foundations of the counterbalancing constraint, and explain why so many analysts find it relevant to contemporary international relations. We then show that this constraint does not apply to the United States today: the concentration of capabilities in the United States is well past the threshold at which counterbalancing becomes prohibitively costly for the other major powers; balancing is exceedingly unlikely to emerge, and will long remain so. Finally, we show why the absence of the counterbalancing constraint is neither overdetermined nor insignificant, though analysts and policymakers have begun to take it for granted.

The Argument for Counterbalancing Constraints

Balance-of-power theory posits that because states residing in global anarchy have an interest in maximizing their long-term odds of survival, they will check great concentrations of power (hegemony) by building up their own capabilities (internal balancing) or aggregating their capabilities in alliances with other states (external balancing).[6] The higher the probability of hegemony, the more likely states are to balance. Leading states by definition represent potential hegemonic threats, and so they must constantly be vigilant, lest their actions, whether or not intended to attain hegemony, provoke counterbalancing by other powers.

Counterbalancing is a constraint to which any leading power must pay heed, for it has the potential to transform the systemic distribution of capabilities. According to the theory, the constraint is generated by a systemic imperative to create a counterpoise, either by augmenting the power of a single state until it becomes a peer rival to the hegemon, or through a military alliance or alignment that aggregates capabilities roughly commensurate with those of the hegemon. Counterbalancing uses or seeks to build up real resources and capabilities to match, check, or block another state's use of such capabilities to advance its security interests. As Christopher Layne observes, "[T]he concept of balancing expresses the idea of a counterweight, specifically, the ability to generate sufficient material capabilities to match—or offset—those of a would-be, or actual, hegemon."[7]

Though powerful, the counterbalancing constraint is provoked only by circumstances surrounding hegemony. Balance-of-power theory is often applied loosely, but its main implications concern real or potential hegemons.[8] To be sure, the constraint emerges in specific relationships between specific states, and is often entangled with particular

---

[6] We focus on the neorealist formulation of balance-of-power theory first set forth in Waltz, *Theory of International Politics*, although we are sensitive to the findings in the voluminous research that has appeared since that book's publication. For particularly helpful discussions of this literature that establish the links between Waltz's theory and the classical literature on the balance of power, see Levy and Thompson, "Hegemonic Threats"; Jack S. Levy, "Balances and Balancing: Concepts, Propositions and Research Design," in *Realism and the Balancing of Power: A New Debate*, ed. John A. Vasquez and Colin Elman (Saddle River, N.J.: Prentice-Hall, 2003); and Richard Little, *The Balance of Power in International Relations: Metaphors, Myths, and Models* (Cambridge: Cambridge University Press, 2007).

[7] Christopher Layne, "The War on Terrorism and the Balance of Power," in *Balance of Power: Theory and Practice in the 21st Century*, ed. T. V. Paul, James J. Wirtz, and Michel Fortmann (Stanford, Calif.: Stanford University Press, 2004), 106.

[8] Many other kinds of power-acquisition strategies may fall under the purview of different theories, such as security dilemma theory. For discussions, see Charles L. Glaser, "The Security Dilemma Revisited," *World Politics* 50 (1997); and Ken Booth and Nicholas Wheeler, *The Security Dilemma: Fear, Cooperation, and Trust in World Politics* (Houndmills: Palgrave Macmillan, 2007). The classical theory also applies to "hegemonic threats" that may emanate from an alliance of states threatening dominance—not an implication that

clashes of interests, but it is systemic in nature. Counterbalancing is action taken to check a concentration of power in the system. It is action, moreover, that would not have been taken in the absence of an actual or potential hegemon. It follows that "balancing is a great-power phenomenon, because only great powers can prevent one among them from attaining geopolitical predominance."[9]

Counterbalancing is a theoretical source of realism's trademark emphasis on prudence and restraint, and figures prominently in the writings of nonrealist scholars as well.[10] If decision-makers ignore it, realists warn, the result may be self-defeating foreign policy crusades, driven by domestic, ideological, or psychological biases. When counseling restraint in the face of temptation, realists generally argue that even if the likelihood of counterbalancing is not evident to policymakers, it is always latent in any international system. An enduring tragedy of great power politics, they stress, is that it is precisely when decision-makers believe they can ignore counterbalancing constraints that they are most likely to call them forth with overambitious foreign policies.

Given the centuries-old theoretical pedigree of this argument, it is little wonder that realists and other scholars reached for it when the Soviet Union's demise in 1991 rapidly shifted power toward the United States. Throughout the 1990s, commentators warned that the transition from bipolarity to what they expected to be a brief unipolar moment had primed the international system for counterbalancing.[11] As the unipolar "moment" stretched into the 2000s, scholars continued

---

is relevant to the current debate. See Little, *Balance of Power*, chap, 1. For more on why balancing has to be defined rigorously, see Stephen Brooks and William Wohlforth, "Striking the Balance," *International Security* 30 (2005–6).

[9] Layne, "War on Terrorism," 106. As Randall Schweller further clarifies, "If two states are merely building arms for the purpose of independent action against third parties, they are not balancing. Indeed, state A may be building up its military power and even targeting another state B and still not be balancing against B, that is trying to match B's overall capabilities to prevent B from invading A or its vital interests. Instead, the purpose of A's actions may be coercive diplomacy: to gain bargaining leverage with B." *Unanswered Threats: Political Constraints on the Balance of Power* (Princeton: Princeton University Press, 2006), 9.

[10] Robert Keohane, for example, argues, "Multilateral military action endorsed by the permanent members of the Security Council is much less likely to generate counterbalancing coalitions." "Multilateral Coercive Diplomacy: Not 'Myths of Empire,' " November 2002, Columbia International Affairs Online (CIAOnet.org). Similar examples include Joseph Nye, "The Limits of American Power," *Political Science Quarterly* 117 (2003); Ikenberry, "The Rise of China"; and Cronin, "The Paradox of Hegemony."

[11] See, e.g., Christopher Layne, "The Unipolar Illusion: Why New Great Powers Will Arise," *International Security* 14 (1993); Layne, "From Preponderance to Offshore Balancing: America's Future Grand Strategy," *International Security* 22 (1997); and Kenneth Waltz, "Evaluating Theories," *American Political Science Review* 91 (1997).

to express confidence that counterbalancing was in the offing. Thus, Layne warned that "the Iraq War may come to be seen as a pivotal geopolitical event that heralded the beginning of serious counter-hegemonic balancing against the United States."[12]

This confidence is without foundation. In this chapter, we assess the argument for a counterbalancing constraint on the terms most favorable to it: we assume that nothing has changed in international politics since the eighteenth-century heyday of realpolitik *except* for variables that have always been central to balance-of-power theory. We thus set aside all the other changes in international politics that might militate against balancing, including nuclear deterrence, the spread of democracy, globalization, and the declining benefits of territorial conquest. Even so, the reemergence of counterbalancing dynamics remains exceedingly improbable. That is, the variables that drive balance-of-power theory itself are now configured so as to render the balancing constraint so improbable as to render it inoperative.

Chief among these variables is the distribution of material capabilities. In the next several sections, we examine the current unipolar distribution of capabilities, show that it renders the balancing constraint inoperative, and assess the validity of our argument by examining China's economic growth, military programs, and strategic behavior.

The Distribution of Capabilities

"Nothing has ever existed like this disparity of power; nothing," historian Paul Kennedy observes: "I have returned to all of the comparative defense spending and military personnel statistics over the past 500 years that I compiled in *The Rise and Fall of the Great Powers,* and no other nation comes close."[13] Though assessments of U.S. power have changed since those words were written in 2002, they remain true. Even when capabilities are understood broadly to include economic, technological, and other wellsprings of national power, they are concentrated in the United States to a degree never before experienced in

---

[12] Layne, "War on Terrorism," 119. Similarly, Kenneth Waltz warned in 2002, "The United States cannot prevent a new balance of power from forming. It can hasten its coming as it has been earnestly doing." Waltz in Ikenberry, *America Unrivaled,* 64; see also Art, "Striking the Balance"; and Christopher Layne, *The Peace of Illusions: American Grand Strategy from 1940 to the Present* (Ithaca, N.Y.: Cornell University Press, 2006).

[13] Kennedy, "The Eagle Has Landed."

the history of the modern system of states and thus never contemplated by balance-of-power theorists.

The United States spends more on defense than all the other major military powers combined, and most of those powers are its allies. Its massive investments in the human, institutional, and technological requisites of military power, cumulated over many decades, make any effort to match U.S. capabilities even more daunting than the gross spending numbers imply. Military research and development (R&D) may best capture the scale of the long-term investments that give the United States a dramatic qualitative edge in military capabilities. As table 2.1 shows, in 2004 U.S. military R&D expenditures were more than six times greater than those of Germany, Japan, France, and Britain combined. By some estimates over half the military R&D expenditures in the world are American.[14] And this disparity has been sustained for decades: over the past 30 years, for example, the United States has invested over three times more than the entire European Union on military R&D.[15]

These vast commitments have created a preeminence in military capabilities vis-à-vis all the other major powers that is unique after the seventeenth century. While other powers could contest U.S. forces near their homelands, especially over issues on which nuclear deterrence is credible, the United States is and will long remain the only state capable of projecting major military power globally.[16] This capacity arises from "command of the commons"—that is, unassailable military dominance over the sea, air, and space. As Barry Posen puts it,

> Command of the commons is the key military enabler of the U.S. global power position. It allows the United States to exploit more fully other sources of power, including its own economic and military might as well

[14] Calculated from the SIPRI military expenditures database (www.sipri.org) for 1998. In that year, U.S. military R&D spending accounted for over 75 percent of total spending by the countries listed in table 2.1.

[15] Another and perhaps even longer-term predictor of military power is what Björn Hagelin calls "science and technology-based military innovation," an area where the United States' lead is, if anything, even more marked. See "Science and Technology Based Military Innovation in the United States and Europe," in *SIPRI Yearbook 2004: Armaments, Disarmament, and International Security* (Oxford: Oxford University Press, 2004).

[16] Sustained U.S. investment in nuclear capabilities, against the backdrop of Russian decline and Chinese stasis, may even have undermined the standard calculus of deterrence; see Keir A. Lieber and Daryl G. Press, "The End of MAD? The Nuclear Dimension of U.S. Primacy," *International Security* 30 (2006).

TABLE 2.1
Defense Expenditures by the Major Powers, 2006

	Defense expenditures ($ billion)	% Great power defense expenditures	% World defense expenditures	Defense expenditures % of GDP	Defense R&D expenditures ($ billion)
United States	528.6	65.6	46	4.1	75.5
China	49.5	6.1	4	2	n.a.
Japan	43.9	5.4	4	1	1.1
Germany	36.9	4.6	3	1.4	1.1
Russia	34.7	4.3	3	4.1	n.a.
France	53	6.6	5	2.5	3.9
Britain	59.2	7.3	5	2.7	4.4

Sources: Stockholm International Peace Research Institute, "The 15 Major Spending Countries in 2006," http://www.sipri.org/contents/milap/milex/mex_data_index.html (consulted November 8, 2007); Stockholm International Peace Research Institute Military Expenditure Database, http://www.sipri.org/contents/milap/milex/mex_database1.html (consulted November 8, 2007); Organization for Economic Co-operation and Development, *OECD Main Science and Technology Indicators 2006*, No. 2 (Paris: OECD, 2007).

Note: Defense expenditures as a percentage of GDP are 2005 estimates; R&D expenditures are for 2004.

as the economic and military might of its allies. Command of the commons also helps the United States to weaken its adversaries, by restricting their access to economic, military and political assistance. . . . Command of the commons provides the United States with more useful military potential for a hegemonic foreign policy than any other offshore power has ever had.[17]

Posen's study of American military primacy ratifies Kennedy's emphasis on the historical importance of the economic foundations of national power. It is the combination of military and economic potential that sets the United States apart from its predecessors at the top of the international system (fig. 2.1). Previous leading states were either great commercial and naval powers or great military powers on land, never both. The British Empire in its heyday and the United States during the Cold War, for example, shared the world with other powers that

[17] Barry Posen, "Command of the Commons: The Military Foundation of U.S. Hegemony," *International Security* 28 (2003): 9.

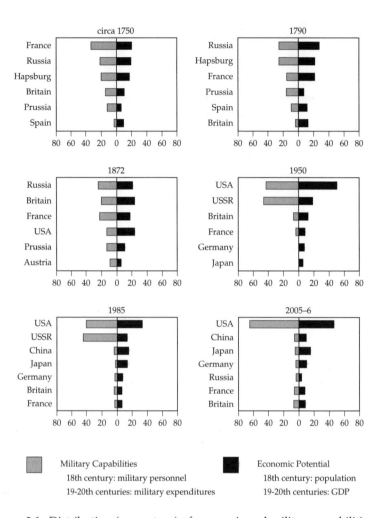

Figure 2.1. Distribution (percentage) of economic and military capabilities among the major powers, seventeenth–twenty-first centuries. *Sources*: Eighteenth-century data: Paul M. Kennedy, *The Rise and Fall of the Great Powers: Economic Change and Military Conflict from 1500 to 2000* (New York: Random House, 1987). GDP, 1870–1985: Angus Maddison, *Monitoring the World Economy, 1820–1992* (Paris: OECD, 1995). GDP, 2005–6: International Monetary Fund, World Economic Outlook Database, April 2007. Military expenditures, 1872–1985: J. David Singer and Melvin Small, "National Material Capabilities Data, 1816–1985," computer file (Ann Arbor, Mich.: Inter-University Consortium for Political and Social Research). Military Expenditures, 2005–6: Stockholm International Peace Research Institute (SIPRI), database on military expenditures, http://first.sipri.org. *Note*: Until 1985, China used the Soviet material product system of national accounts. The 1985 figure for China's GDP is Maddison's estimate, based on a PPP-style formula. The 2005–6 figure is based on market exchange rates.

matched or exceeded them in some areas. Even at the height of the Pax Britannica, the United Kingdom was outspent, outmanned, and outgunned by both France and Russia. Similarly, at the dawn of the Cold War the United States was dominant economically as well as in air and naval capabilities. But the Soviet Union retained overall military parity, and thanks to geography and investment in land power it had a superior ability to seize territory in Eurasia.

The United States' share of world GDP in 2006, 27.5 percent, surpassed that of any leading state in modern history, with the sole exception of its own position after 1945 (when World War II had temporarily depressed every other major economy). The size of the U.S. economy means that its massive military capabilities required roughly 4 percent of its GDP in 2005, far less than the nearly 10 percent it averaged over the peak years of the Cold War, 1950–70, and the burden borne by most of the major powers of the past.[18] As Kennedy sums up, "Being Number One at great cost is one thing; being the world's single superpower on the cheap is astonishing."[19]

The only other economy big and rich enough to generate military capabilities on the American scale is that of the European Union, whose 27 member states have a combined GDP larger than that of the United States. To realize that potential, however, Brussels would have to wield Europe's aggregate economic output with the same strategic purpose as the United States, a unitary state. A superpower's military force could be purchased only at the price of a frontal assault on European nations' core sovereignty. Balance-of-power theory assumes that states seek to preserve their security and autonomy, and, as Jolyon Howorth and Anand Menon point out, "[F]undamental to an understanding of the EU is an appreciation of the fact that such considerations are as present *within* it as they are in its dealings with the outside world."[20] Neither the authority nor the ability to act decisively in Europe's name exists even in monetary matters, to say nothing of foreign and defense policy.[21] Ultimate authority rests with the member states, all 27 of which must agree to any decision on defense and security

[18] Calculated from *Budget of the United States Government Fiscal Year 2005: Historical Tables* (Washington, D.C.: United States Government Printing Office, 2005).

[19] Kennedy, "The Eagle Has Landed."

[20] Jolyon Howorth and Anand Menon, "Complexity and International Institutions: Why the European Union Isn't Balancing the United States," manuscript, Yale University.

[21] Kathleen R. McNamara and Sophie Meunier, "Between National Sovereignty and International Power: What External Voice for the Euro?" *International Affairs* 78 (2002): 849.

TABLE 2.2
Economic Indicators for the Major Powers, 2006

	GDP, current prices ($ billion)	% Great power GDP, current prices	% World GDP, current prices	GDP per capita, current prices	Public debt (% GDP)	Hours worked (per person in employment)	Productivity ($ GDP per hour worked)
United States	13,245	46.1	27.5	44,190	64.7	1,804	48.3
China	2,630	9.2	5.5	2,001	22.1	n.a.	n.a.
Japan	4,367	15.2	9.1	34,188	176.2	1,784	34.4
Germany	2,897	10.1	6	35,204	66.8	1,436	44
Russia	979	3.4	2	6,856	8	n.a.	n.a.
France	2,232	7.8	4.6	35,404	64.7	1,564	49
Britain	2,374	8.3	4.9	39,213	42.2	1,669	40.1

Sources: International Monetary Fund, World Economic Outlook Database, April 2007, http://www.imf.org/external/pubs/ft/weo/2007/01/data/index.aspx (consulted November 8, 2007); Central Intelligence Agency, CIA World Factbook, https://www.cia.gov/library/publications/the-world-factbook/ (consulted November 8, 2007); Organization for Economic Co-operation and Development, "OECD Employment Outlook 2007, Statistical Annex," http://www.oecd.org/dataoecd/29/27/38749309.pdf (consulted November 8, 2007); Organization for Economic Co-operation and Development, "OECD Compendium of Productivity Indicators 2006," http://www.oecd.org/dataoecd/4/22/37574961.pdf (consulted November 8, 2007)

Note: Data for U.S. public debt are from 2005. Productivity estimates are from 2005.

policy. This requirement of unanimity "places profound limits on the potential for decisive EU security policies."[22]

American primacy is also rooted in the county's position as the world's leading technological power. The United States remains dominant globally in overall R&D investments, high-technology production, commercial innovation, and higher education (table 2.3).

Despite the weight of this evidence, elite perceptions of U.S. power had shifted toward pessimism by the middle of the first decade of this century. As we noted in chapter 1, this was partly the result of an Iraq-induced doubt about the utility of material predominance, a doubt redolent of the post-Vietnam mood. In retrospect, many assessments of U.S. economic and technological prowess from the 1990s were overly optimistic; by the next decade important potential vulnerabilities were evident. In particular, chronically imbalanced domestic finances and accelerating public debt convinced some analysts that the United

---

[22] Howorth and Menon, "Complexity and International Institutions," 9.

TABLE 2.3
Science and Technology Indicators for the Major Powers, 2003–6.

	High Tech production ($ millions) (2003) [a]	% World high tech production (2003)	Gross domestic expenditure on R&D ($ Million PPP) (2006)	# of triadic patent families (2005) [b]	Science and engineering doctoral degrees (2003) [c]	PCs per 1000 people (2004)	Internet access per 1000 people (2005)	Secure internet servers [d] per million people (2006)
United States	1,351,048.7	39	343,747.5	16,368	26,891	762.2	630 [e]	869.2
China	423,825.9	12	115,196.9	433	8,153	40.9	85.1	0.4
Japan	376,250.1	11	130,745.4	15,239	7,581	541.6	667.5	331.9
Germany	146,494	4	62,493.2	6,266	10,796	545.3	454.7	348.6
Russia	n.a.	n.a.	16,668.7	49	10,409	104.3	152.3	3.2
France	136,665.7	4	40,392	2,463	6,890	495.7	429.6	96.5
Britain	116,200.2	3	35,171.10	1,588	8,810	599.8	473.5	561.5

Sources: World Bank, World Development Indicators 2007, http://go.worldbank.org/3JU2HA60D0 (consulted November 8, 2007); Organization for Economic Co-operation and Development, "OECD Main Science and Technology Indicators 2007/1," http://www.oecd.org/document/33/0,3343,en_2649_34451_1901082_1_1_1,00.html (consulted November 8, 2007); National Science Board, "Science and Engineering Indicators 2006, Volume 2," http://nsf.gov/statistics/seind06/pdf/volume2.pdf (consulted November 8, 2007).

[a] In 1997 dollars.

[b] Triadic Patent Families represent attempts to receive patents for an invention in the United States, Europe, and Japan. See <http://www.nsf.gov/statistics/seind06/c6/c6g.htm>.

[c] The data for China is from 2001, the data for France is from 2002, and the data for Russia is from 2000.

[d] Secure internet servers use encryption technology in internet transactions. See www.netcraft.com.

[e] Data is from 2004.

States once again confronted a competitiveness crisis.[23] If concerns continue to mount, this will count as the fourth such crisis since 1945; the first three occurred during the 1950s (Sputnik), the 1970s (Vietnam and stagflation), and the 1980s (the Soviet threat and Japan's challenge). None of these crises, however, shifted the international system's structure: multipolarity did not return in the 1960s, 1970s, or early 1990s, and each scare over competitiveness ended with the American position of primacy retained or strengthened.[24]

Our review of the evidence of U.S. predominance is not meant to suggest that the United States lacks vulnerabilities or causes for concern. In fact, it confronts a number of significant vulnerabilities; of course, this is also true of the other major powers.[25] The point is that adverse trends for the United States will not cause a polarity shift in the near future. If we take a long view of U.S. competitiveness and the prospects for relative declines in economic and technological dominance, one takeaway stands out: relative power shifts slowly. The United States has accounted for a quarter to a third of global output for over a century. No other economy will match its combination of wealth, size, technological capacity, and productivity in the foreseeable future (tables 2.2 and 2.3).

The depth, scale, and projected longevity of the U.S. lead in each critical dimension of power are noteworthy. But what truly distinguishes the current distribution of capabilities is American dominance

[23] Even the most vociferous critics of "fiscal overstretch" stress that the U.S. budget deficits are primarily due to domestic policy choices, not external burdens. See Niall Ferguson and Lawrence Kotlikoff, "Going Critical: American Power and the Consequences of Fiscal Overstretch," *National Interest* 73 (2003).

[24] See the discussion in Fareed Zakaria, "How Long Will America Lead the World?" *Newsweek*, June 12, 2006, 44–45.

[25] Population aging is a prominent example in this regard. It has become commonplace for analysts to note that U.S. fiscal prospects and economic growth will suffer due to the aging of the U.S. population and the high costs associated with this transition, which is correct; what tends to be overlooked is that population aging will negatively affect the other great powers to a much greater extent. In a comprehensive analysis, Mark Haas demonstrates that global population aging will "be a potent force for the continuation of U.S. power dominance, both economic and military. . . . Although the United States is growing older, it is doing so to a lesser extent and less quickly than all the other great powers. Consequently, the economic and fiscal costs for the United States created by social aging (although staggering, especially for health care) will be significantly lower for it than for potential competitors. Global aging is therefore not only likely to extend U.S. hegemony (because the other major powers will lack the resources necessary to overtake the United States' economic and military lead), but deepen it as these other states are likely to fall even further behind the United States." "A Geriatric Peace? The Future of U.S. Power in a World of Aging Populations," *International Security* 32 (2007): 126–27.

in all of them simultaneously. The chief lesson of Kennedy's 500-year survey of leading powers is that nothing remotely similar ever occurred in the historical experience that informs modern international relations theory. The implication is both simple and underappreciated: the counterbalancing constraint is inoperative and will remain so until the distribution of capabilities changes fundamentally. The next section explains why.

UNIPOLARITY AND THE COUNTERBALANCING CONSTRAINT

The main feature of the distribution of capabilities today is thus unprecedented American primacy.[26] While many acknowledge this fact, few appreciate one of its major consequences: that neither balance-of-power theory nor historical experiences of the balancing constraint applies to the United States today. Balance-of-power theory predicts that states will try to prevent the *rise* of a hegemon; it tells us nothing about what will happen once a country establishes such a position. All the historical experience of balancing from the seventeenth century until 1991 concerns efforts to check a rising power from upsetting the status quo. Consequently, for three centuries no balance-of-power theorist ever developed propositions about a system in which hegemony *is* the status quo. While both history and balance-of-power theory suggest that a rising potential hegemon needs to be concerned about the counterbalancing constraint, neither yields this implication for a hegemon already firmly established. On the contrary, both theory and historical experience suggest that when hegemony is the status quo, the obstacles to balancing are magnified. In the subsections that follow, we consider how the current unipolar system affects external balancing (alliance formation), internal balancing (generating power domestically), and the opportunity cost of balancing.

External Balancing

The main systemic obstacles to external balancing are coordination— a ubiquitous difficulty in international relations—and the collective action problem, which is even more formidable. Collective goods theory

---

[26] The paragraphs that follow build on and develop arguments and research presented in Wohlforth, "Stability of Unipolar World"; Wohlforth, "U.S. Strategy"; and Stephen G. Brooks and William C. Wohlforth, "American Primacy in Perspective," *Foreign Affairs* 81 (2002).

predicts that counterbalancing alliances will be hard to form and make effective.[27] A balancing constraint against a prospective hegemon can be enjoyed by states that do not contribute to it; one state's security benefit does not prevent others from benefiting as well. The result is a powerful incentive to free ride. States are tempted to stand aside and pass the balancing buck to others. Hence it is little wonder that John Mearsheimer's review of two centuries' experience leads him to conclude that "great powers seem clearly to prefer buck-passing to balancing."[28]

The collective action problem feeds into the coordination challenges that beset any cooperative endeavor among states. Each prospective balancer is a self-interested actor seeking to minimize costs and risks and maximize the degree to which the alliance's strategy complements the actor's other preferences. Even when they agree on the need to balance, states tend to disagree on how burdens should be shared and what strategy should be followed. Allies tend to splinter over who gets to lead and set strategy. Except for those few alliances lucky enough to be able to balance a hegemon without a great deal of strategic coordination, effective alliances demand that members' decisions on national security be shaped by their collective purpose. Leadership in an alliance of sovereign states with roughly equal capabilities is usually so contentious an issue that it is never really settled, which leads to strategic incoherence.

The sheer size and comprehensiveness of the power gap favoring the United States, moreover, raises still higher the coordination and collective action barriers to external balancing. The greater and more comprehensive the hegemon's lead, the larger and more strategically coherent the coalition needed to check it. As figure 2.1 illustrates, the power gaps that balancing efforts had to overcome in the past were much narrower, and yet the barriers loomed large. They are far more formidable now given the long road prospective balancers would have to travel to produce a credible check on American power.

A comparison to history's most successful power-aggregating alliance, NATO, is instructive. NATO's ability to overcome the perennial

[27] Mancur Olson, *The Logic of Collective Action: Public Goods and the Theory of Groups* (Cambridge: Harvard University Press, 1965); Glen H. Snyder, *Alliance Politics* (Ithaca, N.Y.: Cornell University Press, 1997)

[28] John J. Mearsheimer, *The Tragedy of Great Power Politics* (New York: Norton, 2001), 160. A comprehensive test of balance-of-power theory in eight historical international systems over 2,000 years found the collective action problem to be a ubiquitous cause of balancing failure even in "most likely" cases. See William C. Wohlforth et al., "Testing Balance of Power Theory in World History," *European Journal of International Relations* 13 (2007).

obstacles to balancing in the Cold War hinged on two conditions: it confronted a one-dimensional superpower that was competitive mainly in conventional land power; and U.S. leadership within the coalition allowed Washington to overcome coordination problems and absorb the costs and risks of free riding by others. Those advantages do not apply to the would-be members of a countercoalition against U.S. power today. There is no obvious leader of a hypothetical coalition, nor would that coalition posses the latent power advantage NATO enjoyed.

Today's unipolar system, in short, multiplies the problems that complicated the balancing efforts of the past. Organizing collective action to check a rising power is hard enough; fashioning a durable, coherent coalition against a well-established hegemon is a tougher order of business. All of the difficulties of overthrowing a ramified status quo now work for, rather than against, the hegemon. Several of the major powers are longtime allies of the United States and derive substantial benefits from their position. Attempting to balance would put those benefits at risk, and Washington has ample opportunities to exploit the free-rider problem by playing divide and rule.

Internal Balancing

Just as the theory of collective goods predicts chronic challenges to external balancing, another major body of social science theory generates the same expectation regarding internal balancing. The new institutionalism in economics, sociology, and political science leads to the expectation that increasing returns, path dependence, and other domestic-level institutional lags will present major obstacles to internal balancing via domestic self-strengthening reforms.[29] Emulating the hegemon is hard, successfully doing so is harder, and extracting and allocating the resources needed to close the gap is harder still. The experience of the states that tried to contain revolutionary and Napoleonic France is the best known of dozens of cases illustrating the challenges to emulating the power-generating practices of a prospective hegemon.[30] As Randall Schweller has argued, domestic impediments to the-

---

[29] Douglass C. North, *Institutions, Institutional Change, and Economic Performance* (Cambridge: Cambridge University Press, 1990); Walter W. Powell and Paul J. DiMaggio, *The New Institutionalism in Organizational Analysis* (Chicago: University of Chicago Press, 1991); James G. March and Johan Olsen, *Rediscovering Institutions: The Organizational Basis of Politics* (New York: Free Press, 1989); Kathleen Thelen, "Historical Institutionalism in Comparative Politics," *Annual Review of Political Science* 2 (1999).

[30] For examples from eight international systems over two millennia, see Kaufman, Little, and Wohlforth, *Balance of Power*

oretically optimal power-generating policies are "the main reason why states have so infrequently balanced efficiently and in a timely fashion against dangerous threats."[31]

Needless to say, some states have in the past overcome domestic obstacles, generating the power needed to check a hegemon. But the bigger and more comprehensive the power gap, the harder this task becomes. Today's prospective internal balancers thus face a much higher bar than their predecessors.

Path dependency also makes internal balancing far more challenging than it was in the past. Many of today's possible balancers chose domestic and foreign policies long ago on the assumption of U.S. leadership and alliance. They built particular kinds of military establishments and defense industries; created particular national security institutions; fostered particular sets of ideas about national identity; and made particular commitments to domestic constituencies. The difficulty of weapons development today and the increasing returns in defense production make a reversal of course very difficult economically, socially, and politically.

The very same arguments apply in reverse to the hegemon. Consider, for example, high-technology military capabilities. An important feature of the current international security landscape is the absence of competition on this crucial dimension of power. The United States' massive commitment to R&D in general and military-related R&D in particular presents ever higher barriers to entry into this competition. The trend since the collapse of the Soviet Union's military industrial complex has been a steady *widening* of the U.S. lead.[32] This dramatic advantage is not restricted to military weaponry; the United States is also in a class by itself in collecting, processing, and distributing information on the battlefield. To reverse the momentum in this state of affairs would require Herculean efforts.

Opportunity Costs

A final impediment to balancing is the opportunity cost of using resources and bending strategy toward countering the system's strongest state. Some fortunate balancers may find that their efforts to counter the hegemon complement their other foreign policy objectives. But

---

[31] Schweller, *Unanswered Threats*, 11.

[32] See Stockholm International Peace Research Institute, *SIPRI Yearbook 2004–5*, chap. 9.

most are not so lucky; the resources they use for balancing often cannot be used for other purposes. Many are less fortunate still, and find that balancing undermines other core interests. Here, we will discuss only opportunity costs for pursuing security interests, but this analysis can easily be extended to other core interests as well.[33]

A state's willingness to pay for balancing is conditioned by the proportion of its security problems that would be addressed by checking systemic hegemony. The smaller this proportion is, the higher the opportunity cost—and thus the lower the probability—of balancing. More specifically, the more important are local security issues compared to the benefit of checking hegemony, the greater is the opportunity cost of balancing. Two features of the current international system increase the relative importance of local security concerns and thus increase the opportunity costs of checking the systemic hegemon.

First is geography. The costs and challenges of moving military forces over long distances mean that countries generally pose greater threats to their neighbors than to states farther away. Neighbors are also more likely to have more potential clashes of interest with each other than with distant states. The Atlantic and Pacific oceans separate the United States from the Eurasian landmass, where all the prospective balancers reside. When the putative hegemon and most of the potential balancers are close neighbors—as they were in the classic balancing episodes in modern European history—systemic and local imperatives more readily reinforce each other, meaning that balancing the hegemon is less likely to come at the expense of addressing local security challenges. In contrast, when the hegemon lies far offshore and the prospective balancers are close neighbors, as in the current system, local imperatives loom larger, and the counterbalancing strategy loses appeal.

Second is the number of lesser states relative to great powers. The previous section showed that the current international system is characterized by an unprecedented hegemony within the great-power subsystem. Also important is the extraordinary proliferation of medium and minor powers. The dramatic increase in the number of states over the

[33] A notable example in this regard concerns China. As we discuss in chapter 4, Chinese leaders are acutely aware that their effort to increase China's economic capacity, and thus its share of the global distribution of power, is intimately tied to its ability to maintain open access to economic globalization. In turn, they recognize that any broad-based challenge to U.S. security policy is dangerous because it places such access to economic globalization in jeopardy, in light of Washington's status as globalization's key actor—both politically and economically.

last half-century means that there are many more with at least some offensive military capability and occasionally significant defensive capability.[34] Each great power has to think about more (and, in some cases, more capable) states than did their predecessors in most previous international systems. The result is again to increase the significance of local security issues and decrease the salience of systemic balance.

The high relative salience of local security issues in today's unipolar system raises the opportunity costs of systemic balancing. In many cases, the capabilities needed to check U.S. power are ill suited for local security challenges. As we shall discuss in more detail in chapter 3, when states face trade-offs between purchasing capabilities that might constrain the United States as opposed to those more useful for dealing with more immediate local problems, most opt for the latter most of the time.

Even more important are the direct local security costs of systemic balancing. With great powers other than the United States clustered in and around Eurasia, efforts to produce systemic balance are likely to stoke local security dilemmas and generate compensating efforts by neighbors long before they materially reduce U.S. preponderance. Moreover, such efforts may have the perverse effect of pushing neighboring powers closer to the United States.

Assessing the China Challenge

China is widely viewed as the country with the greatest potential to challenge the United States and, therefore, the argument we have presented here. More than any other single indicator, estimates of China's GDP measured using purchasing power parity (PPP) have fueled this perception.[35] As figure 2.2 makes clear, the widely used World Bank PPP exchange rate produces an estimate of China's economic size that is double the market exchange rate (MER).

Which measure is right? One answer is that the choice matters less than may first appear. The key to national power, after all, is not size but size *and* wealth.[36] Aggregating a lot of poor people into one economy does not make it capable of generating power internationally. PPP estimates, for example, show that India had a much larger economy

---

[34] Numerical measures of this shift are presented in Wohlforth, "U.S. Strategy."

[35] Avery Goldstein, *Rising to the Challenge: China's Grand Strategy and International Security* (Stanford, Calif.: Stanford University Press, 2005), 72.

[36] Ashley J. Tellis, Janice Bially, Christopher Layne, and Melissa McPherson, *Measuring National Power in the Postindustrial Age* (Santa Monica, Calif.: RAND, 2003).

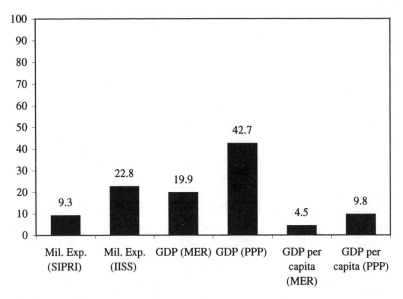

Figure 2.2. Military expenditures and GDP in China as a percentage of U.S. figures, 2006. *Sources*: SIPRI Military Expenditure Database; International Institute for Strategic Studies, *The Military Balance*, 2007; International Monetary Fund, World Economic Outlook Database, April 2007. World Bank, *2005 International Comparison Program, Preliminary Results* (December 2007). *Note*: Data for GDP PPP estimates are 2005; all other data 2006.

than Great Britain in the mid-–nineteenth century, obviously not a good measure of their relative capabilities.[37] Even by PPP estimates, the gap in per capita GDP remains massive, with China at $7,600 and the United States at $43,400 (see fig. 2.2).

The difference between estimates based on MER and PPP nevertheless remains important, for it affects expectations of the speed with which China might be capable of counterbalancing the United States. Using the PPP estimate as a baseline and extrapolating current growth rates into the future, many analysts project that the overall size of China's economy will rapidly approach that of the United States. Of course, such estimates ignore the many challenges that China faces, including the rapid aging of its population.[38] Even setting those reservations aside, these forecasts are based on unsound analysis.

[37] Angus Maddison, *Monitoring the World Economy* (Paris: Development Centre of the Organisation for Economic Co-operation and Development, 1995).

[38] See Susan L. Shirk, *China: Fragile Superpower* (New York: Oxford University Press, 2007).

PPP adjusts GDP figures to account for differences in relative prices, which are often acute between countries at different stages of development. Although the prices of many manufactured products tend to be equalized by international trade, the price of labor is not, and therefore labor-intensive products and services tend to be relatively cheap in poor countries. PPP corrects for this by using prices for a locally selected basket of goods to adjust the exchange rate for converting local currency into dollars. Economists agree that, properly applied, this method provides better estimates of comparative living standards. But forecasts of the future balance of power are not about living standards. They are about China's presence as a great power in international politics. As one analysis of China's military potential stresses, "From an external perspective, comparisons of GDP at market exchange rates are often the most useful. They better reflect the purchasing power of households and businesses on international markets. GDP at market exchange rates also provides a better check on borrowing capacity and the role of a country in international financial markets than does GDP at purchasing power parity exchange rates."[39]

No one knows how much to discount the PPP numbers for the purposes of comparing national power. What is certain, economist Albert Keidel notes, is that one should not "use projections of national accounting growth rates from a PPP base. This common practice seriously inflates estimates of China's future economic size—exaggerating the speed with which China's economy will overtake that of the U.S. in total size."[40] Projections must take into account the fact that growth will cause prices to converge with international norms and thus the PPP to converge with the market exchange rate. Adjusting for that convergence, Keidel estimates that it will take until 2050 for China's total economic size to equal the United States, and for per capita GDP in China to reach Spain's per capita GDP in 2000.[41]

In sum, while rapid economic growth makes China an increasingly important actor in world politics, it still has a long way to go before it can contest American dominance in all key measures of power. This

---

[39] Keith Crane, Roger Cliff, Evan S. Medeiros, James C. Mulvenon, and William H. Overholt, *Modernizing China's Military: Opportunities and Constraints* (Santa Monica, Calif.: RAND, 2005), 16.

[40] See the discussion in Albert Keidel, "Prospects for Continued High Economic Growth in China," Carnegie Endowment for International Peace, PSRI international Forum on China's Development, November 10–11, 2004.

[41] Ibid., 6–8.

conclusion is confirmed by China's behavior and the assessments of its leadership. None of China's external alignments can be considered counterbalancing. The only other major power with which China has concluded formal partnership agreements is Russia. As we discuss in detail in chapter 3, the Sino-Russian strategic partnership is propelled primarily by economics and regional security interests and is not well explained as a counterbalancing alignment. Neither Chinese nor Russian officials, nor experts on the two countries' foreign policies, describe the partnership in such terms.

Some scholars do describe China's growing military expenditures as counterbalancing.[42] But it is only possible to reach this conclusion if balancing is defined so expansively as to include any effort by any state to enhance its military capacity.[43] There is no doubt that China is improving its military, and little doubt that it will continue to do so, at least until competing demands on the state budget determine otherwise. After all, the People's Liberation Army starts from a primitive technological and organizational base.[44] Any military leadership would want to upgrade that force.

China's military expenditures are a small fraction of the American commitment, and this ratio is not sensitive to the means of estimating it (see fig. 2.2). With a rapidly growing economy, China can afford to spend more on defense. The result of such expenditures over time may be new challenges for U.S. military operations in what Barry Posen calls the "contested zones" in or near China.[45] The extent of these challenges depends on what the United States, Japan, Taiwan, and others do in response to China's efforts. But the main point is that China's current level of effort is nowhere near adequate to constitute counterbalancing—that is, to affect the United States' overall military primacy and its command of the commons.

With a smaller and much less advanced economy and a comparatively antiquated and inefficient military force, China cannot affect the overall military gap vis-à-vis the United States unless it is able to devote a substantially greater proportion of its comparatively smaller economic resources to defense than does the United States. Compared to China, the United States has and will long have a dramatic relative

[42] See, e.g., Layne, *The Peace of Illusions*; and Art, "Striking the Balance," 178–80.

[43] See Brooks and Wohlforth, "Striking the Balance," 186–91.

[44] Crane et. al., *Modernizing China's Military*.

[45] Posen, "Command of the Commons"; Thomas J. Christensen, "Posing Problems without Catching Up," *International Security* 25 (2001).

advantage in its ability to convert wealth to military power because of its massive investment over decades in the accumulation of the skills and infrastructure necessary to produce and use advanced weaponry.[46] Yet China consistently devotes a *smaller* proportion of its GDP to defense than the United States does. Again, this conclusion is not sensitive to the measure used (see table 2.1). Given that China is not even working as hard as the United States at generating military power, we cannot describe its behavior as counterbalancing.

Why isn't China counterbalancing U.S. power? According to experts on Chinese foreign and defense policy, its reasons are exactly those our argument predicts. Avery Goldstein concludes that China shifted in the mid-1990s toward its current grand strategy—the key element of which involves avoiding any direct challenge to the United States— precisely "because it recognizes just how weak it is relative to the U.S. and its allies. As such, China's strategy reflects its attempt to play a weak hand well. The U.S., by contrast, holds most of the high cards." As he stresses, after the mid-1990s there was a clear recognition in China that

> contrary to the belief when the Cold War ended, the world was not quickly going to become multipolar. Instead, unipolarity would last for decades, with the U.S. remaining the world's sole superpower. . . . Although China's economic and military capabilities were growing as a result of the reform program in place since 1979, it still lagged far behind the world's leading states, especially the U.S. Perhaps most significantly, China's leaders . . . more clearly recognized just how far they had to go before their armed forces were in the same league as those of the U.S. and its allies.[47]

[46] For further discussion, see Stephen Brooks, *Producing Security: Multinational Corporations, Globalization, and the Changing Calculus of Conflict* (Princeton: Princeton University Press, 2005), 237–39.

[47] Avery Goldstein, "China's Grand Strategy and U.S. Foreign Policy," Foreign Policy Research Institute, November 27, 2005; available at www.fpri.org. See the related analysis in Goldstein, *Rising to the Challenge*. Peter Gries's review of recent Chinese analysts writings on the United States reaches the exact same finding as Goldstein: "While many Chinese have convinced themselves that U.S. power predominance cannot last, they do grudgingly acknowledge the world's current unipolar nature. This view represents a dramatic shift from the early 1990s, when many Chinese held out hope for a multipolar international system. . . . While some elements of resistance remain, Chinese strategy today has largely shifted away from balancing and towards bandwagoning." See "China Eyes the Hegemon," *Orbis* 49 (2005): 406. Reported Chinese government assessments of overall economic, military, technological, scientific, and other elements of power (what Chinese analysts call "comprehensive national power") are consistent with the analysis

China's experience of unipolarity's first decade—an experience that led its leaders to reorient their foreign policy toward a peaceful rise—exemplifies the importance of the high expected general and opportunity costs of balancing under unipolarity. As Goldstein underscores, Chinese leaders recognized that

[e]ven though China remained economically and militarily outclassed in the first half of the 1990s, its growing capabilities had already begun to prompt others to debate "China's rise" and led some to react in ways that could damage China's interests. In the U.S., there was new talk about a "China threat" and what might have to be done about it. Among China's immediate neighbors, especially those in Southeast Asia, there was new concern about China's assertive posture towards resolving maritime and territorial disputes, and some wondered what this might portend about the role an even more powerful China would play in coming decades. Against this background, China's leaders were alarmed by Washington's efforts in the mid-1990s to update its Cold War–vintage alliances with Australia and Japan, as well as enhanced U.S. military cooperation with the nations of Southeast Asia—trends that Beijing worried might be the beginnings of an American-led regional effort to contain China.[48]

Summary and Net Assessment

We have argued that the larger, more comprehensive, and more entrenched the hegemon's lead, the more formidable the collective action and coordination barriers to balancing, and the higher the likely domestic, autonomy, and opportunity costs of pursuing this strategy. Given the current distribution of capabilities, we would thus not expect the counterbalancing constraint to be operative. The contours of China's behavior on the international scene—no counterbalancing, a peaceful rise, avoiding the focused enmity of the United States—are consistent with our argument. The consensus view of experts on China's foreign relations is that the strategic reasoning behind this behavior is also exactly as our argument would expect. And, of course, none

---

presented here. See the discussion in Robert J. Art, *A Grand Strategy for America* (Ithaca, N.Y.: Cornell University Press, 2003), 243–44.

[48] Testimony of Avery Goldstein before the U.S.-China Economic and Security Review Commission, July 21, 2005, available at http://www.uscc.gov/hearings/2005hearings/hr05_07_21_22.php (consulted September 19, 2007).

45

of the other major powers is trying to counterbalance U.S. power. But then, by historical standards the United States is not working very hard to keep its lead. And the core findings about the size and comprehensiveness of the U.S. lead apply to both extant and, as best as it can be measured, latent power. Hence, prospective counterbalancers can be far more certain of the likely cost and ultimate outcome of a concerted effort to rein in U.S. power than any of their counterparts over the last three centuries.

To assess realist balance-of-power theory on its most favorable possible terms, we remained as close as possible to the basic logic of the theory. Although our argument in this chapter "structural" in that it derives causal effects from the distribution of capabilities, it departs from standard interpretations of neorealism in two respects. First, we conceptualize power broadly, to include geography, technology, the distinction between latent and manifest power, commensurability (the degree to which the leading state leads in all key elements of power), and other elements of state capability. Although these aspects of the distribution of capabilities appear in a great many applications of balance-of-power theory and realism more generally, Kenneth Waltz excluded all of them from *Theory of International Politics*. The inclusiveness of one's concept of power is a measurement issue, not a theoretical one. With the right measures, a much broader conception of power and, hence, of structure can be employed that nonetheless treats power as a resource states use to pursue their ends.

Second, as we have stressed throughout this chapter, our approach to structural explanation is probabilisitic, not deterministic. We treat the distribution of power as a variable that makes certain kinds of outcomes highly likely or unlikely rather than inevitable or impossible.[49] By contrast, the approach to structural explanation that flows from Waltz's theory, at least in the eyes of its critics, must be deterministic. That is, even if structural effects are subtle and operate over the long run, they must follow inexorably from structure. For years, scholars have contended that merely showing that the behavioral patterns Waltz sought to explain do not flow deterministically from the distribution of power is fatal to the theory. Formal modelers are unable to derive from the premises of Waltz's theory (anarchy, the distribution

---

[49] Elsewhere we have outlined the theoretical difference between analyzing "material" variables in a probabilistic versus a deterministic manner. See Stephen G. Brooks and William C. Wohlforth, "New versus Old Thinking in Qualitative Research," *International Security* 26 (2002).

of power, and the assumed preference for unit survival) an equilibrium prediction of any of the structural effects he identifies without adding additional specifications of actors' preferences.[50] Constructivists similarly argue that the behavioral consequences Waltz derived from his simple structural theory actually depend on further unstated assumptions about states' identities.[51]

In keeping with this established scholarly tradition of critiquing Waltz, a common response to our argument is thus that counterbalancing the United States is not ruled out by unipolarity.[52] It *could* happen. If China, Russia, and the EU formed an all-Eurasia alliance against the United States, if the EU abolished the sovereignty of its constituent 27 governments and instituted a superstate and a military buildup, if China were to continue growing at 12 percent annually yet also extract 20 percent of GDP for the military, balance might be restored to the world. These objections reinforce rather than undermine our argument. For us, the question is not whether certain outcomes are impossible or inevitable, but rather how unipolarity influences their likelihood.

Because debates about Waltz's particular approach to modeling the effects of power distributions cast such a long shadow, we must be very clear about where our argument fits in. Existing treatments of unipolarity that employ a strict "power as resources" approach are mapped out on table 2.4.[53] The prediction advanced by Waltz and by Layne that unipolarity inevitably begets balancing falls in the northwesternmost, deterministic/narrow box. Wohlforth's initial explanation for the absence of counterbalancing under unipolarity is similarly framed deterministically, but it relies on a definition of power that includes geography and so belongs in the northeastern box. In this book,

---

[50] See, e.g., Robert Powell, *In the Shadow of Power: States and Strategies in International Politics* (Princeton: Princeton University Press, 1999); R. Harrison Wagner, "Bargaining and War, *American Journal of Political Science* 44 (2000).

[51] Wendt, *Social Theory.*

[52] See, e.g., Kier Lieber and Gerard Alexander, "Waiting for Balancing: Why the World Is Not Pushing Back," *International Security* 30 (2005).

[53] The table is embarrassingly self-referential because for the purposes of this discussion we have excluded treatments that include non-"material" elements such as threat perceptions and domestic institutions in their explanatory scheme. See, e.g., Walt, "World Off-Balance"; and Michael Mastanduno, "Preserving the Unipolar Moment: Realist Theories and U.S. Grand Strategy after the Cold War," in *Unipolar Politics: Realism and State Strategies after the Cold War,* ed. Ethan B. Kapstein and Michael Mastanduno (New York: Columbia University Press, 1999).

Table 2.4
Approaches to Unipolarity

	Measurement of power	
Explanatory style	Narrow	Broad
Determinism	Counterbalancing (Waltz 2000; Layne 1993; 2006)	No counterbalancing (Wohlforth 1999; 2002)
Probabilism		Counterbalancing highly improbable (Brooks and Wohlforth 2002; 2008).

Note: Studies referred to are Kenneth N. Waltz, "Structural realism after the Cold War," *International Security* 25 (2000); Christopher Layne, "The Unipolar Illusion: Why New great Powers Will Arise," *International Security* 14 (1993), and The Peace of Illusions: American Grand Strategy from 1940 to the Present (Ithaca, N.Y.: Cornell University Press, 2006); Stephen G. Brooks and William C. Wohlforth, "American Primacy in Perspective," *Foreign Affairs* 81 (2002).

we strictly employ the probabilistic approach, as we did in an earlier collaborative article.[54]

Attempts to check the leading state's power, in sum, are theoretically possible in any international system. But behavior that is possible may be patently self-defeating and hence highly improbable. Even if we examine only causal factors that are featured in balance-of-power theory itself, it is clear that counterbalancing is highly improbable today. The plain fact is that balance-of-power theorists never contemplated a unipolar system. Applying the theory to such a system essentially reverses its implications for constraints on the leading state. The balancing constraint may well work on the leading state up to a threshold of hegemony or unipolarity.[55] Once a state passes this threshold, however, the causal arrows reverse: the stronger the leading state is and the more entrenched its dominance, the more improbable and thus less constraining counterbalancing dynamics are.

Why the Absence of Counterbalancing Matters

Realists will perceive important stakes in the contest between our power-based explanation for the absence of counterbalancing under

[54] See Brooks and Wohlforth, "American Primacy in Perspective," esp. 24–25, 27, 30.

[55] The "unipolar threshold" is discussed further in Wohlforth, "U.S. Strategy"; it is applied in eight different international systems in Kaufman, Little, and Wohlforth, *Balance of Power*.

unipolarity and the conventional balance-of-power wisdom. But others may well doubt that counterhegemonic balancing has any relevance to a world in which economic globalization, nuclear deterrence among most major powers, the spread of democracy, changing collective ideas, international institutions, and other factors work together to reduce the probability of major war among great powers to a historically low level. As Robert Jervis argues, because these factors produce something of a security community among the major powers (China and Russia are important partial exceptions, in his view), the question of how they constrain the United States "will not map on the classical form of the balance of power because this phenomenon was driven by the fear of war, and the ultimate sanction against a hegemon was the use of force. The other members of the Community do have reason to fear the United States, but not invasion from it, and they may want to oppose it, but force is not among the relevant tools."[56]

If counterbalancing is driven only by the fear of invasion and loss of sovereign statehood at the hands of the hegemon, then even the strictest realist might doubt its relevance to states with secure second-strike capability. By realist lights, nuclear deterrence should be credible concerning states' commitments to preserve their core territorial security. Why then do so many realists and other analysts continue to assume that counterbalancing remains relevant today? The answer is that in practice most realist scholars assume—but do not, in general, explicitly state—that states balance against nonexistential security threats.

According to the theory, balancing to prevent hegemony is not an end in itself but a means to security and autonomy. Kenneth Waltz contends that "balancing is a strategy for survival, a way of attempting to maintain a state's autonomous way of life."[57] If balancing is only a strategy for survival, then it applies only to concentrations of power that might threaten the survival of other great powers. If it also concerns autonomy, then it can be expected to occur in response to concentrations of power that fall well short of the capability to conquer the other great powers. Waltz appears to equate the two, implying that balancing for autonomy is synonymous with balancing for survival.

This kind of ambiguity is typical of balance-of-power theorists, who frequently claim that the theory is driven by the assumption that states maximize their security and yet define hegemony as a concentration

[56] Robert Jervis, *American Foreign Policy in a New Era* (London: Routledge, 2005), 31.
[57] Waltz, "Structural Realism," 64.

of power that would put one state in a position to "dominate" or "lay down the law to"—rather than simply "conquer"—the other great powers. Although in past eras it may not have been necessary to make a distinction between survival and autonomy as motivations, it is necessary today. Most theoreticians appear to employ a broader definition of security that encompasses autonomy and other interests. From their comprehensive survey of balance-of-power theory, for example, Levy and Thompson derive the proposition that it predicts counterbalancing against "concentrations of power that would put one state in a position to dominate over the rest."[58] Most theoretical writings over the last three centuries appear to define hegemony as a concentration of power that threatens not just other great powers' "core security"—that is, their prospects for survival as sovereign territorial units—but also and much more immediately their capacity autonomously to resolve less existentially important "secondary security" issues, and even preferences not directly related to security, such as prestige or status. While they are not always as explicit about it as they could be, the analysts who employ balance-of-power theory to contemporary international politics are being consistent with this practice.[59]

This discussion helps to explain why so many analysts and practitioners think counterbalancing is potentially such a powerful constraint on the United States, and why they believe it continues to matter in a world where the threat of great power wars for survival is extremely low. But there are analysts who insist that counterbalancing only applies when the survival of great powers is at stake. They may well doubt the importance of our finding that balancing is so improbable because it is so costly. For some, the question is this: Do states actually balance against hegemonic threats to security interests other than simple survival? At stake is whether there are empirical grounds for concluding that states such as Russia and China would try to balance the United States today if it were not so prohibitively costly.

The subsections that follow review historical evidence from the multi- and bipolar eras in order to address this question. We show, first, that counterbalancing constrained even a major power that presented a comparatively low probability threat to the core security of its peers: Great Britain during its heyday in the international system. Second, we examine the most instructive case of all, the latter Cold

---

[58] See Levy and Thompson, "Hegemonic Threats," for relevant citations and analysis.

[59] Especially clear about this is Josef Joffe. See *Überpower: The Imperial Temptation of America* (New York: Norton, 2006).

War, when nuclear deterrence rendered core security threats more unlikely than in any earlier period.

Counterbalancing an "Offshore Power": The British Case

IR scholarship portrays Britain as a hegemon and as a balancer, but rarely as a victim of counterbalancing itself. In fact, as figure 2.1 shows, Britain never held a position of primacy remotely resembling that of the United States in the Cold War, to say nothing of unipolarity.[60] Given its comparatively modest power potential, offshore location, and relatively limited commitment to land power, Britain arguably presented a less direct threat to the core security of other major powers than did such continental behemoths as France, Russia, and Germany. Nevertheless, for most of its career at the top of the international heap, powerful rivals proved willing and able to impose tight counterbalancing constraints on London's freedom of action. And they frequently did so to counter British threats to their status, imperial interests, or general autonomy rather than to their core security.

France and Russia exemplify different manifestations of this constraint. Throughout the eighteenth century, France was always within plausible reach of naval power commensurate with Britain's. All it would take was a few years of successful domestic reform and improved finances, or the reduction of continental constraints on French power, for Paris to be in a position to reconstitute a fleet and constrain Britain's growing global empire.[61] France quickly ramped up naval power and challenged Britain in the periphery on three noteworthy occasions: in 1754–63, when a series of French efforts to contain and roll back recent British gains in all three regions of the empire—the Caribbean, North America, and India—culminated in the Seven Years' War; again in 1776–84, when France intervened decisively on the side of rebellious American colonists, blockaded Gibraltar, and sent a naval squadron and troops to aid the Indian states of Maratha and Mysore against the Raj; and yet again in 1798–1801, when Napoleon invaded

---

[60] See, for a comprehensive analysis, Patrick Karl O'Brien and Armand Clesse, eds., *Two Hegemonies: Britain, 1846–1914, and the United States, 1941–2001* (Burlington, Vt.: Ashgate, 2002). O'Brien summarizes the book's implications: The idea of British hegemony is a "myth": the United States is "the sole example of geopolitical hegemony since the fall of Rome."

[61] Paul M. Kennedy, *The Rise and Fall of British Naval Mastery* (London: Macmillan, 1983).

Egypt to carry the rivalry with Britain out to the empire.[62] In each case, Britain ultimately emerged with most of its possessions intact (the United States being an important exception), but the aggregate effect in London was powerful, as British ministers were constantly compelled to frame policy with a view toward potential French-inspired military constraints throughout the empire.[63]

And after the defeat of France in 1815, Russia stepped into the breach as a new hegemonic rival with the means and motive to contest British positions in the periphery.[64] To be sure, constraining Britain in the periphery was hard for Russia. How does an elephant strike a whale? The only route was via expansion in Asia, which drove the celebrated Anglo-Russian "great game" in the nineteenth century. British leaders assumed that they could not bear the governance costs of sustaining their empire if the local populations became truly rebellious. If Russian power advanced close enough to the frontiers of empire to communicate with and aid potentially rebellious locals, a tipping point could quickly be reached that would make Britain's entire position in Asia untenable. Hence, St. Petersburg possessed potent if unwieldy means to constrain Britain in Asia.

The counterbalancing constraint operated in the core as well. Throughout the first half of the eighteenth century, Britain and France shared leadership in western Europe first as allies and later as rivals. Both arrangements exercised a powerful constraint on Britain's options on the Continent. London operated under the assumption that it had to rein in demands on a range of European issues lest the French turn again toward direct struggle with Britain.[65] Similarly, Britain's victory

---

[62] On each of these episodes, see, inter alia, Jeremy Black, *Eighteenth Century Britain, 1688–1783* (London: Palgrave, 2001), chap. 15; Karl Schweitzer, "The Seven Years' War: A System Perspective," in *The Origins of War in Early Modern Europe*, ed. Jeremy Black (Edinburgh: John Donald, 1987); and Edward Ingram, *Commitment to Empire: Prophecies of the Great Game in Asia, 1797–1800* (Oxford: Clarendon Press, 1981).

[63] See Paul W. Schroeder, *The Transformation of European Politics* (London: Oxford University Press, 1993); Jeremy Black, "Enduring Rivalries: Britain and France," in *Great Power Rivalries*, ed. William R. Thompson (Columbia: University of South Carolina Press, 1999); and Jeremy Black, *Natural and Necessary Enemies: Anglo-French Relations in the Eighteenth Century* (Athens: University of Georgia Press, 1986).

[64] See, especially, Malcolm Yapp, *Strategies of British India: Britain, Iran, and Afghanistan, 1798–1850* (Oxford: Clarendon Press, 1980); and David Gillard, *The Struggle for Asia, 1828–1914: A Study in British and Russian Imperialism* (London: Methuen, 1977).

[65] Historians debate whether Britain had other options, with some arguing that wily Parisian diplomacy played the key role in "transferring control of European diplomacy from Britain to France," while others hold that "British policy was in tune with national resources." The key is that the operational assessment in London was that policy was

over Napoleon in 1814 also showcased Russia's unsurpassed military capabilities. Britain and Russia consequently shared leadership in Europe, while contesting it elsewhere.[66] The net effect was that Britain was strongly constrained in Europe, where concern over potential counterbalancing demanded deference to Russia's strategic priorities in key areas.[67] As in the case of Britain's co-leadership with France a century before, this outwardly amicable relationship came with substantial constraints on British action. The alternative to deferring to St. Petersburg might result in that empire's formidable firepower being arrayed directly against British continental interests.

In the twentieth century, finally, a new powerhouse rival stepped in: Germany. Although German strategists often framed their desire to counterbalance Britain—in the social Darwinist language of the day—as a struggle for survival, historians overwhelmingly assign far greater weight to the craving for status and autonomy.[68] To attain a "place in the sun" alongside (or in place of) Britain, the German leadership, having already surpassed Britain's industrial and military power, fatefully chose to mount a full-scale challenge to its naval primacy.[69]

The bottom line is that even though Britain's offshore location, modest investments in land power, and comparatively modest power potential reduced its salience as a threat to the core security of other great powers, it nonetheless periodically faced a counterbalancing constraint that restricted its freedom of action for most of its two centuries as a leading power. Indeed, much of the evidence for the significance of this constraint comes not from what other powers actually did but from what British leaders chose not to do. Britain, after all, is the realists' main example of a leading state that wisely restrained itself in the

---

strongly constrained by potential rivalry with France. See the discussion in Black, *Natural and Necessary Enemies*, chap. 1.

[66] Schroeder, *Transformation of European Politics* and his *Austria, Britain, and the Crimean War: The Destruction of the European Concert* (Ithaca, N.Y.: Cornell University Press, 1972); Schroeder, "The 19th Century International System: Changes in the Structure," *World Politics* 39 (1986) Schroeder, "Did the Vienna Settlement Rest on a Balance of Power?" *American Historical Review* 97 (1992); and Richard Elrod, "The Concert of Europe: A Fresh Look at an International System," *World Politics* 28 (1976).

[67] See Schroeder, *Transformation of European Politics* for examples.

[68] As Layne puts it, "German leaders were concerned that unless Germany developed countervailing power, its independence and interests in international politics would be circumscribed by Britain." Layne, "The Unipolar Illusion," 123. See, e.g., Paul M. Kennedy, *The Rise of the Anglo-German Antagonism, 1860–1914* (Boston: G. Allen and Unwin, 1980).

[69] Ivo Lambi, *The Navy and German Power Politics, 1862–1914* (Boston: G. Allen and Unwin, 1984).

face of temptation precisely in order to avoid exacerbating the counter-balancing constraint.[70] London frequently deferred to potent rivals—a penchant that came to be called the "tradition of appeasement" in British foreign policy.[71]

The Latter Cold War

We have shown how counterbalancing worked in the untypical case of an offshore naval power, Britain. Although counterbalancing is far from an iron law, it nevertheless amounted to a very important constraint on British security policy. The evidence from this case suggests that when it is feasible at acceptable cost, states will engage in counterbalancing even when the problem of concentrated power does not present direct and plausible threats to core security. In other words, states that can be relatively optimistic about their core security will nonetheless face incentives to balance to protect secondary security and nonsecurity interests, and are also more likely to pursue counterbalancing when it does not cost too much. But ambiguity persists, because, prior to the advent of nuclear deterrence, it was usually possible to connect indirectly the pursuit of autonomy, status, or other secondary objectives with the "ultimate" goal of state survival. If power concentrated in the hands of one state threatened other states' autonomous capacity to resolve secondary or local security issues today, the argument went, perhaps it could affect their very survival in the distant future.

The latter Cold War, therefore, is an important case. Like Britain and Russia in the nineteenth century, the two superpowers were relatively secure against each other's conventional forces. With the acquisition of secure second-strike capabilities by the 1960s, however, the nuclear argument for insecurity could be turned on its head into a powerful argument for ultimate security. Thus, the core security imperative for balancing greatly weakened as the Cold War matured.[72] Yet, in the "new

---

[70] See, for example, Layne, "From Preponderance to Offshore Balancing."

[71] Paul M. Kennedy, *Strategy and Diplomacy, 1870–1945: Eight Studies* (London: G. Allen and Unwin, 1983); Britain's pre-1914 attempt to maintain détente with imperial Germany is an important case in point. See Sean M. Lynn-Jones, "Détente and Deterrence: Anglo-German Relations, 1911–1914," in *Military Strategy and the Origins of the First World War*, ed. Steven E. Miller, Sean M. Lynn-Jones, and Stephen Van Evera (Cambridge: MIT Press, 1991).

[72] This contention is reflected in the contemporary scholarly literature. A majority of scholars writing in the latter Cold War era assumed that security imperatives worked for

Cold War" of the late 1970s and early 1980s, the two superpowers proved willing to expend tremendous resources to counterbalance each other. This effort is particularly striking for Soviets, who devoted up to a third of their economic output to the generation of military power.[73] Why these frantic efforts to counterbalance U.S. capabilities even when the USSR's core security was safe under the umbrella of some 10,000 deliverable warheads? The historical literature focuses on two intertwined motivations, neither related to the Soviet Union's core security: ideology and status.[74] The importance of formal superpower parity for the Soviets showed up in numerous diplomatic exchanges under Khrushchev, but its relative significance in generating constraints is clearest under Brezhnev. American decision-makers perceived this clearly, even as they negotiated the détente-era agreements that formalized superpower parity. Subsequent memoir evidence backs up this impression.[75] Thus, it was clear that détente and status were linked. What was not clear was how the formal parity enshrined in détente was to be reconciled with continued real status inequality between the two principals.

Part of the problem was that Moscow remained a one-dimensional superpower whose claim to parity was based mainly on military

cooperation; and hence that competitive behavior had to be explained by other factors. Security-centric neorealists themselves explained most of the superpowers' competitive expansionism after 1960 as a result of domestic politics or ideology. See, e.g., Stephen M. Walt, "The Case for Finite Containment: Analyzing U.S. Grand Strategy," *International Security* 14 (1989); and Barry Posen and Stephen Van Evera, "Defense Policy of the Reagan Administration: Departure from Containment," in *Conventional Forces and American Defense Policy,* ed. Steven Miller (Princeton: Princeton University Press, 1986). In addition, many analysts viewed the latter Cold War as a weak two-power concert, threatened intermittently by ideology and domestic impulses. See, e.g., Roger E. Kanet and Edward A. Kolodziej, eds., *The Cold War as Cooperation* (London: Macmillan, 1991); and Allen Lynch, *The Cold War Is Over—Again* (Boulder, Colo. Westview, 1992).

[73] For a review of key treatments and new evidence, see Mark Harrison, "How Much Did the Soviets Really Spend on Defence? New Evidence from the Close of the Brezhnev Era," Warwick Economic Research Papers No. 662, University of Warwick, January 2003.

[74] See Odd Arne Westad, *The Global Cold War* (Cambridge: Cambridge University Press, 2005); and, for an earlier treatment, William C. Wohlforth, *Elusive Balance: Power and Perceptions during the Cold War* (Ithaca, N.Y.: Cornell University Press, 1993), chaps. 5–8. Primary evidence is presented in the various publications of the Carter-Brezhnev project, discussed below.

[75] For contemporary evidence and U.S. perceptions, see Wohlforth, *Elusive Balance,* chap. 7. Memoirs that attest to the importance of "equality and equal security" include G. M. Kornienko, *Kholodnaia voina—svidetel'svto ee uchastnika* (Moscow: Mezhdundarodnye otnosheniia, 1994); Georgy Arbatov, *The System: An Insider's Life in Soviet Politics* (New York: Times Books, 1993); and Anatoly Dobrynin, *In Confidence* (New York: Random House, 1995).

power. Matching the United States in overall wealth or technological prowess was out of the question, but there was one area where the Soviets were somewhat competitive: the Third World. Given Soviet ideology and ongoing revolutionary turmoil in the Third World, checking the United States in that area was a plausible option—though it did run the risk of eliciting a forceful U.S. response. This is exactly what happened in the sequence of events that destroyed détente and set in motion the last round of the Cold War.

Neither the available documents nor the recollections of Brezhnev's aides paint a picture of a leadership taking on the United States for world primacy.[76] Instead, they reveal all the classic signs of "status dissonance"; that is, dissatisfaction with an inferior position brought about by the attainment of parity in some important dimension but not others. The issue was a modest enhancement in Moscow's position, made possible by a fortuitous combination of opportunity and means. Brezhnev and his aides sought to translate the détente-era declarations of parity and equality into reality by emulating the status-superior power. Even as they remained firmly committed to maintaining comprehensive military parity with the United States, they also built a blue water navy and sought to compete for influence outside traditional Soviet spheres of influence.

Soviet success in containing and even (in the short term) rolling back U.S. power in Vietnam contributed to a sense of optimism that the feat could be repeated elsewhere.[77] This was the context for a series of Soviet moves in Africa, Europe, Southeast Asia, and eventually Central Asia. The selection of targets for expanded Soviet presence was affected by ideology and events on the ground—generally the coming

[76] Most responsible for this finding is the Carter-Brezhnev Project, sponsored by the Center for Foreign Policy Development, at the Thomas J. Watson Jr. Institute for International Studies, Brown University; the National Security Archive; and the Cold War International History Project, which declassified scores of important documents, and organized a series of critical oral history conferences. A key publication of the Project is Odd Arne Westad, ed., *The Fall of Détente: Soviet-American Relations in the Carter Years* (Oslo: Scandinavian University Press, 1997). Westad's summary of the new evidence on the Horn conflict is typical: "The main foreign policy aim for Soviet involvement in Africa was to score a series of inexpensive victories in what was perceived as a global contest with Washington for influence and positions in the Third World." "Moscow and the Angolan Crisis, 1974–76: A New Pattern of Intervention," Cold War International History Project, *Bulletin* 8–9 (1996–97): 21.

[77] Ilya V. Gaiduk, *Confronting Vietnam: Soviet Policy toward the Indochina Conflict, 1954–1963* (Washington, D.C.: Woodrow Wilson Center Press, 2003); and Gaiduk, *The Soviet Union and the Vietnam War* (Chicago: I. R. Dee, 1996).

to power of Marxist-Leninist parties in the wake of the last round of decolonization—but the larger aim was to increase the Soviet Union's general presence and influence globally, provide a counterweight to what was still seen to be a superior U.S. global position, and to contribute to the acquisition of a full superpower's portfolio. Though important, intervention in the developing world was only a small part (measured in terms of resources) of Moscow's counterbalancing effort. Arguably more important (and certainly more expensive) was the Soviet Union's comprehensive drive to maintain overall military parity with the United States.[78]

The problem was that against the backdrop of the Soviet Union's massive military programs, the new moves in the Third World had the effect of slowly shifting the Carter cabinet in favor of National Security Adviser Brzezinski's hawkish view of a "Soviet thrust toward global preeminence."[79] The result was a dramatic intensification of the Cold War rivalry, as each side proved willing to allow the contest over prestige to infuse the central strategic relationship. In short, each superpower was willing to accept the acknowledged costs and risks of renewed competition in order to balance the other, even though each could rely on a robust nuclear deterrence for its core security. Because each possessed sufficient power to make the costs of counterbalancing bearable, each was willing to undertake it.

The last round of the Cold War was extremely expensive. The two superpowers expended enormous resources to contain each other. Talk in the 1980s of American decline was inflated, but it had a basis in reality: the United States was seeking to contain and intimidate—and it was itself being contained by—what appeared to be a formidably capable superpower. And what drove the two sides to absorb such costs were issues divorced in important ways from either state's core security concerns.

In sum, two leading states that presented comparatively low-probability threats to the existential security of other great powers nonetheless faced counterbalancing constraints. This lends credence to the counterfactual argument that even a nuclear-armed China or Russia

---

[78] For a comprehensive assessment, see Carmel Davis, "Power vs. Threat: Explanations of U.S. Balancing against the Soviet Union after 1976," Ph.D. diss., Department of Political Science, University of Pennsylvania, 2004.

[79] Zbigniew Brzezinski, *Power and Principle* (New York: Farrar, Straus and Giroux, 1983), 148.

would counterbalance the United States if it had the material wherewithal to do so.

Conclusion

The counterbalancing constraint is less likely to emerge than at any
time since the modern international system took shape in the seventeenth century. Were it not so prohibitively costly, other great powers
likely would seek to balance U.S. power. To gauge the significance of
this conclusion, imagine what U.S. security policy over the past 15
years would have been like in a world with the counterbalancing constraint. In contemplating the use of force to pursue its objectives—as
in the 2001 invasion of Afghanistan or the 1991 Persian Gulf War—
American policymakers would have had to factor in the prospect of
military intervention by another great power, either before or after the
deployment of U.S. military power.

The Cold War experience provides a clear indication of the difference the absence of this constraint made in both 1991 and 2001. In the
1991 Gulf War, U.S. freedom of action was greatly enhanced by the
Soviet Union's economic freefall in the years preceding the conflict,
which meant that it was not in a position to support Iraq despite having a friendship treaty with it. By comparison, the potential for direct
or indirect Soviet intervention was a significant constraint on the use
of American force in the Middle East following 1973 oil embargo.[80] As
for Afghanistan, it became a graveyard for Soviet forces in the late
1980s in significant part because the United States provided substantial
backing to the military opposition to Soviet rule. The 2001 U.S. invasion of Afghanistan would have been much more problematic if Russia
had decided to return the favor by helping the Taliban; not only did
Russia fail to do so, but it actually provided crucial assistance to U.S.
forces by sharing intelligence and also by facilitating the creation of
new American bases in the region.

---

[80] To be clear, the Soviets did not actively engage in efforts to constrain U.S. policy in
this instance. However, U.S. policymakers did consider the use of force in the Middle
East in 1973 but decided that it would be impractical and dangerous in part due to fears
about how the Soviets would respond. See the discussion of recently released British
documents on this issue in Glenn Frankel, "U.S. Mulled Seizing Oil Fields In '73," *Washington Post*, January 1, 2004, available at http://www.washingtonpost.com/ac2/
wp-dyn/A46321–2003Dec31 (consulted September 19, 2007).

The same basic pattern holds for all of the recent cases where Washington has used or threatened force, including the 2003 invasion of Iraq and the interventions in the Balkans and Kosovo in the mid-1990s. In all of these cases, U.S. policy would have been greatly complicated, to say the least, had it faced the prospect of opposition from another great power, or group of such powers, capable of using military capabilities to constrain it.

Realism, Balance-of-Threat Theory, and the "Soft Balancing" Constraint

CHAPTER 2 SHOWED THAT UNDER unipolarity, counterbalancing is too costly to arise as a systemic constraint on the United States.[1] Many analysts believe that the dynamics of countervailing power are still present, but operate at a lower, less comprehensive level than in the typical conception of balancing. *Soft balancing* is the term that has emerged to describe this new form of balancing, which is contrasted with traditional "hard" counterbalancing. T. V. Paul's analysis is emblematic of the more general argument:

> Traditional balance of power theory . . . fails to explain state behavior in the post–Cold War era. . . . Major powers such as China, Russia, France, Germany, India, and Russia have not responded with significant increases in their defense spending. Nor have they formed military coalitions to countervail U.S. power, as traditional balance of power theory would expect. . . . Hard balancing no longer has an appeal for second-tier powers because they do not believe, as least as of now, that the United States is a threat to their sovereign existence. They are, however, worried about the unilateralism and interventionist tendencies in U.S. foreign policy, especially since September 11, 2001, and they have resorted to less threatening soft-balancing measures to achieve their objective of constraining the power of the United States without unnecessarily provoking retribution. Thus, if balancing implies restraining the power and threatening behavior of the hegemonic actor, strategies other than military buildups and alliance formation should be included.[2]

---

[1] The case material in this chapter is adapted from Stephen G. Brooks and William C. Wohlforth, "Hard Times for Soft Balancing," *International Security* 30 (2005).

[2] T. V. Paul, "Soft Balancing in the Age of U.S. Primacy," *International Security* 30 (2005): 52–53, 71. Elsewhere, Paul emphasizes that "soft balancing involves tacit balancing short of formal alliances. It occurs when states generally develop ententes or limited security understandings with one another to balance a potentially threatening state or a rising power. Soft balancing is often based on a limited arms buildup, ad hoc cooperative exercises, or collaboration in regional or international institutions." "The Enduring Axioms of Balance of Power Theory," in *Balance of Power Revisited: Theory and Practice in*

Lower-level efforts at balancing by great powers have emerged as the systemic constraint most frequently cited in scholarly discussions of American foreign policy. This idea of soft balancing seems so plausible and has achieved such salience in large part because it is rooted in balance-of-threat theory—a second important realist approach that, according to many scholars, has more explanatory power than traditional balance-of-power theory.[3]

As its name suggests, balance-of-threat theory predicts that states will balance against threats; threat, in turn, is driven by a combination of three key variables: aggregate power, geography, and perceptions of aggressive intentions.[4] The theory's originator, Stephen Walt, contends that it explains recent actions by great powers that have had the effect of constraining U.S. security policy.[5] As Walt applies the theory to the United States, changes in just one independent variable, perceptions of intentions, have major consequences for the recent behavior of the great powers.[6] Robert Pape has written in greatest detail about the perception of intentions in applying balance-of-threat theory to contemporary great-power relations. Pape stresses that "the Bush strategy of aggressive unilateralism is changing the United States' long-enjoyed reputation for benign intent and giving other major powers reason to fear its power. . . . Major powers are already engaging in the early stages of balancing behavior against the United States."[7] According to Pape, Walt, and numerous other analysts, this dynamic creates a strong conditional constraint on U.S. security policy: if the "United States acts in ways that fuel global concerns about U.S. power" and undermine its long-standing reputation for benign

---

the Twenty-First Century, ed. T. V. Paul and James J. Wirtz (Stanford, Calif.: Stanford University Press, 2004), 3.

[3] Michael Mastanduno makes this case specifically with respect to U.S. foreign policy under unipolarity in "Preserving the Unipolar Moment."

[4] Stephen M. Walt, *The Origins of Alliances* (Ithaca, N.Y.: Cornell University Press, 1987), 22–26. Walt delineates a fourth independent variable—offensive power—but this variable can be seen as an element of aggregate power and is often not treated separately when applying balance-of-threat theory to specific cases, including by Walt himself; see, e.g., *Taming American Power: The Global Response to U.S. Primacy* (New York: Norton, 2005), 132.

[5] See Walt, *Taming American Power,* 126–32.

[6] As Walt concludes, "There are clear signs that U.S. power is making other states uncomfortable and encouraging them to search for various ways to limit U.S. dominance. . . . Whether such efforts will grow in number and in significance, however, will depend largely on what the United States chooses to do. . . . In particular, will most states see U.S. intentions as comparatively benign, or will they believe that U.S. intentions are aggressive?" *Taming American Power,* 141.

[7] Pape, "Soft Balancing against the United States," 9.

intent, "efforts to balance the United States will increase and the United States will find itself increasingly isolated."[8] According to some analysts, such balancing efforts by other powers could escalate to the level of traditional counterbalancing.[9]

Unpopular U.S. policies have doubtless exacerbated the inclination of governments and their publics to resent the leading power.[10] Other major powers do undertake actions that impede U.S. goals in foreign policy, including military security. These actions matter, and U.S. policymakers would prefer they not occur. Yet labeling them "soft balancing" prejudges the open question of whether they are the outgrowth of balancing dynamics. Answering that question is important: if balance-of-threat theory is right and recent constraining actions are indeed a direct outgrowth of concern about U.S. power and intentions, then the United States faces the prospect of more, and more intense, efforts to constrain its power in response to its security policy.

In short, the existence of constraining actions is uncontested; what explains them needs to be debated. In this chapter, we pit balance-of-threat theory against our argument that unipolarity renders balancing inoperative. At first blush, this exercise may seem unnecessary. We

[8] Walt, *Taming American Power*, 132, 141. In addition to those works already cited, see also Walt, "World Off Balance"; Josef Joffe, "Defying History and Theory: The United States as the 'Last Superpower,' " in Ikenberry, *America Unrivaled*; Robert A. Pape, "Soft Balancing: How States Pursue Security in a Unipolar World," paper presented to the American Political Science Association Annual Convention, Chicago, September 2–4, 2004; Erik Voeten, "Resisting the Lonely Superpower: Responses of States in the United Nations to U.S. Dominance," *Journal of Politics* 66 (2004); Josef Joffe, "Gulliver Unbound: Can America Rule the World?" Twentieth Annual John Boynthon Lecture, Centre of Independent Studies, August 5, 2003, www.cis.org.au/events/jbl/josef_joffe.html (consulted September 19, 2007); Stephen M. Walt, "Can the United States Be Balanced? If So, How?" paper presented to the American Political Science Association Annual Convention, Chicago, September 2–4, 2004; Christopher Layne, "America as European Hegemon," *National Interest* 72 (2003); Bradley A. Thayer, "The Pax Americana and the Middle East: U.S. Grand Strategic Interests in the Region after September 11," *Mideast Security and Policy Studies* (Begin-Sadat Center for Strategic Studies, Bar-Ilan University) 56 (2003).

[9] Pape, for example, notes that if "the unipolar leader pursues aggressive unilateral military policies that change how most of the world's major powers view its intentions, one should expect, first, soft balancing and, if the unipolar leader's aggressive policies do not abate, increasingly intense balancing efforts that could evolve into hard balancing." "Soft Balancing against the United States," 18.

[10] Peter J. Katzenstein and Robert O. Keohane, eds., *Anti-Americanisms in World Politics* (Ithaca, N.Y.: Cornell University Press, 2007); Andrew Kohut and Bruce Stokes, *America against the World: How We Are Different and Why We Are Disliked* (New York: Times Books, 2006).

showed in the previous chapter that the expected costs of counterbalancing are exceptionally high under unipolarity. Lower levels of balancing also entail costs, particularly if we consider the opportunity cost of constraining the United States in terms of other objectives a country may have. After all, hemming in the United States is not the only motivation of other states. They seek economic growth, local security, and other objectives that may be compromised by attempts to constrain the United States, especially if they provoke retaliation. And the wider the power gap, the harder it is for any state to check the United States single-handedly, greatly increasing the need for any would-be soft-balancer to recruit other states also willing to confront the trade-offs inherent in constraining U.S. security policy.

Bringing into view the opportunity cost of constraining the United States—something theorists of soft balancing have neglected—leads us to expect that other great powers will try to constrain the United States only when doing so is compatible with their valued objectives. Given this expectation, what general patterns of evidence do we find? To buttress the balance-of-threat argument, analysts highlight four cases from the past decade: Russian assistance to Iranian nuclear efforts; Russia's strategic partnership with China; enhanced military coordination among members of the European Union; and French, German, and Russian opposition to the U.S.-led war in Iraq. Advocates of the argument may well offer additional cases, but collectively they represent a small fraction of the opportunities the major powers have had over the course of that decade to act to restrain U.S. power. Each of those forgone opportunities weighs against the balance-of-threat argument. Moreover, all of the great powers that played a role in these four cases also cooperate extensively with the United States on matters central to the national security concerns of all parties.[11] Indeed, sometimes they cooperate in ways that enable U.S. policies they officially oppose, as in Germany's decision to assist the invasion of Iraq by providing the Pentagon with a copy of Saddam Hussein's plan to defend Baghdad.

In short, as in the case of balance-of-power theory, if balance of threat were not already so influential a theory, little in great-power relations over the last 15 years would call it to mind. But analysts are strongly attached to the balancing metaphor and prone to see any correlation

[11] See, for example, Kristin Archick, "US-EU Cooperation against Terrorism," Congressional Research Service Report, July 12, 2005.

between leaders' discontent with the United States, or with unipolarity more generally, and constraining actions as evidence that balancing is in play and poised to become more significant. In this chapter, we therefore test the argument for balance-of-threat constraints against our own view, that balancing dynamics are not ready to be triggered by any slip in other governments' estimate of the benignity of U.S. intentions. The theoretical stakes are straightforward: if our argument is right, then *all* theories of balancing constraints are irrelevant for the United States in today's unipolar world. This conclusion is of more than purely academic interest; it has profound implications for policy. If the balance-of-threat argument is valid, then the United States confronts a nightmare scenario: absent a dramatic effort to shore up its reputation for benign intentions, other major powers may be willing to absorb the costs and bear the trade-offs to consistently check America.

Does the logic of a balance-of-threat theory trump our argument? Examining the cases most likely to support the former, we find no evidence that it does. Constraining the United States is not the only motivation of other states, and there is no evidence that it is a motivation strong enough to trump other state objectives when they conflict with it. Our overall conclusion is that the other great powers will act to impede the United States only when doing so is compatible with other valued objectives. There is thus no indication that, in the years ahead, constraining actions will increase linearly in response to U.S. security policy. This does not mean that the United States will be spared all barriers put up by other great powers; however, their emergence is contingent on factors particular to other societies. As in chapter 2, we thus conclude that balancing is an inoperative constraint on U.S. security policy.

The Argument for Balance-of-Threat Constraints

The argument for balance-of-threat constraints rests on two general premises, each of which can be challenged. The first is that the United States has encountered more, or more significant, constraining actions in recent years. Of course, the United States has long had to contend with efforts to counter its objectives, not just from competitors but from allies as well. Consider, for example, what happened in the decade that followed the Cuban missile crisis in 1962: France defected from NATO's military command; the United States was unable to obtain assistance from its major European allies in conducting the Vietnam War; Germany, Japan, and other countries stubbornly resisted a devaluation of their currencies; and France sought to undermine the Bretton Woods system by purchasing large amounts of gold from the U.S. Treasury. These actions all took place in the shadow of the Cold War, a reference point for judging their significance. In their bipolar standoff, the United States and the Soviet Union provided each other with a yardstick for measuring the significance of changes in policy by other states. In today's unipolar system, by contrast, no comparable reference point exists for assessing the consequences of policies. For this reason, it is harder to judge whether U.S. security policy faces high or rising constraints from other great powers.

The second premise underlying the balance-of-threat argument concerns the perceptions of intentions as an explanation for recent behavior by great powers. As noted previously, although balance-of-threat theory highlights three independent variables—aggregate power, geography, and perceptions of intentions—only the latter, according to analysts, can explain the recent pattern of constraining actions against the United States. The United States' geographic position is a constant, not a variable. And although the U.S. share of aggregate power has grown in recent years, Pape underscores that "[b]ecause a unipolar leader is already stronger than all individual second-ranked powers, additional increments of power are unlikely to significantly increase its ability to become a global hegemon. For this reason, although the leading state's relative power gains are viewed with suspicion, they are ultimately of secondary importance."[12] Pape consequently focuses on perceptions of intentions:

> The United States has long been a remarkable exception to the rule that states balance against superior power. Aside from the Soviet Union, major powers have rarely balanced against it. The key reason is not the United States' overwhelming power relative to other major powers, which has varied over time and so cannot explain this nearly constant pattern. Rather, until recently the United States enjoyed a robust reputation for nonaggressive intentions towards major powers and lesser states beyond its own hemisphere.[13]

---

[12] Pape, "Soft Balancing against the United States," 14. Pape uses the term *global hegemony* to describe a preponderance far greater than our own definition of unipolarity.

[13] Ibid., 9. In his analysis, Walt also highlights the perceptions of intentions: "The United States does not want to give up its position of primacy and cannot alter its geo-

Although Pape, Walt, and others believe that perceptions of U.S. intentions have recently changed, have they shifted sufficiently to influence other states? In a unipolar system, Pape argues, even a very small change in perception of intentions can significantly increase the likelihood of balancing:

> Perceptions of the most powerful state's intentions are more important in unipolar than in multipolar worlds. . . . The overwhelming power of the unipolar leader means that even a modest change in how others perceive the aggressiveness of its intentions can significantly increase the fear that it would make a bid for global hegemony. . . . The logic of unipolarity would suggest the more aggressive the intentions of the unipolar hegemon, the more intense the balancing by second-ranked states.[14]

This assertion ignores all of the barriers to balancing set forth in chapter 2. Most notably, Pape does not consider geography, even though it is a key factor in balance-of-threat theory. In the current international system, geography clearly mitigates perceptions of threats from the United States and exacerbates second-ranked states' perceptions of threats from each other. Even if we accept Pape's core contention, it remains unclear whether perceptions have changed enough to overcome the influence of geography on the likelihood of balancing by other great powers. Moreover, it is also possible that great powers' perceptions of U.S. intentions have not, in fact, changed at all. Lieber and Alexander underscore that other great powers have no reason to fear that U.S. intentions toward them have changed, given that the focus of U.S. security policy in recent years has been terrorists and a small number of "rogue" states.[15] Regardless, the crucial point is that perceptions of intentions have always been hard to measure, and detecting a subtle shift in this variable that can be linked to policy is a difficult exercise.[16]

---

graphic location, but it can pay close attention to how others perceive its intentions." *Taming American Power*, 132.

[14] Ibid., 14–15, 18. To be sure, scholars continue to debate this logic. Layne, for example, sees it this way: "In unipolar systems there is no clear distinction between balancing against threat or against power, because the threat inheres in the hegemon's power. In a unipolar world, others must worry about the hegemon's capabilities (which, more or less, are knowable), not its intentions (which are difficult to ascertain and always subject to change)." "War on Terrorism," 119.

[15] Lieber and Alexander, "Waiting for Balancing."

[16] As Mastanduno observes, balance-of-threat theory has yet fully to confront "the conceptual and empirical challenges of studying images, intentions and perceptions of threat in relations among states." "Preserving the Unipolar Moment," 168.

In sum, although one can take issue with each premise underlying the balance-of-threat argument—that great power actions in the later part of the unipolar era have constrained U.S. security policy to a greater extent than during the earlier part of this period, and that perceptions of U.S. intentions have shifted in ways that can explain this increase—we will accept them for the purpose of evaluating the argument on its most favorable terms. In the analysis that follows, we will examine the key empirical question at hand: how do the causal mechanisms of balance-of-threat theory figure in the cases soft-balancing theorists themselves single out? In keeping with the intellectual history of balance-of-power theory, balance-of-threat theory is systemic when applied to the United States. Balancing is action taken to check a potential hegemon. If the argument for balance-of-threat constraints is to have the explanatory and predictive punch its proponents advertise, it must be connected to this same underlying causal mechanism. That is, for the argument to be valid, the emergence of constraining actions must be linked causally to the systemic concentration of power in the United States.

Although evaluating the balance-of-threat argument seems straightforward, its proponents do not themselves supply the conceptual tools to distinguish behavior that is an outgrowth of systemic balancing from an alternative that we might call "unipolar politics as usual." Specifying this alternative explanation is the purpose of the next section.

Specifying the Alternative Explanation

The balancing metaphor encourages analysts to interpret any behavior that complicates U.S. foreign policy as an effort to check U.S. power. This tendency is reinforced by the assumption, which underlies much realist thinking, that states' interest in security dominates all other interests. Soft-balancing theorists agree that the United States presents at most a notional threat to the territorial security of other major powers, and thus that the motives for counterbalancing must have to do with secondary issues of security.[17] Although they acknowledge that the security interest in balancing is not existential and thus not presumptively prior to other possible interests, proponents of the argument for

[17] See, e.g., Pape, "Soft Balancing against the United States"; and Joffe, *Überpower*.

67

balance-of-threat constraints do not take the next logical step of considering the significance of other state interests and the trade-offs between them and secondary security interests.[18] Our argument, by contrast, brings into focus the costs and trade-offs inherent in any such behavior, and therefore the crucial importance of considering other factors besides a security-driven reaction to U.S. power leading to constraints on the United States.

Of the myriad aims states might pursue, we address four that scholars agree are both important and clearly distinguishable—conceptually and empirically—from the security interest highlighted in balance-of-threat theory.[19]

ECONOMIC INTEREST

The quest for economic growth is a nearly universal interest with no necessary connection to the concerns over security that drive balance-of-threat theory. Governments may undertake actions for economic gain—either for the country as a whole or for powerful interest groups—that have nothing to do with a hegemon on the horizon and yet hamper the conduct of U.S. foreign policy.

REGIONAL SECURITY CONCERNS

Regional coordination of policy is more common now than in the past for many reasons unconnected to U.S. primacy: a vast increase in the number of states; a consequent increase in the number of weak or failed states; and the rise of transnational security challenges such as organized crime, terrorism, drug trafficking, and refugee flows. Major powers frequently face incentives to enhance their capabilities—often through collaboration with other regional states—in response to these local or regional concerns. These efforts may result in shifts in relative power—and perhaps in reduced U.S. freedom of action—even if they are unrelated to constraining U.S. power.

---

[18] An important strand of argument within realist theory is that as the threat to a state's core survival become less probable, a rational state will become less willing to maximize military security when doing so has a high cost in terms of other state priorities like economic capacity; see Stephen Brooks, "Dueling Realisms," *International Organization* 1997.

[19] To make the analysis tractable, we do not examine some potentially important state aims, such as prestige/status and other "milieu goals," that are often hard to distinguish from secondary security interests and interest in autonomy.

POLICY DISPUTES AND BARGAINING

Other states may undertake actions that constrain the United States not in response to the threat to security inherent in U.S. power, but because they disagree with specific U.S. policies. Governments may resist a policy because they consider it ill suited to the problem at hand, for example, and not because they think opposition will constrain U.S. power. Given the reasonable expectation of future differences of view on policy, and therefore the expectation of future bargaining over policy, states may take actions intended to increase their leverage over the long term.

DOMESTIC POLITICAL INCENTIVES

Opposing the United States may be a winning strategy domestically even for leaders with no general interest in constraining U.S. power. Only domestic opposition that is an outgrowth of the systemic concentration of power in the United States can be thought of as a manifestation of the balancing imperative. All other ways in which the domestic politics of other countries feed actions that complicate matters for the United States fall outside the logic of the balance-of-threat theory. In particular, the argument does not encompass actions that are manifestations of historical experiences or political or cultural understandings—either for the nation as a whole or for individual political parties or groups—and are unconnected with the rise of unipolarity.

Criteria for Testing the Argument for Balance-of-Threat Constraints

To the degree that these four explanations account for actions that constrain U.S. foreign policy, our argument for the absence of balancing is supported and the argument for balance-of-threat constraints is weakened. It would be surprising to find no evidence consistent with the latter. Just as unlikely would be evidence that checking U.S. power is the only explanation in play. The real issue is relative salience. For each case, checking U.S. power could explain a majority of the variance; an important part, but not a majority of the variance; little variance; or essentially no variance at all.

Determining the relative strength of the various explanations, however, is no easy task. The key cases cited by analysts are quite recent, so reliable inside information can be scarce. The chief putative balancing powers—France, Russia, and China—are not known for the transparency of their executive decision-making. And public rhetoric presents difficult analytical challenges, for a government with an interest in balancing may not want to advertise it. At the same time, all four explanations may generate balancing rhetoric from policymakers, creating prima facie evidence for soft balancing. Leaders motivated chiefly by domestic political considerations are hardly likely to say so; they may detect domestic political advantage in touting a threat from U.S. power even if it is not the real issue. In turn, leaders who have sincere differences with the United States over policy may talk up balancing to help build a coalition to increase their bargaining leverage. Being seen by Washington as a potential balancer has risks, to be sure, but it also holds out the promise of magnifying one's bargaining power and any concessions one might make. Governments that pursue relative economic advantages for themselves or their constituents may find it convenient to cloak their actions in high-minded talk about checking U.S. power. And the United States is so prominent on the global stage that it is a convenient focal point for other states that seek to cooperate on regional security.

Balancing talk, moreover, is often as cheap as it is useful. A state can rationally be expected to address an issue only to the degree that it has the capability to do so. Actors and observers expect France to play a far more substantial role in resolving a conflict in the Balkans than in North Korea—and vice versa for China. Yet because of the United States' globe-girdling capabilities, critical U.S. involvement is likely to be expected in both cases. This illustrates the immense gap between the set of issues the United States might rationally be expected to address seriously and the corresponding sets of the other great powers. As a result, there are issues over which they can take positions without expecting to be compelled to bear the costs of their resolution.

Finally, other governments may well see complications for U.S. security policy as a bonus side effect of actions undertaken for reasons having little to do with U.S. power. A leader's satisfaction with a policy that restricts U.S. power does not demonstrate that restricting it is the underlying purpose of the policy. From a rhetorical standpoint, this may be a distinction without a difference; from an explanatory standpoint, however, it is crucial.

Ultimately, rhetoric is a poor indicator of the explanatory power of balance-of-threat theory. For it to be taken seriously, there must be evidence for its current explanatory value.[20] Otherwise, the theory is providing not an explanation but an expectation. Although some uncertainty will always attend judgments about such recent events, there are observable implications of the differences between the balance-of-threat argument and the alternative we advance.

There is an overarching guideline that allows us to assess the competing arguments: policymakers' willingness to accept trade-offs between constraints on the United States and other valued objectives. The balance-of-threat argument is not about preferences but about behavior. Many politicians in France, Russia, China, and other putative balancing states periodically express a preference for what they often call "multipolarity" (although by this they usually mean multilateralism). They also express a desire for mutually beneficial partnerships with the United States, robust economic growth, prosperity, and many other values. The question our argument raises is this: What other priorities are they willing to sacrifice to put limits on the United States? If our argument is correct, then constraining actions by great powers will emerge only when they are compatible with other state priorities. Put another way, our argument is that these actions are best explained by factors that are unrelated to U.S. power.

Testing the Balancing Explanation against Unipolar Politics as Usual

We now evaluate the relative strength of the balance-of-threat explanation compared with our alternative in the cases highlighted by proponents of the former—a procedure strongly biased in its favor. Our general argument is that unipolarity makes balancing so costly as to render the dynamics of balancing inoperative. The evidence of the last 15 years is consistent with this view: no traditional counterbalancing and almost no low-level, "quasi" or "soft" balancing. Normal practice in social science would be to pit our argument against balance-of-threat theory in explaining this pattern or in accounting for a randomly

---

[20] On this falsifiability issue, see, in particular, Lieber and Alexander, "Waiting for Balancing."

selected set of cases within it. We would thus seek to determine how well balance-of-threat theory fares against our explanation of typical great-power interactions under unipolarity—that is, interactions with no evidence of balancing of any kind. Instead, we have chosen to pit our argument against balance-of-threat theory only in the cases its advocates have selected as evidence.

Thus, we limit our examination to cases where the causal mechanisms of balance-of-threat theory ought to be strongly in play. These instances have attracted analysts' attention because they share three key characteristics: coordination among two or more states in areas directly related to security; the involvement of at least one great power; and state actions that make it harder for Washington to advance its security interests.

The Sino-Russian "Strategic Partnership"

In some respects, Russia's strategic partnership with China appears the strongest case of the argument for balance-of-threat constraints in action.[21] It is a treaty-governed relationship that has resulted in a net shift in the distribution of military power against the United States. Russia's own military is unable to use much of the output of its defense industry. To the extent that its strategic partnership with China permits the transfer of some of this output to a military that can use it more effectively, the net effect is a shift in relative power. In addition, Russia-China cooperation includes a regional security organization that excludes the United States—the Shanghai Cooperation Organization (SCO). Moreover, both governments have periodically expressed a strong desire to limit U.S. involvement in their regions.

In the end, however, checking U.S. power plays, at best, a marginal role in the Sino-Russian partnership. Although officials in Beijing and Moscow may see a welcome bonus in complications for U.S. security policy that emerge from their partnership, analysts should not confuse side effects with important causes. Let us consider each of the three elements of the partnership, in ascending order of importance: the diplomatic relationship, the SCO, and the arms sales.

Although Russian and Chinese leaders periodically describe their diplomatic partnership as an expression of their preference for a

---

[21] Analyses that treat these partnerships in balancing terms include Paul, "Enduring Axioms"; Walt, "Can the United States Be Balanced?" and Joffe, "Defying History and Theory."

multipolar world, there is little evidence that checking the United States is the driving force behind it. Rhetoric notwithstanding, the policies are crafted to avoid trading off the parties' partnership against their key bilateral relationships with the United States. The Russia-China Treaty on Good-Neighborliness, Friendship, and Cooperation, signed in 2001, capped more than a decade of improving bilateral ties, but it lacks anything resembling a mutual defense clause.[22] While the treaty obligates the signatories in a general sense to maintain the global equilibrium and to consult each other in the event of threats to security, neither it nor any other public Sino-Russian agreement entails any observable commitment to counter U.S. power. No mutual undertaking in accordance with the partnership has involved significant costs in the countries' relationships with the United States.[23]

Russian and Chinese leaders have frequently used SCO gatherings to express their preference for a multipolar world, and both they and their authoritarian partners in Central Asia sometimes portray the organization as a bulwark against U.S. and European pressure on democratization and human rights. Given the rhetoric, it is hardly surprising that some observers see the SCO as a coordinating mechanism for balancing U.S. power in the region.[24] Yet an examination of the organization's real activities undermines this interpretation.[25] Balance-of-threat theory does not encompass the causes that actually got the SCO up and running. The organization's main initial goal was confidence building among the new states in the region, especially by resolving old Soviet-Chinese border disputes. China further sought to stabilize and secure its borders from Islamic extremism, a factor that threatened not only

[22] For a detailed analysis of the treaty, see Elizabeth Wishnick, "Russia and China: Brothers Again?" *Asian Survey* 41 (2001).

[23] Ample evidence and analysis on this score is presented in the chapters on Russia, India, and China in Richard J. Ellings and Aaron Friedberg with Michael Wills, eds., *Strategic Asia, 2002–03: Asian Aftershocks* (Seattle: National Bureau of Asian Research, 2003). On China's grand strategy and its implications for balancing see Avery Goldstein, "An Emerging China's Grand Strategy," in *International Relations Theory and the Asia Pacific*, ed. G. John Ikenberry and Michael Mastanduno (New York: Columbia University Press, 2002); and Alastair Iain Johnston, "Is China a Status Quo Power?" *International Security* 27 (2003).

[24] See, for example, Sergei Blagov, "Russia Seeking to Strengthen Regional Organizations to Counterbalance Western Influence," *Eurasia Insight*, December 4, 2002, at Eurasianet.org; and Ariel Cohen, "The U.S. Challenge at the Shanghai Summit," Heritage Foundation WebMemo No. 1124, June 13, 2006, available at http://www.heritage.org/Research/RussiaandEurasia/wm1124.cfm (consulted September 19, 2007).

[25] See Kathleen Collins and William C. Wohlforth, "Central Asia: Defying 'Great Game' Expectations," in *Strategic Asia, 2003–04: Fragility and Crisis*, ed. Richard J. Ellings

post-Soviet Central Asia but also the restive Xinjiang region of western China. China feared that the Uighur separatists were receiving funding and arms from Uighurs in its neighboring states, as well as from Afghanistan. Russia shared the common threat of an increasingly Islamicized Chechen separatist movement. Uzbekistan joined the SCO in 2001 as it sought a common forum for responding to the Islamic Movement of Uzbekistan (IMU)—a transnational guerilla threat.[26] The SCO signed a declaration on June 15, 2001, expanding its mission in the region and focused increasingly on terrorist threats, religious extremism, and to a lesser extent, arms and narcotics trafficking. The organization announced the creation of a counterterrorism center in Bishkek, Kygyzstan, known as the Regional Anti-Terrorism Structure (RATS), but the project stalled and few assets were invested or resources committed.[27]

Thus, the main issue that China, Russia, and the Central Asian states agreed upon that warranted an upgrading of the organization was counterterrorism. Having coordinated the SCO around this issue, however, the members were unable to assemble the capabilities required to address it. This shortcoming was made brutally evident after the terrorist attacks of September 11, 2001, when U.S.-led Operation Enduring Freedom quickly toppled the ruling Taliban in Afghanistan and weakened the IMU—the very threats whose rise had just begun to provide the SCO's raison d'être. The U.S. deployment to Afghanistan created a contradiction between the SCO's rhetorical role as a balancing mechanism and its operational role as a regional security organization. At least initially, China and Russia resolved the contradiction by strongly supporting the United States in the war on terror.

In ensuing years, member states again sought to position the SCO as central to the region's security. This effort was buttressed by the downturn in Uzbekistan's security ties with the United States and NATO in response to Western criticisms of Tashkent's violent suppression of a domestic demonstration.[28] The SCO officially called upon

---

and Aaron Friedberg with Michael Wills (Seattle: National Bureau of Asian Research, 2004).

[26] Interview with senior analyst, Institute of Strategic Studies, Tashkent, Uzbekistan, August 2002, reported in Collins and Wohlforth, "Central Asia."

[27] "Declaration of the Establishment of the Shanghai Cooperation Organization, June 15, 2001," http://www.sectsco.org/html/00088.html (consulted October 10, 2007).

[28] John C. K. Daly, Kurt H. Meppen, Vladimir Socor, and S. Frederick Starr, "Anatomy of a Crisis: U.S.-Uzbekistan Relations, 2001–2005," Silk Road Paper, Central Asia–Caucusus Institute Silk Road Studies Program, February 2006, http://www.silkroadstudies.org/new/inside/publications/0602Uzbek.pdf (consulted September 19, 2007).

the United States to announce a deadline for ending its military presence in the region. The anti-U.S. political message had to remain subtle, however, given Russian and especially Chinese leaders' interest in avoiding a confrontation with the United States, continued differences between the two great powers and between Uzbekistan and Kazakhstan, and developing ties between Kazakhstan and the United States. On the ground, meanwhile, the real activity centered on counterterrorism. The RATS slowly took on substance, sponsoring joint counterterror exercises involving units from Russia, China, and other member states, and creating an intelligence database on terrorist activities in the region. As Celeste Wallander sums up, "[T]he SCO is a successful regional organization, but other than the rhetoric against U.S. unilateralism and against liberalization, its successes do not threaten U.S. interests."[29] Pragmatic regional security cooperation remained the SCO's real operational focus, with the organization's political utility a welcome bonus.

The real core of Russia's relationship with China, however, is not the diplomatic partnerships but extensive military coproduction arrangements and major arms sales. Yet Russia's fundamental interest in these exports is not checking U.S. power but rather a desperate need to slow the decline of its military industrial complex. Between 1992 and 1998, Russia experienced what was probably the steepest peacetime decline in military power by any major state in history.[30] Weapons procurement and spending declined dramatically after 1991, and by 2000 only 20 percent of Russia's operational weapons stocks were modern, compared with 60–80 percent in NATO countries.[31] Given the collapse of domestic orders (in 2001, only 10 percent of Russian defense firms received state orders), Russia's defense sector possesses massive excess capacity.[32] Against a backdrop of massive competing demands for new

[29] Celeste A. Wallander, "Russia: The Domestic Sources of a Less-Than-Grand Strategy," in *Strategic Asia, 2007–08*, ed. Richard J. Ellings and Michael Wills, eds. (Seattle: National Bureau of Asian Research, 2007).

[30] Christopher Hill, "Russian Defense Spending," in United States Congress, Joint Economic Committee, *Russia's Uncertain Economic Future* (Washington, D.C.: United States Government Printing Office, 2002), 168. An excellent overview of the defense sector's dilemmas is Christopher Davis, "Country Survey XV: The Defence Sector in the Economy of a Declining Superpower: Soviet Union and Russia, 1965–2001," *Defence Peace and Economics* 13 (2002).

[31] "Only 20% of Russian Arms Are Modern," Radio Free Europe Radio Liberty, *Daily Report*, May 21, 2001.

[32] Kevin P. O'Prey, "Arms Exports and Russia's Defense Industries: Issues for the U.S. Congress," in Joint Economic Committee, *Russia's Uncertain Economic Future*. See also

resources (dismal maintenance and training, dire personnel problems, and overall inefficiency), increased defense outlays after 2001 did little to alter the fact that even a downsized Soviet-scale defense sector is too big for Russia.[33]

Arms sales are a lifeline for a military industry producing less than one-third of its 1992 output, and rapidly losing technological competitiveness. Even more immediately, exports aid a defense sector that supplies income and welfare services to hundreds of thousands of workers and their families, provides the economic lifeblood of dozens of cities, and enriches numerous managers and public officials. Military industry represents one of the few high-technology sectors in which Russians remain competitive, and they perceive a strong overall commercial interest in promoting exports. The evidence concerning Russia's major arms relationships overwhelmingly indicates that Moscow's eagerness to sell weaponry to Beijing is only indirectly and marginally connected to the issue of U.S. hegemony.

Bringing in India—which for a brief period near the turn of the century was sometimes touted as the third member of an anti-Western "Asian triangle"—further weakens the balance-of-threat argument. Many Russian analysts regard their country's partnership with India as a hedge against rising Chinese power in Asia. Russia has tended to sell India more advanced weapons systems than it exports to China, and the agreements on the joint design and production of weapons that Russia has signed with India also tend to be deeper and more comprehensive than the arrangements that Moscow has made with Beijing. Russian officials are quick to cite these facts when questioned by domestic critics who accuse them of mortgaging Russia's security through the arms transfers to China. Needless to say, Moscow's interest in marketing military hardware (and nuclear technology) to New Delhi was undiminished after India moved to develop an entirely new cooperative security relationship with the United States in the second half of the George W. Bush presidency.

The argument for balance-of-threat constraints fails to explain the arms transfers—the materially most significant aspect of the Sino-Russian partnership. What makes the argument superficially applicable to

---

Johnson's Russia List, No. 9125, August 3, 2005; "Ministry Source: 40 Percent of Russian Defense Industry Enterprises Losing Money," Interfax-AVN.

[33] Julian Cooper, "Developments in the Russian Arms Industry," *SIPRI Yearbook: Armaments, Disarmament, and International Security 2006* (Stockholm: SIPRI, 2006), appendix 9C, available at http://yearbook2006.sipri.org/chap9/app9c (consulted September 19, 2007); Stephen J. Blank, "Potemkin's Treadmill: Russian Military Modernization," in *Mil-*

the case is not that China wants to import weapons. If the Chinese obtained weaponry from Israel or South Africa, it would hardly attract so much attention. The arms sales seem so significant because they come from Russia, suggesting interstate cooperation to balance U.S. capabilities. But the evidence shows that if the United States were to cut its defense outlays by two-thirds tomorrow, Moscow's interest in arms sales would be undiminished.

The Moscow-Tehran Connection

Analysts commonly interpret great power support for states that are opponents of the United States as evidence for the argument for balance-of-threat constraints. Russia's relationship with Iran is the most prominent case in point.[34] Russia has assisted Iran's nuclear program, cooperated in space technology and other high-technology areas, sold large quantities of military hardware (Iran is Russia's third largest customer, after China and India), and pursued a general policy of engagement with Iran. Such policies helped to buttress Iran against pressure from Washington for nearly a decade.

There is scant evidence, however, that the relationship is driven by an effort to check U.S. power. Regional security concerns and economic incentives have remained consistently at the forefront. Russia has numerous reasons besides constraining U.S. power to seek good relations with Iran. Nuclear sales, technology transfers, and other moves that bolster Iran are part of an engagement strategy that is itself driven by Moscow's need for Iranian cooperation in resolving regional issues surrounding the exploitation of petroleum and other natural resources in the Caspian. Even regional analysts who stress the importance of geopolitics do not accord balancing the United States a significant role in explaining the Moscow-Tehran connection.[35] As in the China case, Moscow has no incentive to alienate Tehran. At the same time, the two states remained at loggerheads on local issues throughout the 1990s and early in the next decade, placing limits on the scope and depth of their cooperation.

---

itary Modernization in an Era of Uncertainty, ed. Ashley J. Tellis and Michael Wills (Seattle: National Bureau of Asian Research, 2005), 175–205.

[34] See, for example, Pape, "Soft Balancing against the United States," 42–43; Walt, *Taming American Power*, 128; and Walt, "Can the United States Be Balanced?"

[35] See, for example, Carol R. Saivetz, "Perspectives on the Caspian Sea Dilemma: Russian Policies since the Soviet Demise," *Eurasian Geography and Economics* 44 (2003); Gawdat Bahgat, "Pipeline Diplomacy: The Geopolitics of the Caspian Sea Region," *Interna-*

Russia's arms sales to Iran buttress this general strategy of engagement, but, as with China and India, economic incentives loom large, for all the reasons noted above. Nuclear cooperation attracts the most attention from analysts. From the early 1990s on, Russia was the only major power openly cooperating with Iran in this area, defying occasionally intense pressure from Washington. A major problem with the balance-of-threat interpretation is that Russian experts are virtually unanimous in regarding the Moscow-Tehran nuclear connection as driven principally by economic concerns. No one in Russia can explain how the country's security would benefit from Iran's nuclearization. Russia's official policy is that proliferation of weapons of mass destruction "is the main threat of the 21st century."[36] The commercial interests in play are substantial enough, however, to induce Moscow to set a relatively high bar for proof of an increase in the risk of proliferation caused by its relationship with Tehran.

Nuclear technology is a declining asset inherited from the Soviet Union that figures importantly in Russia's small share of high-technology exports. With abundant hydrocarbon-fueled electrical generation capacity and declining demand compared to Soviet times, the domestic market for nuclear technology has dried up. Foreign sales are vital to sustaining essentially half of the atomic energy ministry's activities, and Iran is a major market.[37] Viktor Mikhailov, Russia's atomic energy minister when the agreement with Iran was initiated, summed up the motivation succinctly: "What could Russia have brought onto world markets? We only had one strength: our scientific and technical potential. Our only chance was broad cooperation in the sphere of peaceful nuclear energy."[38]

---

tional Studies Perspectives 3 (2002); and Douglas W. Blum, "Perspectives on the Caspian Sea Dilemma: A Framing Comment," *Eurasian Geography and Economics* 44 (2003).

[36] Transcript of Putin's BBC interview on June 22, 2003, reprinted in Johnson's Russia List, No. 7236, June 24, 2003, http://www.cdi.org/russia/johnson/7236-8.cfm (consulted September 19, 2007).

[37] See Celeste A. Wallander, "Russia's Interest in Trading with the 'Axis of Evil,' " PONARS Policy Memo 248, Center for Strategic and International Studies, October 1, 2002, http://www.csis.org/index.php?option=com_csis_pubs&task=view&id=2254 (consulted September 19, 2007); testimony for "Russia's Policies toward the Axis of Evil: Money and Geopolitics in Iraq and Iran," Hearing before the House Committee on International Relations, February 26, 2003. For a general analysis of the problems facing Russia's nuclear industry and its interest in foreign sales, see Igor Khripunov, "MINATOM: Time for Crucial Decisions," *Problems of Post-Communism* 48 (2001).

[38] Vladimir A. Orlov and Alexander Vinnikov, "The Great Guessing Game: Russia and the Iranian Nuclear Issue," *Washington Quarterly* 28 (2005): 51.

Large sums of money for the ministry and associated firms are at stake. Russia's construction of Iran's Bushehr reactor alone is worth up to $1 billion; reprocessing fuel is also lucrative; and more reactor projects are planned. And the Iranians, Russians stress, pay cash. Boosters of these deals claim that the total value of the long-term relationship could exceed $8 billion and involve orders for more than 300 Russian companies. Moreover, significant numbers of high-technology jobs—many located in politically crucial and economically strapped regions of Russia—are involved.[39] The Russian atomic energy ministry remains a formidable interest group in Moscow politics, and its lobbyists work hard to make the case publicly and in the corridors of the Kremlin that the nuclear sector is critical to Russia's modernization.[40]

Russia's substantive foreign policy behavior is consistent with this analysis. When the economic and regional security incentives for engaging Iran appear to contradict Russia's general antiproliferation stance, the latter wins. The extent of Iran's nuclear weapons-related programs came to the fore in 2002–3, and they turned out to have been based not on the Russian project but on purchases from the transnational nuclear proliferation network run from Pakistan by A. Q. Khan, as well as indigenous efforts. In response to the new evidence, Moscow recalibrated its policy in 2003. If the balance-of-threat argument was valid in this case, it is precisely at this time when Russian concerns about U.S. power should have been especially high, inducing Moscow to increase, not decrease, the scope of its nuclear cooperation with Iran. And yet at this time, Russia reaffirmed its commitment to nonproliferation and its desire to see Iran submit to robust International Atomic Energy Agency (IAEA) inspections. To allay potential IAEA concerns regarding the Bushehr reactor, Russia secured a deal with Iran on returning all fuel to Russia for reprocessing. The Russians also pressured Tehran to sign and implement the IAEA additional protocol in 2003, which imposed further restrictions and openness on the Iranian program. Although Iran left the protocol in 2005 and U.S. and European concerns about its overall nuclear program increased, these did not

[39] Russia's atomic energy ministry claims that the Bushehr contract alone will secure 20,000 jobs and involve work at over 300 Russian companies; see Anatoly Andreev, "Mirnyi Atom dlia Bushera," *Trud*, December 27, 2002, 1. For more on Russia's role in proliferation in Asia, see Bates Gill, "Proliferation," in Ellings and Friedberg, *Strategic Asia, 2003–04*.

[40] Though the nuclear issue gets most of the attention, a very similar constellation of interests lies behind Russia's arms sales to Iran. Tor Bukkvoll, "Arming the Ayatollahs: Economic Lobbies in Russia's Iran Policy," *Problems of Post-Communism* 49 (2002).

concern Russia's nuclear project, resulting in diminished diplomatic pressure on Moscow.

Russia's ongoing reluctance to adopt an American-style hard line on Iran's nuclear program is the result of the same regional security and especially economic incentives. In expressing their reservations concerning further pressuring Tehran, President Putin and other top government officials stressed that if Russia backed away from its contract with the Iranians, American or European companies might exploit the opening. As Putin put it, "We will protest against using the theme of nuclear weapons proliferation against Iran as an instrument for forcing Russian companies out of the Iranian market."[41] Moscow demanded guarantees that international efforts to compel Iran to comply with IAEA strictures do not come at the expense of Russia's commercial interests. Nor do the makers of Russian foreign policy want to forgo the diplomatic dividends of their position as the great power with the best ties to Tehran, unless Iranian recalcitrance vis-à-vis the IAEA forces them to.[42]

In short, there is no basis for concluding that Russia's relationship with Iran is driven by an effort to check U.S. power. Regional security concerns figure crucially in the larger diplomatic relationship, while economic incentives are the driver behind nuclear cooperation.

The European Union's Cooperation on Defense

In recent years, member states have made concerted efforts to enhance the European Union's Security and Defense Policy (ESDP), including the development of a 60,000-man rapid reaction force, a new security strategy, a defense agency to support efforts to improve military capability, and the formation of 1,500-man "battle groups" capable of higher-intensity operations.[43] European officials sometimes justify these efforts by stressing that they will lay the foundation for a larger EU role in regional and global security, implicitly reducing U.S. influence. For many analysts, this is a clear example of balancing behavior.[44] The evidence, however, does not support such an interpretation.

---

[41] Quoted in Orlov and Vinnikov, "The Great Guessing Game," 59.

[42] See Alexei Arbatov, "Russia and the Iranian Nuclear Crisis," Carnegie Endowment for International Peace, May 23, 2006. Available at http://www.carnegieendowment.org.

[43] For a comprehensive analysis, see Nicole Gnesotto, ed., *EU Security and Defense Policy: The First Five Years (1999–2004)* (Paris: European Union Institute for Security Studies, 2005).

[44] See, for example, Barry R. Posen, "European Union Security and Defense Policy: Response to Unipolarity?" *Security Studies* 15 (2006); Robert Art, "Striking the Balance," *Inter-*

The origins of the ESDP lie well before the onset of the foreign policy changes in the Bush administration that analysts such as Pape and Walt regard as having enhanced incentives to balance U.S. power. Experts and decision-makers believe the key impetus is not U.S. power, but the need to deal with the prospect of the United States' decreased presence in Europe and reduced willingness to solve Balkans-style problems for its European allies.[45] For example, in explaining the origins of the ESDP, the director of the European Union's Institute for Security Studies, Nicole Gnesotto, notes that "because American involvement in crises that were not vital for America was no longer guaranteed, . . . the Europeans had to organize themselves to assume their share of responsibility in crisis management and, in doing so, maintain or even enhance the United States' interest within the Alliance."[46] Similarly, Charles Kupchan stresses:

> There is no better way to get the Europeans to take on more defense responsibilities than to confront them with the prospect of an America that is losing interest in being the guarantor of European security. It is anything but happenstance that Europe redoubled efforts to forge a common defense policy just after the close of NATO's war on Kosovo. The Europeans are scared—and justifiably so—that America will not show up the next time war breaks out somewhere in Europe's periphery. And they are aware that they can either prepare now for that eventuality—or be left in the lurch.[47]

For many of the key member governments, notably the United Kingdom, the corrosive effects of European military weakness on the transatlantic alliance provided the impetus for enhancing EU capabilities. Most analysts thus concur that EU defense cooperation can go forward only if it is seen as complementary to the alliance with the United States. That is, some degree of U.S. support is a necessary condition of the ESDP's progress. Indeed, the forces that the Europeans are seeking

---

national Security 30 (2005): 180–83; Art, "Europe Hedges its Security Bets," in Paul, Wirtz, and Fortmann, *Balance of Power Revisited*; Walt, "Can the United States Be Balanced?"; Joffe, "Defying History and Theory"; and Layne, "America as European Hegemon."

[45] Significantly, even some proponents of the balance-of-threat argument grant this point: for example, in discussing "Europe's gradual effort to create a genuine European defense capability," Walt stresses that "the original motivation for this policy was not anti-American." *Taming American Power*, 129.

[46] Nicole Gnesotto, "ESDP: Results and Prospects," in Gnesotto, *EU Security*, 25.

[47] Charles Kupchan, *The End of the American Era: U.S. Foreign Policy and the Geopolitics of the Twenty-first Century* (New York: Knopf, 2002), 152.

to create complement, rather than compete with, U.S. capabilities because they provide additional units for dealing with small contingencies or peacekeeping missions abroad.[48] As Jolyon Howorth summarizes the key founding documents of the ESDP:

> There is little room for ambiguity in these statements: one objective of ESDP is to relieve the US army from regional crisis management responsibilities in Europe (and possibly elsewhere) in order to allow Washington to make better use of its military in more strategically significant parts of the world. This may be a partnership which the US is unsure it welcomes but that is another matter. ... If a conceptual term from IR were to be applied to this approach, it would be bandwagoning and not balancing.[49]

The prospect of increasing EU military capabilities may well have become more popular among European policymakers in recent years, perhaps in part in reaction to U.S. power.[50] However, any effort to create capabilities that might constrain the United States involves financial and other costs that many member states are still reluctant to bear. Both the rapid reaction force and the battle groups are not standing forces but rather pools of national units on which the EU can draw if the Council of Europe decides unanimously to use military force. And as Robert Cooper points out, "There is no member state for which EDSP is central to its security policy."[51] Indeed, Howorth and Menon emphasize that "there is absolutely no evidence to suggest that member states are planning to entrust the Union with territorial defense."[52] Even if all currently envisioned forces materialize according to plan, they will create little serious ability to constrain the United States. As Howorth notes, "The concern that European force generation might come to rival the US military is a not uncommon one among US commentators. The problem is that it is simply devoid of any empirical

[48] Indicative of this is that from 2004 onward, the EU has focused on small, 1,500-man battle groups, which are deployable quickly but are only capable of small operations or the initial phase of large operations. See Jolyon Howorth and Anand Menon, "Complexity and International Institutions: Why the European Union Isn't Balancing the United States," manuscript, Yale University, 18–19.

[49] Jolyon Howorth, "The European Security and Defence Policy: Neither Hard nor Soft Power Balancing—Just Policy-Making (or Is It Just 'Muddling Through'?)," paper presented to the American Political Science Association Annual Meeting, Philadelphia, August 31, 2006, 7.

[50] For this argument, see Art, "Striking the Balance," 181–82.

[51] In Gnesotto, *EU Security,* 189.

[52] Howorth and Menon, "Complexity and International Institutions," 17.

reality. . . . Even in the most 'muscular' of the various theoretical scenarios for the future of the ESDP there is no suggestion of the EU developing military capacity which could remotely aspire to rival or compete with the US military."[53]

To this point, far from sacrificing other preferences to create capabilities that might constrain the United States, the Europeans may be sacrificing limited resources that could be useful for countering U.S. power to create capabilities that largely complement those of the United States.[54] Unless European publics assume a much greater willingness to pursue higher defense expenditures, making the rapid reaction contingent into a credible force will have to come at the expense of developing advanced systems capable of competing with or displacing those fielded by U.S. forces. In the opinion of most military analysts, the most likely trajectory—even if all goes well for the EU's current plans—is actually a widening of the gap in high-intensity military capabilities in favor of the United States.[55]

In sum, regional security needs, not checking U.S. power, best explain EU defense cooperation. There is also no indication of an enhanced European willingness in recent years to bear the economic costs to develop military capabilities that could reduce the growing gap with the United States.

Opposition to the Iraq War

Unlike Russia's Asian partnerships, opposition to the U.S. invasion of Iraq did not entail measurable shifts in military power. It nonetheless seemed tailor-made for the balance-of-threat argument.[56] On a policy it declared vital to its national security, the United States faced opposition from key allies. The opposition was not haphazard but coordinated in elaborate diplomatic exchanges. The leaders of France, the

[53] Howorth, "European Security and Defence," 8. For more, see Jolyon Howorth, *The Security and Defence Policy in the European Union* (New York: Palgrave Macmillan, 2007).

[54] For an analysis that captures this trade-off, see Bastian Giegerich, "Not Such a Soft Power: The External Deployment of European Forces," *Survival* 46 (2004).

[55] See, for example, Hans-Christian Hagman, "EU Crisis Management Capabilities," paper presented to the conference "The European Union—Its Role and Power in the Emerging International System," Woodrow Wilson School, Princeton University, October 3–5, 2003; and Julian Lindley-French, "In the Shadow of Locarno? Why European Defense Is Failing," *International Affairs* 78 (2002).

[56] See, for example, Pape, "Soft Balancing against the United States," 29–32; Paul, "Soft Balancing," 64–70; and Walt, *Taming American Power*, 130–131.

linchpin of the "coalition of the unwilling," made a point of describing their policy as part of an overall preference for a multipolar world.

Nevertheless, to explain what happened by referring to balance-of-threat theory oversimplifies and misrepresents what occurred. Security concerns about the United States played no discernable role for some of the principal actors in the drama. For others, strategic calculations that superficially resemble balancing, but actually stem from a different logic, interacted in complex ways with other incentives that also pushed toward constraining the United States. Even a generous rendering of the balance-of-threat argument would accord such balancing at best a minor role.[57]

GERMANY AND TURKEY

A central link in the complex chain of events that ended in the failure of the U.S. attempt to achieve a second UN Security Council resolution authorizing the invasion of Iraq was Germany's uncompromising opposition to U.S. policy and, as a consequence, a brief but dramatic shift in post–Cold War Franco-German relations. For the first time in more than a decade, Berlin was the supplicant in the relationship, which presented Paris with an attractive opportunity to regain its status as the EU's driver just as it was expanding to include a raft of new Central European member states.[58] This shift originated in German domestic politics.

To be sure, Chancellor Schröder expressed doubts about the wisdom of invading Iraq long before Germany's election campaign got under way in the summer of 2002. But his need to recapture elements of his political base soon pointed toward taking an especially strong stand on the issue. Running on a dismal economic record and having alienated his left-wing supporters with tough economic proposals and controversial military commitments abroad, Schröder was facing near-

---

[57] In reconstructing interallied disputes over Iraq, the best extant account is Philip H., Gordon and Jeremy Shapiro, *Allies at War: America, Europe, and the Crisis over Iraq* (New York: McGraw-Hill, 2004). Other accounts and chronologies that were critical in constructing this case study included Elizabeth Pond, *Friendly Fire: The Near-Death of the Transatlantic Alliance* (Washington, D.C.: Brookings Institution Press and European Union Studies Association, 2003); Gustav Lindstrom and Burkhardt Schmidt, eds., "One Year On: Lessons from Iraq," Challiot Paper No. 68, EU Institute for Security Studies, March 2004; John Peterson, "Europe, America, Iraq: Worst Ever, Ever Worsening?" *Journal of Common Market Studies* 42 (2004); David Allen and Michael Smith, "External Policy Developments," *Journal of Common Market Studies* 42 (2004); and "The Divided West," parts 1–3, *Financial Times*, May 27–30, 2003.

[58] Pond, *Friendly Fire*, chap. 3.

certain defeat as the political season began to ramp up. His political advisers told him that his reelection hinged on recapturing two left-wing constituencies: core Social Democratic Party (SPD) activists, and left-wing voters in eastern Germany who were defecting to the pacifist and anti-American Party of Democratic Socialism (the successor party of the former Communists).[59] Both of these constituencies had long-standing preferences against war in general: not anti–Iraq War or anti–unilateral war, but *antiwar*. The strength of antiwar preferences (which are unrelated to U.S. power and existed long before the onset of unipolarity) in these constituencies key to Schröder's reelection helps to explain why he adopted the position on Iraq that he did.

In this political environment, along came what one Schröder operative called "the miracle" of Vice President Dick Cheney's August 26 speech calling for preventive war in Iraq and questioning a UN-based approach.[60] The speech gave the Schröder team a chance to relaunch its reelection bid on an uncompromising antiwar platform. The campaign's tenor and dynamic changed immediately. As antiwar passions mounted, economic issues, on which the Christian Democrats' Edmund Stoiber had been campaigning effectively, receded into the background. Political incentives pushed Schröder toward an increasingly uncompromising antiwar stand. Even after President Bush moved away from Cheney's initial stance and took the Iraq matter to the UN, Schröder adopted a hard-line position, declaring his refusal to support the use of force even if sanctioned by the Security Council. Yet, as strident as he became on Iraq, Schröder never expressed his opposition in balancing or multipolar terms, sticking to a script of opposition on strategic grounds combined with a general posture as a principled socialist heroically standing up to a U.S. president who embodied everything German leftists loathe.[61]

A second link in the story of constraining the United States on Iraq was Turkey's decision not to permit the U.S. military to use its territory for an assault on Saddam Hussein's army.[62] In hindsight, the decision did not undermine the invasion's operational effectiveness, but this

[59] Martin Walker, "The Winter of Germany's Discontent," *World Policy Journal* 19 (2002–3).

[60] Ibid.

[61] See, e.g., Jeffrey Herf, "The Perfect Storm and After: Retrospect and Prospect for American-German Relations," American Institute for Contemporary German Studies, http://www.aicgs.org/analysis/c/herfc.aspx (consulted October 10, 2007).

[62] See Pape, "Soft Balancing against the United States"; and Walt, "Can the United States Be Balanced?"

was not clear at the time. Accordingly, many analysts view the Turks' decision as an example of balancing. In this case, however, long-standing domestic political dynamics were even more dominant than in Germany, for they overwhelmed a strategic decision to support the United States. Of key importance here was Turkey's baleful experience of the 1990–91 Persian Gulf War, which was widely perceived as an economic disaster for the Turks. Also significant was Turkey's concern that upsetting the status quo in Iraq could alter the political equation regarding the Iraqi Kurds, whose independence might incite conationals in Turkey itself. These two historical legacies help to explain why any Turkish government would have had to bargain hard for strong guarantees from the United States to reassure a public that was skeptical about the consequences of another war in the region. Negotiations with Turkey followed three tracks: political (regarding the degree of autonomy for Iraqi Kurds and the fate of Iraqis of Turkish descent); military (concerning where Turkish troops could be deployed in Iraq); and economic (compensation for the costs that a war would impose on Turkey).

Although the details of the economic package were never fully worked out, Prime Minister Tayyip Erdogan and the leadership of his Islamist Justice and Development Party ultimately supported a three-track deal to allow the United States to use Turkey as a staging ground for the invasion of Iraq and submitted a resolution to parliament asking their members to support it.[63] Erdogan and the party leadership calculated that supporting the Bush administration would best secure Turkey's interests in postwar Iraq while maximizing the economic benefits. Both the powerful Turkish military and the opposition Republican People's Party, however, opted to free ride and let the ruling party suffer the domestic political costs of pushing through the measure, assuming, as did Erdogan and most analysts, that it would pass. In the event, it did win a majority under standard rules. But under Turkish parliamentary rules, the 19 abstentions meant that the resolution failed by three votes to win the necessary simple majority of those present. News accounts note that some parliamentarians' ignorance of this rule may have affected their votes.[64] Immediately thereafter, top generals who had previously opted to free ride sought to reverse the decision.

[63] Mustafa Kibaroglu, "Turkey Says No," *Bulletin of the Atomic Scientists* 59 (2003).
[64] "A Pivotal Nation Goes into a Spin," *Economist*, March 8, 2003, 41. See also Gordon and Shapiro, *Allies at War*.

By the time these machinations got under way, however, the rapid advance of U.S. and British forces in Iraq radically devalued the importance of the Turkish invasion route.

In sum, the behavior of both Germany and Turkey can be largely traced to long-standing domestic political dynamics that are unrelated to the concentration of power in the United States. Russia and France are far more complex actors in this case because both had stated preferences for multipolarity, general policies of buttressing the role of the UN Security Council and thus the bargaining value of their veto power in that body, economic interests in play in Iraq, and sincere policy differences with the United States over costs and benefits of a war and its relation to the war on terrorism. The interaction among these dynamics was complicated. How does the balance-of-threat explanation fit into this mosaic?

RUSSIA

President Putin and his top foreign policy aides were reluctant to take the lead in any coalition constraining the Bush administration, having just entered a period in which close cooperation with the United States was highly valued.[65] At the same time, they were inclined to maintain their existing policy on Iraq, under which Russia reaped rich economic rewards. Russian firms profited handsomely under the UN's oil-for-food program, and Saddam Hussein also offered longer-term inducements that Russia could realize only if sanctions were withdrawn: a major development contract with Russia's Lukoil (valued at some $12 billion) and the prospect of settling Iraq's state debt to Russia of about $8 billion. As long as there was some possibility that the Iraq issue could be settled with the Baathist regime in power, Russia had incentives to position itself to reap these promised rewards.

Putin's initial response to these mixed incentives was to keep his options open with strategic ambiguity. While Foreign Minister Igor Ivanov made strong statements in opposition to U.S. pronouncements, Putin authorized official contacts with Iraqi opposition figures and chose to support UN Security Council Resolution 1441 in November, which warned Iraq of "serious consequences" if it did not meet its disarmament obligations. Meanwhile, U.S. officials sought Russian support by offering inducements—honoring Iraqi contracts with Russian

---

[65] See William C. Wohlforth, "Russia," in Ellings and Friedberg, *Strategic Asia, 2002–03*; and Thomas M. Nichols, "Russia's Turn West: Sea Change or Opportunism?" *World*

oil companies, and promising Russia a role in the postwar stabilization—which the United States could deliver only after a regime change in Baghdad. Putin's most trusted aides reportedly worked hard to reach an agreement with Bush administration officials.[66] But as long as Putin remained uncertain of U.S. resolve and ability to prevail, he risked more by aligning himself with the United States than by standing aloof. If Hussein survived the crisis—perhaps by satisfying the world that Iraq had disarmed—Putin would lose the economic benefits Baghdad offered, having gained nothing. Pressuring Baghdad to disarm in accordance with Resolution 1441 thus had three overlapping benefits: it maintained the prestige of the Security Council (Russia's favored forum); it did not foreclose the possibility of cooperation with the United States if Hussein proved recalcitrant; and it maintained Russia's potentially profitable position in case the crisis was resolved without a full-scale invasion of Iraq.

Ultimately, Russia chose to align with France and Germany in opposing a second UN resolution authorizing an invasion. In intense diplomatic exchanges in January and February 2003, President Jacques Chirac convinced Putin that France (with Germany) would lead the campaign. With such longtime U.S. allies taking the lead, Putin could expect that the diplomatic costs of opposing Washington would be minor. Given the relatively low expected costs, other factors argued in favor of Putin's decision. In particular, Putin appears to have considered an invasion to be an unwise and potentially very costly strategic move that would ill serve the war on terror.[67]

Putin worked hard to ensure that his tack toward Europe did not come at the expense of a working strategic partnership with the United States. As his foreign policy aide Sergei Prikhodko put it, "Our partnership with the United States is not a hostage of the Iraq crisis. There are far too many common values and common tasks both short term and long term. . . . Our co-operation never stopped, even during the Iraq crisis."[68] This was not just rhetoric; concrete cooperation continued on intelligence sharing, nuclear arms control, NATO expansion,

---

Policy Journal 19 (2002–3). On Putin's strategy and maneuverings on Iraq, see Wohlforth, "Russia's Soft Balancing Act," in Ellings and Friedberg, *Strategic Asia, 2003–04.*

[66] Pavel Felgenhauer, "New Détente to Die Young," *Moscow Times*, May 29, 2003, 9.

[67] Reports suggest that Russia's intelligence services were feeding Putin wildly exaggerated estimates of Iraq's prospects in a war with U.S. forces. See Sergei Karaganov, "Crisis Lessons," *Moscow News*, April 23, 2003, 2.

[68] Quoted in Andrew Jack and Stefan Wagstyl, "Optimism on Russian Postwar Accord with U.S.," *Financial Times*, May 16, 2003, 8.

peacekeeping in Afghanistan, and the multilateral efforts to counter the proliferation threat from North Korea—all of which helped to ensure that Russia would not jeopardize its overall relationship with the United States.[69] And as then National Security Adviser Condoleezza Rice's famous quip "Punish France, ignore Germany, and forgive Russia" indicates, this strategy worked.[70]

FRANCE

The primacy of long-standing domestic political factors in the German and Turkish cases, and Russia's extreme circumspection and unwillingness to face any significant trade-off between constraining the United States on Iraq and other goals, all serve to bring France's role to the fore. Nevertheless, checking U.S. power is notably absent from the three main explanations for French policy that experts highlight.[71]

First was the dispute over policy between the French and U.S. governments. After 9/11, both the United States and France were greatly concerned about the threat of international terrorism and wanted to take decisive steps to reduce it. Concerning Afghanistan, both governments saw forceful expulsion of the Taliban as a valuable step in the effort against terrorism. Regarding the value of invading Iraq, in contrast, French and U.S. policymakers reached dramatically different assessments. While the Bush administration saw the invasion as advancing its foreign policy goals in the Middle East, President Chirac, Foreign Minister Dominique de Villepin, and, indeed, most of the

[69] Pentagon allegations that Russia's intelligence services provided information on U.S. deployments to Saddam Hussein before the U.S. invasion implied that Russia tried to play both sides of the fence. Subsequent reports, however, revealed that the original claims were incorrect. The attack scenarios found in Iraqi archives apparently were written by a hard-line Russian military journalist and given to Russia's ambassador to Baghdad, who handed them off to Saddam's entourage. See "German Paper Sees 'Mix-Up' behind US-Russia Row in Iraq War Plan Case," *Financial Times*, April 24, 2006.

[70] Elaine Sciolino, "French Struggle Now with How to Coexist with Bush," *New York Times*, February 8, 2005, A9.

[71] The following sources were especially helpful in reconstructing French policymaking on Iraq: Gordon and Shapiro, *Allies at War*; Pond, *Friendly Fire*; "The Divided West," parts 1–3; Howorth, "European Security and Defense"; and the conference "The United States and France after the War in Iraq," May 12, 2003, Center for the United States and France, Brookings Institution, Washington, D.C., www.brookings.edu/fp/cusf/events/20030512cusf.htm (consulted September 19, 2007). The assessments in these analyses correspond to those found in the wider literature. Analysts do not see economic incentives as being important in this case; see, for example, Valerie Marcel, "Total in Iraq," U.S.-France Analysis Series, Center for the United States and France, Brookings Institution, Washington D.C., August 2003.

French policy establishment opposed invading Iraq on a variety of grounds, chief among them their expectation that an occupation of Iraq would be so bloody and long as to worsen the problem of Al Qaeda–style terrorism.[72] Given France's large Muslim population and its perceived high exposure to Islamic terrorism, these potential downsides of a contested occupation of Iraq were salient to French policymakers.[73] Hence, at the outset they faced strong incentives to bargain with the United States to alter the Bush administration's policy. Pushing for the issue to be handled in the UN reflected not only France's immediate policy interests, but also its long-term bargaining incentive to maintain the centrality of the Security Council. Once the Bush administration made it clear that it would invade Iraq no matter what, criticizing the Iraq invasion could still be seen as France's optimal response, especially given that the invasion's operational effectiveness did not depend on France's assistance.

Second, informed accounts of French policy highlight European regional dynamics. At a time when the EU faced new challenges resulting from its inclusion of several Central European states, President Chirac could not afford to lose the policy initiative to Chancellor Schröder. Schröder's vulnerability in the face of Washington's ire at his decision made him the supplicant in the bilateral relationship with France, which gave Chirac the opportunity to restart the Franco-German "motor" of the EU with himself in control. Chirac's decision in January to side with Schröder allowed him to co-opt the German leader and restore France to a more commanding role in EU affairs.

[72] See, e.g., "Interview given by M. Jacques Chirac, President of the Republic, to 'TF1' and 'France2,'" March 10, 2003, http://www.elysee.fr/elysee/francais/actualites/a_l_elysee/2003/mars/interview_televisee_sur_l_iraq-page_2–2.4840.html (consulted September 19, 2007); also indicative are the analyses of French counterterror expert Judge Jean-Louis Bruguière. See Bruguière, "Terrorism after the War in Iraq," *US-France Analysis*, May 2003, http://www.brookings.edu/articles/2003/05france_bruguiere.aspx (consulted October 10, 2007). For an excellent general analysis of U.S.-European policy differences on Iraq, see Pond, *Friendly Fire*, chap. 3.

[73] Ex post, the French assessment that the Iraq war would make the terrorism problem worse appears to be right; ex ante, however, this was not entirely clear. It also now seems that by distancing itself from the U.S. policy that it disagreed with, Paris may have been successful in insulating France from the potential downsides of the Iraq invasion that it predicted: indicative in this regard is a recent Program on International Policy Attitudes poll, which found that among the major powers, France is the one most widely viewed worldwide as having a positive influence. "Who Will Lead the World?" April 6, 2005, 1, available at http://www.worldpublicopinion.org/pipa/articles/views_on_countriesregions_bt/114.php?nid=&id=&pnt=114&lb=btvoc (consulted October 17, 2007).

Third, observers agree that long-standing domestic political dynamics played a role in the French president's calculations. For a variety of reasons, the French public has long had an appreciation of standing up to the United States.[74] True to his Gaullist roots, Chirac saw the advantage of playing to this traditional sentiment, particularly given that he had just weathered a touch-and-go reelection in which he won only 19 percent of the vote in the first round.

In the view of most analysts, European regional dynamics and domestic political incentives were important influences on French policy in this case, but they were dominated by policy and bargaining considerations. Had the logic of policy and bargaining pointed toward participation in the war, Chirac would likely have ignored the domestic political incentives. On the other hand, the political and European dimensions may well have tipped the balance in favor of opposition beyond what might have been optimal for policy and bargaining purposes. That, at any rate, is the assessment of numerous French critics of Chirac's and de Villepin's conduct during the crisis.[75] The critical issue, therefore, is to assess the degree to which the balancing explanation captures the general UN Security Council–focused bargaining stance and how this interacted with the more immediate policy concerns swirling around the Iraq issue.

Unlike their counterparts in Moscow and Berlin, Chirac and de Villepin publicly associated their position on Iraq with their preference for a multipolar world. Although the term *multipolarity* as French statesmen use it has many meanings, none matches its definition in political science. If we judge by their public utterances, both men believed that France and the world are better off when key decisions regarding global security are arrived at multilaterally—and that the UN Security Council is an important mechanism in that process.[76] This

[74] Sophie Meunier, "The Distinctiveness of French Anti-Americanism," in Katzenstein and Keohane, *Anti-Americanisms in World Politics.*

[75] See, for example, Lionel Jospin, "The Relationship between France and America," lecture delivered at Harvard University, December 4, 2003; and commentary by French participants at Brookings conference "The United States and France after the War in Iraq."

[76] To cite one example: It was widely reported that the first sentence Chirac uttered in the interview in which he announced his intention to veto the second UNSC resolution was, "We want to live in a multipolar world." In fact, that was the first *clause* he uttered. The remainder of the sentence reads, "i.e. one with a few large groups enjoying as harmonious relations as possible with each another, a world in which Europe, among others, will have its full place, a world in which democracy progresses, hence the fundamental importance for us of the United Nations Organization which provides a

preference fits with France's conception of its identity and foreign policy traditions, but it also merges seamlessly with a rational bargaining strategy vis-à-vis the United States that exploits the fortuitous circumstance of being one of the five veto-wielding permanent members of the Security Council.[77] Given the veto, a policy preference for maintaining the prestige of the Security Council by trying to delegitimize recourse to force without its sanction marginally increases France's influence over the United States. That influence is valuable, given that France is incapable of countering American power or, in most cases, fielding forces of its own to accomplish global missions such as disarming Iraq.

The primary purpose of that bargaining stance, however, is not necessarily to check U.S. power generally but to enhance France's ability to bargain over specific responses to global security issues. In the Iraq case, France's general desire to bolster the Security Council aligned with its real policy preferences on Iraq. Together these incentives pushed Paris toward a position between Germany's outright opposition and the American-British stance. Opposition as categorical as Schröder's would push Washington toward unilateralism and thus weaken the Security Council. In late August, de Villepin repositioned France's policy on Iraq to accept the possibility of the use of force as long as it was channeled through the Security Council. After President Bush put the disarmament of Iraq before the UN in September 2002, France agreed to Security Council Resolution 1441, following hard bargaining to prevent the inclusion of wording that would have given the United States and Britain a green light to topple Hussein without further Security Council say-so.

Chirac's policy may have lured the United States into the web of UN diplomacy, but only by moving France's stance much closer to Washington's and London's and actively preparing to sanction and even participate in a war against Iraq. French policymakers initially assumed that Hussein's recalcitrance would probably lead to a violation of Resolution 1441 and a casus belli. Although it is impossible to know

framework and gives impetus to this democracy and harmony" ("Interview Given by Chirac"). See, for a good example of the foreign minister's thinking, the Alastair Buchan Lecture, 2003, delivered by Foreign Minister Dominique de Villepin, March 27, 2003 at the International Institute for Strategic Studies, http://www.iiss.org/conferences/alastair-buchan/the-alastair-buchan-lecture-2003 (consulted October 17, 2007).

[77] Erik Voeten, "Outside Options and the Logic of Security Council Action," *American Political Science Review* 95 (2001).

whether Chirac was sincere, the evidence suggests that France actively prepared for possible participation in a military action against Iraq, including mobilizing the carrier *Charles de Gaulle,* readying the armed forces, and initiating staff talks with the commander in chief of the U.S. Central Command, General Tommy Franks, on a possible 15,000-man contribution to an allied assault on Iraq. The policy was logical, given Chirac's policy preferences and bargaining interests: France's main hope of pushing Washington and London closer to its preferred policy was by using its influence in the UN Security Council, a route that benefited the longer-term strategy of buttressing the role of that body. Given that bargaining incentives and policy preferences worked in tandem here, France did not face a trade-off between them. It is therefore hard to assign relative weight to each.

These incentives, however, do not always coincide. In one recent case where the two incentives came into conflict—Kosovo—France's position of supporting NATO military action in 1999 was consistent with its immediate policy preferences but not with the long-term bargaining incentive of maintaining the centrality of the UN Security Council. In the Iraq case, even though it served both the general bargaining interest and the immediate policy preference of the French, France's initial policy simply is not consistent with the argument for balance-of-threat constraints because it potentially eased the diplomatic path for a massive exercise and possible expansion of U.S. power.

In January 2003 Chirac learned that the Bush administration was going to go to war regardless of what the UN weapons inspectors uncovered in Iraq. This intelligence exposed a fundamental contradiction between French and U.S.-U.K. policy preferences that had been diplomatically obfuscated until that moment. Chirac strongly preferred containment and inspections as a way of dealing with Iraq, while Bush and Prime Minister Tony Blair just as strongly preferred regime change. The fact that the inspections seemed—to the UN's Hans Blix and the French, at least—to be going so well (which Chirac frankly acknowledged was the result of American and British military pressure) exacerbated the contradictions between the two sides' preferred policies. The realization that the Iraq question was going to be resolved through regime change no matter what the inspectors discovered meant that the French would not participate in the coalition. The only question was how strongly to oppose the Bush administration's decision.

The French leadership much preferred a low-key approach to the Iraq issue. They tried to avoid a public showdown with the United States and the United Kingdom by urging them not to try for a second resolution—in which case, they argued in meetings with Bush officials, the French government would voice disapproval but otherwise stand aside. The Bush administration rejected Chirac's "gentlemen's agreement" out of deference to Blair, who believed that he needed a second Security Council resolution for domestic reasons.[78] But for this unique domestic contingency, a Washington-Paris deal might have been struck, and the most dramatic phase of the interallied dispute avoided. In the event, Chirac decided to work hard to deny the Americans and the British a second resolution, resulting in the well-publicized spectacle of the two sides feverishly lining up allies in the UN, France's veto threat, and the American and British failure to round up a majority in the Security Council.

SUMMARY ASSESSMENT OF THE IRAQ CASE

The argument for balance-of-threat constraints holds that the Bush administration's foreign policy moves increased other great powers' apprehensions of the United States, prompting increased efforts to constrain U.S. power. Our review of the events leading up to the invasion of Iraq shows how mistaken this argument is. For France—the linchpin of the diplomatic coalition that confronted the Bush administration—policy differences, longer-term bargaining incentives, European regional dynamics, and long-standing domestic political incentives all pushed toward constraining the United States in this instance. Even though the French leadership strongly disagreed with the Bush administration over the sagacity of invading Iraq on strategic grounds, the most precedent-breaking aspect of French behavior—the intense campaign against the United States and Britain in the UN Security Council—was something President Chirac tried to avoid. The second UN resolution, and the attendant debate, went forward only because of complex domestic incentives acting on Prime Minister Blair. Proponents of the argument for balance-of-threat constraints are thus wrong to attribute the novel elements in French policy in this case mainly to a shift in French concerns about U.S. power.

[78] This episode is detailed in Gordon and Shapiro, *Allies at War*; see also Howorth "European Security and Defence."

What is true for France also applies to the other key players. The most salient and novel behavior in the Iraq case—especially Chancellor Schröder's fateful decision to oppose the Bush administration categorically—cannot be seen as a response to the underlying power of the United States or to any updated German assessment of the American reputation for benign intentions. Great power behavior during the years immediately following the invasion of Iraq provides further evidence against argument for balance-of-threat constraints. In particular, far from seeking to further distance themselves from the United States, France and Germany rushed to pursue a rapprochement with the Bush administration during this period. Significantly, this move had already gathered substantial momentum even before President Bush and his new secretary of state, Condoleezza Rice, extended a diplomatic olive branch after his 2004 reelection and the subsequent elections of Angela Merkel in Germany and Nicholas Sarkozy in France.

Conclusion: The "Systemic Difference"

Our examination of cases balance-of-threat theorists cite confirms our argument's prediction: that great power constraining actions emerge only when they are compatible with other state priorities unrelated to U.S. power. This finding, combined with the more general dearth of balancing examples, means that there is no empirical basis to the argument for constraints based on balance-of-threat theory.

An influential argument derived from a well-established IR theory thus does not apply to the United States under unipolarity. What are the larger implications of this finding? After all, the great power constraining actions examined in this chapter were real. Nothing in this chapter suggests that the United States need not be concerned about them. The chief difference between the balance-of-threat explanation and the alternative explanation derived from our larger argument is that the former is a systemic constraint while the latter is not. This difference is critical for three reasons.

First is analytical clarity. Of all the complex motivations in play in the Iraq case, the bargaining incentive is closest to what analysts mean by balancing. But the differences between balancing and bargaining are profound. Bargaining—or "normal diplomatic friction, as Lieber and Alexander call it—is ubiquitous in a world of self-interested states.[79] Using the term *balancing* to describe bargaining amounts in practice to equating balancing with international relations writ large. If it becomes another word for bargaining, balancing is meaningless as an analytical concept—something that describes a constant, rather than a variable; a mundane rather than noteworthy development in international politics. Balancing, in short, is a systemic constraint while bargaining is governed by the specific constellation of interests among the states involved in a given issue.

The difference between systemic balancing and a constraint driven by multiple, dyad-specific factors becomes even clearer when one considers that bargaining incentives can sometimes drive states into behavior that is the opposite of balancing. In the Iraq case, for example, France's bargaining interest in maintaining the importance of the UN Security Council led it to follow a policy that held out as a real possibility a UN sanction of a U.S.-led invasion of Iraq. Pursuit of this bargaining incentive led France toward a policy that, in the end, might have abetted and helped to legitimize a potential expansion of U.S. power in the Persian Gulf—that is, the opposite of what one would expect from the argument for balance-of-threat constraints. To call this balancing makes a mockery of the concept.

This episode relates to the second reason for stressing the systemic difference: the argument for balance-of-threat constraints posits a direct and positive link between relative U.S. power and the strength of the restraints on U.S. security policy, while our alternative explanation does not. If it means anything, the balancing argument must predict that less U.S. power and lower involvement will reduce incentives for other states to gain relative power. If our argument is right, however, then there is no reason to expect that reducing either U.S. power or the level of its global engagement would reduce other states' incentives to build up their capabilities. On the contrary, a U.S. withdrawal from the world—as neoisolationists advocate—could easily generate new security dynamics that produce much greater incentives for other powers to increase their capabilities.[80]

The third and most crucial difference concerns the scope and strength of expected future constraining actions by great powers. The constraints conjured up by the balance-of-threat argument are potentially systemwide. If the United States goes too far, the argument goes,

---

[79] Lieber and Alexander, "Waiting for Balancing."

[80] For further discussion of these points, see Brooks and Wohlforth, "Striking the Balance."

it could upset international equilibrium and call forth escalating constraints globally. In contrast, our argument indicates that the United States does not face constraints of such wide scope and potential strength. Other states may take actions that end up impeding U.S. security policy in future years, but this will ultimately depend on a constellation of factors particular to other societies that is unrelated to U.S. power.

Liberalism, Globalization, and the Constraints Derived from Economic Interdependence

LIBERAL INTERNATIONAL THEORY highlights the capacity of international institutions, domestic politics, and economic interdependence to influence international security behavior.[1] We discuss the role of international institutions in chapter 5, and there is a large literature on the domestic political constraints on U.S. security policy, as discussed in chapter 1. This chapter examines the liberal argument concerning how U.S. security policy is influenced by enhanced global economic interdependence—that is, the globalization of trade, finance, and production.

Although interdependence is not limited to the global economy, this is typically how liberal scholars operationalize it when discussing its potential influence on security issues.[2] The signature argument that IR scholars advance regarding constraints on foreign policy is that enhanced economic interdependence changes the degree to which states are open to influence attempts by other states. As David Baldwin emphasizes, as a state becomes more dependent upon the global economy, it exposes itself to a wider range of economic strategies that can be deployed against it by other states.[3] In recent decades, it is evident that U.S. exposure to economic globalization has increased in the trade, finance, and production realms: U.S. exports as a percentage of GDP rose from just under 5.8 percent in 1970 to slightly more than 11.2 percent in 2000; the U.S. outward foreign direct investment (FDI) stock as a percentage of GDP has increased from 7.3 percent in 1970 to 17.1 percent in 2003; and the share of total U.S. long-term securities held by foreigners has increased from 4.8 percent in 1974 to 16.7 percent in 2005.[4] As U.S. international economic exposure has risen, so too has

---

[1] See, for example, Oneal and Russett, "Classical Liberals Were Right," 268–69; and Robert Keohane, "International Liberalism Reconsidered," in *The Economic Limits to Modern Politics*, ed. John Dunn (Cambridge: Cambridge University Press, 1990).

[2] Prominent examples include Rosecrance, *Rise of Trading State*; and Oneal and Russett, "Classical Liberals Were Right."

[3] David A. Baldwin, *Economic Statecraft* (Princeton: Princeton University Press, 1985).

[4] FDI data from Bureau of Economic Analysis; export data from World Bank; finance data from Report on Foreign Portfolio Holdings of U.S. Securities, Department of the Treasury, Federal Reserve Bank of New York, May 2007.

the opportunity cost of reduced access to economic globalization—
something that we would expect, in general, to increase the utility of
economic statecraft strategies.[5]

A number of analysts have indeed argued that the United States has
become increasingly exposed to limits on its security policy as it has
embraced economic globalization to an ever greater extent in recent
decades. Although there is much to the general liberal argument that
enhanced exposure to economic interdependence leads to greater constraints on security policy, the analysis in this chapter shows that it
does not apply to the United States today. This is principally because
of the position the United States occupies in the system. If the U.S.
economy were not so large as a proportion of the system (U.S. GDP
constitutes 27.5 percent of the world total) and did not have such great
importance for the welfare of foreign firms and other states, then much
of the standard liberal argument would likely apply. In large part because the United States occupies such a dominant position in the system and other states are generally much more dependent on it than it
is on them, the United States is in the enviable position of being able
to enhance its economic capacity via enhanced trade, financial, and
production linkages without simultaneously having to face the prospect that other states will increasingly use economic statecraft to hin-
der its security policy.

If the standard liberal view did, in fact, apply to the United States,
we would expect to see an increase in the use of economic statecraft
to influence its security policy as the level of economic interdependence, and U.S. exposure to it, increases. As economic globalization
has accelerated over the past few decades, and as the opportunity cost
of reduced access to the global economy has increased, the use of economic sanctions has indeed sharply increased: there were 117 cases of
economic sanctions from 1970 to 1998, as compared to 53 cases from
1914 to 1969. Significantly, this trend is driven in large part by a much
greater propensity on the part of the United States to use economic
sanctions as a tool of foreign policy: unilateral U.S. sanctions account
for more than half (62 out of 117) of the cases of economic sanctions
from 1970 to 1998.[6] Yet even as the United States has become ever more

---

[5] What is at issue here is not the absolute effectiveness of economic statecraft throughout history, but rather the effectiveness of this foreign policy tool relative to the past and
also to other foreign policy instruments. The point here is that there are theoretical
grounds for concluding that the potential utility of economic statecraft strategies will
increase as the opportunity cost of constrained access to the global economy increases.

[6] Data from Gary Clyde Hufbauer, "Trade as a Weapon," paper presented at the
Fred J. Hansen Institute for World Peace, San Diego State University, April 1999, avail-

linked to the international economy and ever more willing to use economic sanctions against others, over the last three decades no state has ever attempted to use economic sanctions against the United States in order to influence its security policy.[7]

Looking beyond economic sanctions, it is hard to identify documented cases in which other states have employed *any* form of economic leverage against the United States in order to influence its security policy. Instead, we find numerous forgone opportunities to take actions of this kind. For example, despite the intensity of the dispute over the Iraq War between the United States and European powers such as France and Germany, there was no European effort to alter the nature of negotiations with Washington regarding the WTO.[8] And although there were some efforts by European consumer groups to initiate a boycott of U.S. products in light of the Iraq controversy, these boycott efforts operated independently of government actions and, moreover, they were not widespread and did not produce significant results.[9]

Even the strongest champions of the view that the standard liberal argument does apply to the United States today have trouble identifying cases in which other states have undertaken economic leverage policies in order to alter U.S. security policy. For example, the scholar most responsible for calling attention to the ways economic globalization enhances the ability of other states to use cutoffs of military supplies as a tool for influencing U.S. foreign policy cannot identify a single actual case of this happening.[10] Of course, economic leverage may

---

able at http://www.iie.com/publications/papers/paper.cfm?ResearchID=342 (consulted September 19, 2007).

[7] This is the conclusion from a comprehensive analysis of economic sanctions by a research team at the Institute of International Economics; see Gary Clyde Hufbauer, Jefferey J. Schott, and Kimberly Ann Elliott, *Economic Sanctions Reconsidered*, 3rd ed. (Washington, D.C.: Institute of International Economics, 2005). The last documented case of economic sanctions used against the United States to influence its security policy is the Arab League / OPEC restriction of oil supplies sent to the United States from October 1973 to March 1974; for an overview, see Gary Clyde Hufbauer, Jefferey J. Schott and Kimberly Ann Elliott, *Economic Sanctions Reconsidered* (Washington, D.C.: Institute of International Economics, 1985), 465–72.

[8] This case is discussed in more detail in chapter 5.

[9] See the discussion in Katzenstein and Keohane, *Anti-Americanism in World Politics*.

[10] Theodore Moran does identify one hypothetical scenario: that during the 1980s there "was the fear that dovish Japanese political leaders would place conditions on the provision of advanced ceramics from the Kyocera corporation that were used to house the Tomahawk cruise missile guidance system." "Defense Economics and Security," 137. The United States, of course, faces fears of supply cutoffs all the time; the key issue is the likelihood that threat will actually emerge and will impose significant costs. Regarding

be difficult to observe.[11] Yet it is significant that even those analysts who underscore the potential efficacy of economic leverage as a tool for influencing the United States have so much trouble identifying cases of this kind.

This pattern is consistent with the core argument developed in this chapter: that the United States' immense economic size and general importance within the global economy make other states generally much more economically dependent on it than vice versa. The chapter is organized as follows. We begin by outlining the basic features of the liberal argument on interdependence. We then analyze its core theoretical argument that enhanced economic interdependence opens up opportunities for economic statecraft strategies. We successively examine the four key ways that the United States has become increasingly dependent on the global economy in recent decades as economic globalization has accelerated: (1) foreign export market dependence, (2) inward FDI dependence, (3) outward FDI dependence, and (4) financial dependence. We show why these enhanced forms of U.S. dependence on the global economy do not augment the leverage that other states have over U.S. security policy.

The final section of the chapter looks beyond economic statecraft strategies, since enhanced levels of economic interdependence could

---

Kyocera, it is true that it once discontinued making the ceramic package for a key component used by the Pentagon; however, it does not appear that the Japanese government played any role in influencing this decision (see Andrew Pollack, "Japan's Growing Role in Chips Worrying the U.S.," *New York Times*, January 5, 1987). Relatedly, there is a documented case in which "several Japanese electronic companies refused to provide American defense companies with rush orders of key components" just prior to the 1991 Persian Gulf War. In this case, the firms in question did not want to be unable to honor contracts they had with other firms. Ultimately, the U.S. government lobbied the Japanese government to put pressure on the firms; in response to requests from the Japanese government, these firms ultimately did supply the Pentagon with the requested items within a few weeks (suppliers from other countries also contributed needed supplies in the interim). See the discussion of this case in John Eckhouse, "Japan Firms Reportedly Stalled US War Supplies: Pentagon Had to 'Jump through Hoops,' " *San Francisco Chronicle*, April 30, 1991, A1.

[11] For example, even if Arab oil states do not take any direct action, there are many reasons to expect that perceived U.S. oil vulnerability nevertheless constrains the range of security policies that it can adopt toward Saudi Arabia and other key Arab oil exporters (the exact degree to which the United States is vulnerable to oil leverage is a question that requires further research, as we discuss in our concluding chapter). Oil certainly does stand in marked contrast to the economic globalization trends analyzed in this chapter in one key respect: the United States is more dependent on Arab oil-exporting states than vice versa, whereas asymmetries in dependence generally run strongly in the U.S. favor.

potentially limit U.S. security policy in a more indirect manner than is typically emphasized by IR scholars. Specifically, a constraint based in economic interdependence could emerge regardless of any choice by other states to employ economic statecraft. As we show, rising economic interdependence is, for a variety of reasons, very unlikely to engender constraints from nonstate actors, nor is it likely to produce changes in state capabilities that significantly restrict U.S. security policy.

THE ARGUMENT FOR CONSTRAINTS BASED IN ECONOMIC INTERDEPENDENCE

Scholars conceptualize economic interdependence in different ways. In some cases, economic interdependence is conceived in very broad terms—as, essentially, a synonym for economic globalization—and the question is simply whether changes in the global economy can limit state actions. In his classic book on interdependence, for example, Richard Cooper argues that "international economic intercourse both enlarges and confines the freedom of countries to act according to their own lights. It enlarges their freedom by permitting a more economical use of limited resources; it confines their freedom by embedding each country in a matrix of constraints."[12]

Within the literature on international relations, most analysts emphasize the significance of *dependence*; here, the specific focus is on how the global economy makes states more reliant on other states.[13] Scholars advancing this view are divided in large part on the basis of whether they conceptualize economic interdependence as a relationship between pairs of states (which they call a "dyadic" approach) or as a national characteristic derived from the global economy (a "monadic" approach). As David Baldwin notes, "[W]hen an individual state is described as 'dependent,' the obvious question is, 'with respect to whom?' It should specifically be noted that the actor on whom one is dependent may be another state or it may be a rather vague conglomeration of other actors, such as 'other countries,' 'the rest of the world.' "[14]

---

[12] Richard Cooper, *The Economics of Interdependence: Economic Policy in the Atlantic Community* (New York: McGraw-Hill, 1968), 4.

[13] See, for example, Rosecrance, *Rise of Trading State*; Oneal and Russett, "Classical Liberals Were Right"; and Keohane and Nye, *Power and Interdependence*.

[14] David Baldwin, "Interdependence and Power: A Conceptual Analysis," *International Organization* 34 (1980): 496. See also the discussion by Arthur Stein, who notes,

Scholars who view economic interdependence as a national characteristic highlight how it changes the degree to which states are generally dependent on the global economy. Richard Rosecrance, for example, argues in his widely cited study that economic interdependence historically did not have a great influence on the security behavior of the leading states because they could be independent at relatively little cost.[15] Studies that treat interdependence as a relationship between pairs of states focus more on how interdependence creates linkages between states and how breaking these specific linkages can be costly. For example, in their pioneering analysis, Robert Keohane and Joseph Nye stress that "[i]nterdependence, most simply defined, means *mutual* dependence. . . . Our perspective implies that interdependent relationships will always involve costs, since interdependence restricts autonomy."[16] They assert that the general rise of mutual dependence in recent decades—which they note has been driven in significant part by increased economic transactions—can place constraints on states, including the use of military power.[17]

As noted above, the theoretical argument that IR scholars emphasize regarding hindrances on foreign policy is that enhanced economic interdependence changes a state's exposure to economic statecraft strategies. This is far from a hypothetical concern: restricting or putting conditions on economic exchange with a foreign country, or threatening to do so, is a foreign policy tool that recurs throughout history.[18] With respect to trade, governments can employ strategies such as a prohibition on imports, a tariff increase, tariff discrimination, withdrawal of

---

"Most typically, interdependence is conceptualized as a national characteristic derived from international commercial exchange. Nations that export higher proportions of their GNPs are understood to be more open to the world economy—more interdependent— than those selling less abroad. . . . Alternatively, interdependence can be seen as inherently dyadic, as the mutual dependence of pairs of nations. States integrated into the world economy but not part of a bilateral relationship of mutual reliance are not, in this view, interdependent." "Governments, Economic Interdependence, and International Cooperation," in *Behavior, Society, and International Conflict*, ed. Philip Tetlock, Charles Tilly, Robert Jervis, and Jo L. Husbands (New York: Oxford University Press, 1993), 3:257.

[15] Rosecrance, *Rise of Trading State*, 14. As he notes, "States have not until recently had to depend on one another for the necessities of daily existence. In the past, trade was a tactical endeavor, a method used between wars, and one that could easily be sacrificed when military determinants so decreed."

[16] Keohane and Nye, *Power and Interdependence*, 8–9.

[17] Ibid., 9, 27–29.

[18] Much of this history is reviewed in Baldwin, *Economic Statecraft*. For an excellent overview of the range of economic statecraft strategies available to states, see pp. 40–42.

most favored nation treatment, or quotas. With respect to capital, governments can seek to influence the target country in a variety of ways, including freezing its assets or limiting the import or export of capital from it. With respect to outward FDI, a state can pressure the foreign affiliates of its firms to deny inputs to the target country. And with respect to inward FDI, a state can engage in outright expropriation of MNCs from the target country or "partial expropriation" via changes in taxes, depreciation schedules, tariff rates, or other policies that influence the revenue streams of MNCs.[19]

Although analysts regard today's high level of economic interdependence as having significant implications for security affairs, the existing literature does not provide much help in determining whether it actually now restricts U.S. security policy. Despite the fact that there is a massive literature on "globalization," almost all of these examinations are far too general to be of any help for answering the question at hand. Although this literature often discusses U.S. power, constraints on U.S. security policy are not a focus. Moreover, analysts in this literature typically define globalization in very broad terms.[20] Largely for this reason, it is almost impossible to reach anything other than the banal conclusion that globalization augments U.S. power in some ways and undercuts it in others.

More focused, and therefore more relevant, is the large empirical literature that examines how international commerce influences security

[19] This distinction is stressed in Nathan Jensen, "Democratic Governance and Multinational Corporations: Political Regimes and Inflows of Foreign Direct Investment," *International Organization* 57 (2003): 594.

[20] Anthony Giddens defines globalization as "the intensification of worldwide social relations which link distant localities in such a way that local happenings are shaped by events occurring many miles away and vice versa"; Joseph Nye defines it as worldwide networks, with a network being "simply a series of connections of points in a system"; Kenneth Waltz equates globalization with homogenization; Victor Cha sees globalization as the "gradual and ongoing expansion of interaction processes, forms of organization, and forms of cooperation outside the traditional spaces defined by sovereignty"; while for Tony McGrew it is "simply the intensification of global interconnectedness"; for Jean-Marie Guéhenno it is the breakdown of the "separation between domestic and international affairs"; and for Peter Van Ness it is "those human activities that have a reshaping planetary impact." Anthony Giddens, *The Consequences of Modernity* (Stanford, Calif.: Stanford University Press, 1990), 64; Joseph Nye, "The Dependent Colossus," *Foreign Policy* 129 (2002): 74; Kenneth N. Waltz, "Globalization and American Power," *National Interest* 59 (2000): 47; Victor Cha, "Globalization and the Study of International Security," *Journal of Peace Research* 37 (2000): 2; Anthony McGrew, "A Global Society," in *Modernity and Its Futures*, ed. Stuart Hall, David Held, and Tony McGrew (Cambridge, Mass.: Polity Press, 1992), 65; Jean-Marie Guéhenno, "The Impact of Globalisation on Strategy," *Survival* 40 (1998): 6; Peter Van Ness, *Asian Perspective* 23 (1999): 317.

behavior. Yet this literature centers on how commerce influences the overall nature of conflict among states, not on U.S. security policy more specifically.[21] Moreover, almost all of this literature examines how trade influences conflict, even though trade comprises only a minority portion of today's international commerce.

Focusing on the key driver of international commerce in today's global economy—the geographic dispersion of MNC production—Brooks's recent analysis shows that the globalization of production promotes stability among the great powers.[22] Although Brooks's analysis also focuses on the overall pattern of security relations and not U.S. security policy in particular, portions of it do bear on the question at hand. As he shows, the globalization of production has made it impossible for all states, including the great powers, to effectively go it alone in defense production and has also changed the structure of the most advanced states in ways that reduce the economic benefits of conquest. Due to these changes in the economic benefits of conquest and weapons development, he concludes, it has become structurally harder for a great power to "run the tables"—that is, engage in serial conquest, using one instance of conquest as a springboard for the next. Brooks emphasizes that although the United States enjoys a massive advantage in power over other nations, the globalization of production still hinders its ability to run the tables. Although parts of his examination are relevant to understanding whether economic globalization constrains U.S. security policy in other ways, he does not focus on this question. Brooks does find that there is no reason to think that the globalization of production will change the pattern of conflict between

[21] A notable exception is Eugene Gholz and Daryl Press, "The Effects of Wars on Neutral Countries: Why It Doesn't Pay to Preserve the Peace," *Security Studies* 10 (2001). In this article, Gholz and Press focus on the U.S. experience during World War I to evaluate a specific proposition: that increased economic interdependence makes the economies of nonbelligerents vulnerable to the dislocations caused by major wars. Their analysis shows that increased interdependence actually reduces neutrals' vulnerability to third-party wars, which, they maintain, undercuts a recurring rationale for U.S. commitments to uphold the territorial status quo and international security in key regions, notably East Asia and the Middle East.

[22] On trade's secondary status in today's global economy vis-à-vis the globalization of MNC production, see Brooks, *Producing Security,* 16–19. For useful overviews of the literature that focuses on how trade influences conflict, see Katherine Barbieri and Gerald Schneider, "Globalization and Peace: Assessing New Directions in the Study of Trade and Conflict," *Journal of Peace Research* 36 (1999); Susan M. McMillan, "Interdependence and Conflict," *Mershon International Studies* 41 (1997); and Edward Mansfield and Brian Pollins, "The Study of Interdependence and Conflict: Recent Advances, Open Questions, and Directions for Future Research," *Journal of Conflict Resolution* 45 (2001).

the great powers and developing countries—precisely where the bulk of U.S. security policy is now directed—which would seem to suggest that rising levels of economic interdependence will not act as much of a constraint. However, this question needs to be explored in greater depth.

Ultimately, the current literature does not provide much leverage on the question at issue here: does enhanced economic interdependence create limits on U.S. security policy? In the next four sections, we examine the key ways that U.S. dependence on economic globalization has increased in recent decades in order to determine whether other states have gained leverage over U.S. security policy. We will address a series of different arguments; a number are specific and have been advanced directly by scholars, while others are applications of a more general theoretical position.

Dependence Issue Number 1: Foreign Export Markets

If the United States becomes more dependent on a country as an export market, then restricting its access to this particular market would be harmful—perhaps to the point that Washington would consider changing its foreign policy if doing so was a necessary condition for preventing a curtailment of access. What does this hypothetical concern amount to in practice? The key issues are which countries are significant export markets for the United States and, in turn, how likely it is that these countries will actually seek to use this leverage.

Table 4.1 shows the top 20 export markets for the United States. There are only three states—Canada, Mexico, and Japan—that the United States depends upon for more than 5 percent of its total exports. These three countries are all certainly major markets for U.S. products, and it would be very harmful indeed if those products faced restricted access to any of them. But how likely is it that any of them would restrict, or threaten to restrict, access to their markets as a means of influencing U.S. security policy? Given how large the U.S. economy is, it is not surprising that these states are all far more dependent upon the U.S. market than vice versa: as table 4.1 shows, more than 80 percent of Canada's and Mexico's exports are sent to the United States, while the United States absorbs more than one-quarter of Japan's exports. Apart from a U.S. attempt to run the tables militarily, it is hard to fathom any U.S. security policy that would cause any of these three countries to

TABLE 4.1

Top 20 Export Markets for the United States, 2005

Country	Total U.S. exports ($ millions)	Exports as % of total U.S. exports	Foreign exports to U.S.	Total foreign Exports	Foreign exports to U.S. as % of total foreign exports	Dependency on exports to U.S.(%)
Canada	212,192	23.7	294,081	360,136	81.7	57.9
Mexico	120,264	13.4	173,034	214,207	80.8	67.3
Japan	53,265	6.0	138,375	594,941	23.3	17.3
China	41,799	4.7	243,886	761,953	32.0	27.3
United Kingdom	37,569	4.2	50,800	384,365	13.2	9.0
Germany	33,584	3.8	84,967	977,132	8.7	4.9
South Korea	27,135	3.0	43,791	284,418	15.4	12.4
Netherlands	26,288	2.9	14,826	320,065	4.6	1.7
Singapore	20,259	2.3	15,131	229,652	6.6	4.3
France	22,228	2.5	33,848	434,425	7.8	5.3
Taiwan	21,453	2.4	35,103	189,393	18.5	16.1
Belgium	18,562	2.1	13,025	334,206	3.9	1.8
Brazil	15,173	1.7	24,441	116,129	21.0	19.4
Hong Kong	16,319	1.8	9,341	292,119	3.2	1.4
Australia	15,296	1.7	7,291	105,751	6.9	5.2
Switzerland	10,646	1.2	13,004	125,927	10.3	9.1
Malaysia	10,386	1.2	33,693	140,963	23.9	22.7
Italy	11,245	1.3	30,975	373,957	8.3	7.0
India	7,973	0.9	18,819	103,404	18.2	17.3
Israel	8,608	1.0	16,850	42,771	39.4	38.4

Source: Bureau of Economic Analysis on a census basis <www.bea.gov>, except for total foreign country exports from the International Trade Center (UNCTAD / WTO), http://www.intracen.org /applil/TradeCom/TP_EP_CL.aspx?RP=124&YR=2005.

risk the retaliation of curtailed access to the U.S. market, given the economic costs involved. This expectation is only reinforced by the nature of the political relationships they all have with the United States.

Table 4.1 shows that U.S. exports are diversified to a very significant extent, which partly reflects the fact that most foreign markets are very small as compared to the huge volume of U.S. production. What this means is that most of the top 20 export markets for U.S. products are not especially significant when considered on an individual basis. Of course, we need not consider countries individually; a group of countries could also act together to jointly restrict access to U.S. products. However, unless Canada or Mexico can be enticed to join such a coalition—which is unlikely—then a large number of countries would need to act together to be capable of significantly reducing U.S. economic prospects, thereby running into the familiar collective action constraint on coordinated economic restrictions. As various empirical and theoretical studies have shown, cooperation on economic restrictions is very difficult to achieve even among a small group of states.[23]

Reinforcing the collective action problem is the great importance of the huge U.S. market for other countries: all but four of the states noted in table 4.1 depend on the U.S. for at least 7 percent of their total exports. Significantly, these states are all more dependent on the U.S. market than vice versa—often very significantly so, as the last column in table 4.1 shows. This final column simply subtracts the figure in the second column (the percentage of total U.S. exports that go to the foreign country in question) from the figure in the third column (the percentage of the foreign country's total exports that are sent to the United States) and reveals that only three countries come close to having their market be as important to the United States as the U.S. market is to them; in nearly half of the cases, the relative disparity is 15 percent or more. In the end, these other states will have strong reason to fear the prospect of U.S. retaliation if they were to restrict access to their markets.

In sum, it is implausible that foreign governments will undertake, or threaten, a reduction in market access to U.S. goods in order to gain leverage over its security policy.

Dependence Issue Number 2:
Inward FDI and Defense Production

Enhanced levels of both inward FDI and outward FDI can create dependencies that potentially open up avenues for other states to use economic statecraft to constrain U.S. security policy. We will examine

---

[23] See, for example, Michael Mastanduno, *Economic Containment: Cocom and the Politics of East-West Trade* (Ithaca, N.Y.: Cornell University Press, 1992); and Lisa Martin, *Coercive Cooperation* (Princeton: Princeton University Press, 1992).

these two elements of FDI dependency separately, focusing in this section on inward FDI.

Many analysts emphasize that a higher level of inward FDI has great significance for security policy because of how it changes the dynamics of defense production. As noted, Rosecrance underscores that economic interdependence did not have a great influence on the security policies of the leading states until recently because it was long feasible for them to remain economically independent without bearing large costs.[24] In the area of defense production, this has greatly changed in recent decades. The scales have now decisively shifted against a "going it alone" defense production strategy.[25] Beginning in the 1970s, U.S. defense production shifted toward having a high level of internationalization.[26] The globalization of U.S. defense production produced major gains in U.S. weapons systems over the past few decades.[27] However, this augmentation of U.S. military power via globalization carries a key potential downside: as it increasingly relies on non-U.S. companies for defense production, other states may gain leverage they can use to constrain U.S. security policy.

Not surprisingly, numerous scholars and policymakers have advanced concerns about the growing extent to which the Pentagon relies on foreign companies for aspects of weapons production.[28] The core reason for their apprehension is that foreign companies are increasingly buying U.S. high-technology companies that are important elements of the U.S. defense industrial base. Theodore Moran expresses a widespread concern when he warns that "the United States might find itself so dependent on goods, services, and technologies controlled

---

[24] Rosecrance, *Rise of Trading State*, 14.

[25] See the analysis in Brooks, *Producing Security,* chap. 4.

[26] Ibid., 81–99, 126.

[27] Ibid., 100–125, 234–40.

[28] Notable examples include Theodore Moran, "The Globalization of America's Defense Industries," *International Security* 15 (1990); Moran, "Defense Economics and Security"; Moran, "Foreign Acquisition of Critical U.S. Industries: Where Should the United States Draw the Line?" *Washington Quarterly* 16 (1993): 62; Theodore Moran and David Mowery, "Aerospace," *Daedalus* 120 (1991); Raymond Vernon and Ethan Kapstein, "National Needs, Global Resources," *Daedalus* 120 (1991); Aaron Friedberg, "The End of Autonomy: The United States after Five Decades," *Daedalus* 120 (1991); James Kurth, "The Common Defense and World Market," *Daedalus* 120 (1991); J. Nicholas Ziegler, "Semiconductors," *Daedalus* 120 (1991); Susan Tolchin and Martin Tolchin, *Selling Our Security: The Erosion of America's Assets* (New York: Knopf, 1992); and Richard A. Bitzinger, "The Globalization of the Arms Industry: The Next Proliferation Challenge," *International Security* 19 (1994).

by foreign-owned companies located in the United States that the nation literally has to ask permission to pursue policies to advance its own national interests around the world."[29] Of all the voluminous writings on this issue, Moran's provide the most sophisticated and empirically grounded case for taking this warning seriously.[30]

The specific danger for Moran is that "foreign corporations (or their home government) can threaten to issue orders to their U.S.-based affiliates that would delay, place conditions on, exercise blackmail through, or ultimately withhold the goods, services, or technology upon which the United States has become dependent."[31] He emphasizes that during the 1990–93 period alone, foreign corporations bought more than 400 U.S. high-technology companies "in those sectors most crucial for America's civilian as well as defense needs (microelectronics, aerospace, telecommunications, and advanced materials)."[32]

After outlining this general concern, Moran heavily qualifies it: he notes that in "the overwhelming majority of cases" foreign acquisition of U.S. high-technology companies will not, in fact, create a worrying dependency problem for the United States.[33] The reason, he stresses, is that the vast majority of foreign acquisitions of U.S. companies occur in industries with a large number of dispersed suppliers. The real problem is not foreign ownership, but rather "the potential reliance on a few foreign-owned companies. If suppliers are numerous and dispersed at home and abroad, there is no threat from having the sources of supply fall to foreign ownership."[34] Moran argues that a potential dependency problem does not exist "if the largest four firms (or four countries) control less than 50 percent of the market"; in contrast, "if

---

[29] Moran, "Foreign Acquisition," 62.

[30] See Moran, "Foreign Acquisition." This article extends an earlier argument that is outlined in Moran, "Globalization of Defense Industries," 82–83, 85, 95–97. Moran also briefly discusses this basic line of argument on pp. 151–53 of "Defense Economics and Security." A number of other scholars advance arguments that are similar to Moran's; see, for example, Friedberg, "The End of Autonomy"; Bitzinger, "Globalization of Arms Industry"; Vernon and Kapstein, "National Needs, Global Resources," Ziegler, "Semiconductors"; and Tolchin and Tolchin, *Selling Our Security.*

[31] Moran, "Foreign Acquisition," 62.

[32] Ibid., 61.

[33] Ibid., 64; see also p. 62, where Moran notes, "Most of what the Defense Science Board has labeled the foreign 'penetration' of the U.S. industrial base does not involve a loss of control that can be exercised in any meaningful way by those upon whom the United States is becoming dependent for supplies."

[34] Ibid., 62.

they control more than 50 percent of the market, they have the potential to coordinate denial, delay, blackmail, or manipulation." He emphasizes that the vast majority of cases of foreign acquisition do not meet this "4–4–50" threshold: "concentration is lower than four companies or four countries supplying 50 percent of the market."[35]

Factors Lowering the Probability of FDI Leverage Attempts

Even in those relatively rare circumstances where foreign ownership does occur in an industry where suppliers are not numerous and dispersed, a series of overlapping factors neglected in Moran's analysis, in combination, greatly attenuate the significance of the denial strategy he highlights. To begin, the size of the U.S. economy—and its consequent great economic importance for foreign firms—reduces the probability that foreign governments will pursue this strategy and also the probability that foreign MNCs would actually comply with their home governments were such a strategy attempted.

A U.S. presence is now especially valuable for foreign firms for many reasons: (1) the United States is far and away the world's largest market, and having a base within it is important for market-seeking FDI reasons; (2) in significant part because of the United States' high R&D spending—equal to the next seven largest spenders combined—it has very high rates of innovation that foreign firms want to be able to tap; and, relatedly (3) the United States has the highest number of technological personnel and many foreign firms set up a presence there to access them. For these and other reasons, FDI into the United States has surged in recent decades, as table 4.2 shows. The United States is far and away the largest destination for FDI: the next two largest destinations—China and the United Kingdom—are both around half the U.S. level.[36]

Exactly because being based in the United States has become so important for the competitive position of firms, foreign governments will be very reluctant to undertake actions that might threaten the ability of their firms to continue and expand their business activities within the United States. Were any such policies contemplated, moreover, the

---

[35] Ibid., 65.

[36] In 2005, the United Kingdom's inward FDI stock was $817 billion and China's inward FDI stock was $851 billion (with $318 billion based in mainland China and $533 billion based in Hong Kong). Source: UNCTAD, http://stats.unctad.org/FDI.

TABLE 4.2
U.S. Foreign Direct Investment Inward Stock, 1980–2005 (millions of dollars)

1980	83,046
1985	184,615
1990	394,911
1995	535,553
2000	1,238,627
2005	1,625,749

Source: UNCTAD, http://stats.unctad.org/FDI/.

firms in question would undoubtedly resist. Key here is that if a country were to initiate restrictions on its affiliates based in the United States, there is every reason to expect that U.S. policymakers would retaliate against the firms from this country. The rapidity with which U.S. policymakers have decided to employ economic sanctions against other states in recent decades is one telling indicator in this regard. Although the U.S. government might tolerate an isolated experience of supply denial, any widespread supply cutoff would undoubtedly incense U.S. policymakers.

The probability that foreign governments would initiate the denial strategy highlighted by Moran is also reduced by a factor unrelated to the size of the U.S. economy: inward FDI into the United States, in general, and high-technology FDI, in particular, is overwhelmingly concentrated in the hands of U.S. allies. Figure 4.1 shows the 10 countries that have 2 percent or more of the total U.S. inward FDI stock; put together, they account for 87 percent of FDI in the United States. Of these ten countries, only Switzerland and Sweden do not have a formal alliance with the United States.

What is ultimately most important is the amount of FDI in those sectors that are an important element of the defense-industrial base. Leading the list in this regard is the computer/microelectronics sector—an industry in which the U.S. government happens to gather detailed data on the extent of foreign company purchases. Only five countries have more than US$1 billion of FDI in this sector: the United Kingdom, Japan, Netherlands, Canada, and France. All of these countries are allies of the United States. As figure 4.2 reveals, these five

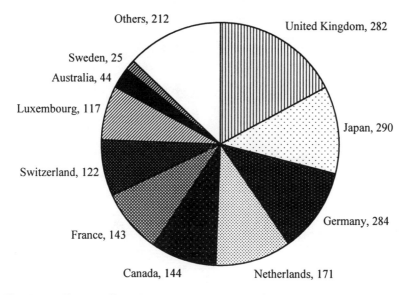

Figure 4.1. Foreign direct investment position in the United States by historical cost basis, 2005 (US$ billions). *Source*: Bureau of Economic Analysis, http://www.bea.gov/bea/di/home/directinv.htm.

countries account for 91 percent of the total amount of U.S. inward FDI in the computer/microelectronic sector.

Also revealing is table 4.3, which shows the breakdown in the total number of purchases of U.S. companies in key defense-industrial sectors since 1990. More specifically, this total is comprised of purchases of U.S. companies in the following sectors: (1) defense-related, (2) advanced materials, (3) lasers, (4) nuclear, (5) propulsion systems, (6) satellites, (7) microelectronics—which includes semiconductors, superconductors, printed circuit boards, process control systems, precision/testing equipment, and search, detection, and navigation systems, and (8) telecommunications—which includes telecommunications equipment, telephone interconnect equipment, messaging systems, cellular communications, satellite communications, and microwave communications. As was the case with purchases in the computer sector, these data show that large-scale purchases of the U.S. defense-industrial base are largely concentrated in the hands of close U.S. allies. In particular, table 4.3 reveals that there are only three countries with more than 100 purchases of U.S. defense-industrial companies during the 1990–2005 period: Canada (220 purchases), the United Kingdom (174 purchases),

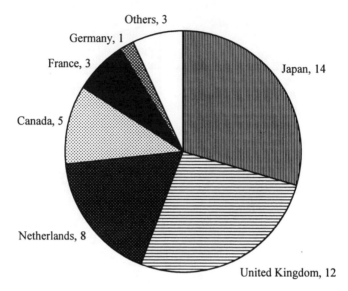

Figure 4.2. Foreign direct investment position in the United States in the computer and electronics product sectors on a historical cost basis, 2005 (US$ billions). *Source*: Bureau of Economic Analysis, http://www.bea.gov/bea/di/home/directinv.htm.

and Japan (115 purchases). These three countries alone account for slightly more than half of the 993 identified purchases of U.S. defense-industrial companies during this period. Only six other countries have more than 25 purchases of U.S. defense-industrial companies during this period, and all but one (Switzerland) have a formal alliance or informal alliance with the United States.[37]

In sum, although Moran is correct that the possibility exists that foreign governments may seek to use defense-related FDI in the United States as leverage, the probability that a wide number of foreign-owned firms in the United States would be subject to the dependency influence he highlights is extremely low.[38]

[37] Taiwan and Singapore have informal alliances with the United States, while Australia, France, and Germany have formal alliances.

[38] Moran certainly does recognize that U.S. policymakers should factor in the "likelihood that the home government of the parent corporation might impose directives on the company that would conflict with U.S. policies" ("Foreign Acquisition," 67). In turn, he notes in passing that "[s]ome home-governments of would-be parent corporations might have a record of closer congruence with U.S. foreign policy goals" (70). However, his analysis does not explore the connection between these two points. He also does

TABLE 4.3

Purchases of U.S. Defense-Industrial Companies by Country, 1990–2005

Canada	220	Norway	7
United Kingdom	174	China	6
Japan	115	Spain	6
Germany	67	Saudi Arabia	5
France	49	Russia	4
Taiwan	40	Austria	3
Switzerland	31	Denmark	3
Singapore	29	Malaysia	3
Australia	28	Pakistan	3
Bermuda	24	Thailand	3
Israel	20	Argentina	2
Netherlands	20	Bahrain	2
Sweden	19	Brazil	2
Finland	18	Luxembourg	2
South Korea	16	U.S. Virgin Islands	1
Belgium	14	South Africa	1
Italy	13	New Zealand	1
Hong Kong	11	Greece	1
India	11	Costa Rica	1
Ireland	8	Cayman Islands	1
Mexico	8	British Virgin Islands	1

Source: SDC Platinum Data—Thomson Financial Database.

Factors Insulating the United States from FDI Leverage Attempts

It is thus implausible that the United States will be subject to an FDI leverage attempt. For two reasons that are overlooked in Moran's analysis, the United States is also extremely unlikely to face any significant restriction on its security policy *even* if foreign governments did attempt to use FDI as leverage in the manner that he posits.

Moran's argument is dependent on the assumption that the United States will be unable to ensure sufficient access to defense inputs that are subject to a supply cutoff. The United States, of course, has the option of offering to pay a large premium to these foreign corporations to get them to continue supplying needed defense inputs from their U.S.-based plants, which may well induce them to cooperate. Even more

---

not discuss that the great importance of the United States for foreign firms reduces the probability that a wide number of foreign-owned firms in the United States would be subject to the dependency influence that he is concerned about.

importantly, the supply base is dynamic, not static. This is a key oversight of Moran's analysis: his proposed 4–4–50 rule is based on an assessment of *current*, not *potential*, supplies.[39] The essence of markets is flexibility; firms jump into market opportunities as they emerge. And the essence of economic globalization is that it has greatly increased the pool of suppliers: it is not simply that the number of potential suppliers has gone up dramatically in recent decades as global markets have expanded, but the ease of identifying them and establishing relationships with them has also concomitantly increased. The point is that if a significant supply disruption occurs, other firms can emerge as producers besides those that are currently engaged in production.[40]

A telling example is the explosion that destroyed the Sumitomo Chemical Company epoxy resin plant in Niihama, Japan, in July 1992. It represented an extreme example of supply concentration, and hence comes close to being a worst-case scenario from Moran's perspective: this one plant produced 65 percent of the world supply of epoxy resin, which is used in the production of semiconductor chips. It demonstrated that semiconductor firms were effectively insulated from a supply shock in significant part because there were alternative suppliers in other countries—many of which were not producing much, or any, epoxy at the time the Niihama plant was destroyed—that were capable of making up for the shortfall in supply.[41]

A second consideration is that over the longer term the U.S. government is also in a position to devote resources to fund the development of new supplier sources to replace inputs from foreign-owned firms that are denying supplies to the United States. If provided with sufficient government assistance, U.S. firms will likely be able to adapt their production to replace specific defense inputs from foreign-based corporations. And although the cost of replacing all non-U.S. suppliers would be massive and likely unbearable, it is very unlikely that anything close to a full replacement strategy would be necessary. Only in very rare circumstances are states likely to overcome coordination

[39] Moran does consider the issue of substitute products that can be used (see ibid., 67–68) after a supply cutoff, but does not consider that other companies can come forward as new suppliers of the original product.

[40] This point is stressed in Brooks, *Producing Security*, 212–13; and Gholz and Press, "Effects of Wars."

[41] For more details on this case, see Brooks, *Producing Security*, 212–13, and the sources cited therein.

problems associated with the implementation of an extensive supply cutoff: in the end, it is implusible that the major sources of U.S.-based FDI would have the opportunity and willingness to jointly seek to deny the United States access to necessary supplies.[42]

Overall Assessment

In sum, Moran is correct that the purchase of U.S. companies that form part of the defense industrial base opens a potential avenue for leverage attempts by foreign governments, but there is no reason to think that this threat can act as a meaningful constraint on U.S. security policy. Recall that even Moran is willing to admit that for the vast bulk of FDI in the United States, the particular concern he raises is not a problem. What he does not recognize is that because the United States is so economically important to foreign firms, there is also a very low likelihood that U.S.-based FDI will be used by foreign governments as leverage. Moreover, the United States is also in a position to be effectively insulated from negative effects even in the low-likelihood event that such a leverage strategy is actually attempted.

Although Moran highlights the purchase of U.S. defense-industrial companies as the prime leverage concern, U.S. weapons production is also highly reliant on inputs from foreign companies located abroad via outsourcing, interfirm alliances, and other international production linkages.[43] The same basic logic just outlined, however, applies to this latter form of dependency as well. The likelihood of the United States facing a considerable cutoff of international production linkages is very low, largely because of the great importance of the U.S. economy and firms for foreign corporations and, more specifically, the degree to which they have undertaken FDI within the United States. Moreover, the potential negative effect of a limited cutoff from international suppliers is minimized for the same reasons stressed above: over the long term, Washington has little reason to worry in large part because the supply base is dynamic, not static, and because the U.S. government can promote alternative suppliers.[44]

[42] For a further discussion of these points, see ibid., 126–28, 213–14.

[43] Ibid., chap. 4.

[44] See also the related discussion in ibid., 210–14, 217–18, which notes that although comprehensive cutoff of the international production linkages that the United States relies upon for defense production would be very harmful, the only conceivable scenario in which it would face such a prospect is if it attempted to militarily "run the tables."

117

Dependence Issue Number 3: Outward FDI

In recent decades, outward FDI has become much more significant as a proportion of the U.S. economy. Any country host to large amounts of U.S. FDI could threaten those assets as a means of influencing U.S. security policy. This is the mirror image of the concern analyzed in the previous section (in which foreign governments seek to influence U.S. security policy by changing the behavior of their firms' foreign affiliates located in the United States). The notion that foreign governments could target U.S. MNCs based within their borders is, in at least one respect, a relatively more plausible concern: a foreign government has the authority to directly take actions harmful to U.S. MNCs, whereas the dynamic discussed in the previous section will only come to pass if foreign MNCs located within the United States actually do what their home governments tell them to. That said, there is no basis for concluding that U.S. security policy will be impeded by threats of foreign governments against the FDI holdings of American MNCs. There are several reasons for this, the two most important of which are directly related to the size of the U.S. economy.

First, other countries are generally very dependent on the U.S. market. Table 4.4 shows the top 25 investment locations for U.S. MNCs (these are the only states for which the total stock of U.S. FDI is at least US$10 billion). As the third column in this table shows, U.S. FDI is generally located in countries that are very dependent on the U.S. market: all but six of these 25 states depend on the United States for at least 7 percent of their total exports. Because these states generally send so much of their exports to the United States, they will be reluctant to threaten U.S. FDI because they will not want to put their overall economic relationship with the United States in jeopardy.

Second, recall that the United States has become the leading base for inward FDI. The last column of table 4.4 shows that for a majority of these states, the United States is home to more than 10 percent of their total FDI. Significantly, the top nine states in table 4.4—which together are home to 61 percent of the U.S. total outward FDI—have a huge percentage of their total FDI based within the United States: all but two of these nine states have at least 25 percent of their total FDI in the United States (the two exceptions, Germany and the United Kingdom, have, respectively, 23 percent and 19 percent). Any state with a

TABLE 4.4

Top 25 Locations for U.S. Foreign Direct Investment, 2005

Country	Stock of U.S. FDI in foreign country ($ millions)	% of total U.S. FDI based in foreign country	Exports of foreign country to U.S. as % of foreign exports	Total FDI stock of foreign country in U.S.	FDI in U.S. as % of total country FDI
United Kingdom	323,796	15.64	13.22	282,457	22.82
Canada	234,831	11.34	81.66	144,033	36.07
Netherlands	181,384	8.76	4.63	170,770	26.63
Australia	113,385	5.48	6.89	44,061	27.68
Bermuda	90,358	4.37	NA	1,517	25.36
Germany	86,319	4.17	8.70	184,213	19.04
Switzerland	83,424	4.03	10.33	122,399	31.01
Japan	75,491	3.65	23.26	190,279	49.22
Mexico	71,423	3.45	80.78	8,653	30.86
Luxembourg	61,615	2.98	3.08	116,736	NA
Ireland	61,596	2.98	26.17	21,898	18.57
France	60,860	2.94	7.79	143,378	16.81
Singapore	48,051	2.32	6.59	2,404	2.17
Spain	43,280	2.09	4.47	7,114	1.87
Hong Kong	37,884	1.83	3.20	2,600	0.55
Belgium	36,733	1.77	3.90	9,712	2.51
Sweden	33,398	1.61	10.65	24,774	12.22
Brazil	32,420	1.57	21.05	2,551	3.57
Italy	25,931	1.25	8.31	7,716	2.63
South Korea	18,759	0.91	15.40	6,203	17.00
China	16,877	0.82	32.01	481	1.04
Taiwan	13,374	0.65	18.53	3,565	3.66
Argentina	13,163	0.64	11.44	NA	NA
Malaysia	9,993	0.48	23.90	410	0.92
Indonesia	9,948	0.48	14.03	NA	NA

Source: BEA on a historical cost basis, http://www.bea.gov/bea/di/home/directinv.htm, except for total foreign country outward FDI stock from UNCTAD on a current price basis, http://stats .unctad.org/FDI/ReportFolders/ReportFolders.aspx, and total foreign country exports from the International Trade Center (UNCTAD/WTO), http://www.intracen.org/appli1/TradeCom/TP_EP_CI .aspx?RP=124&YR=2005.

large amount of FDI invested in the United States will be averse to take actions that threaten the holdings of U.S. MNCs since doing so could result in harmful retaliation.

In addition, a more general point is that if a state were to undertake discriminatory actions against U.S. MNCs, it would in all likelihood harm its chances of attracting FDI in the future. This is significant since the opportunity cost of losing access to MNCs has greatly increased over the past several decades.[45] MNCs do not like unpredictability in policies: FDI is a form of investment that is sensitive to the long-term credibility of commitment of a host government to refrain from major changes in political or economic policies that negatively influence MNCs.[46]

There is thus no basis for concluding that U.S. FDI will be threatened by other states as a means of altering U.S. security policy. In the extremely unlikely event that a threat of this kind did develop, the United States would also likely be insulated from its negative effects to a significant extent. For one thing, its stock of FDI is geographically diversified to a great degree: as table 4.4 shows, the United Kingdom, Canada, the Netherlands, and Australia are the only four countries that are the base for 5 percent or more of the total U.S. FDI stock. Because U.S. FDI is so geographically dispersed, if a threat did emerge to American MNCs' holdings, then it is likely that another country or region where these MNCs already have investments could make up the difference. In addition, the very high level of openness to FDI in today's global economy means that MNCs often have many substitute sites available that they turn to if a particular location becomes untenable.[47] It is only with respect to resource-based FDI that U.S. firms would likely face great difficulty switching from one investment site to another, since many raw materials only exist in a relatively limited number of countries. However, resource-based FDI now accounts for only 7.3 percent of the total U.S. outward FDI stock.[48]

---

[45] Ibid., 39–41.

[46] For an overview of why this is the case, see Jeffrey A. Frieden, "International Investment and Colonial Control: A New Interpretation," *International Organization* 48 (1994).

[47] See the discussion in Brooks, *Producing Security*, 39–42.

[48] This FDI figure is on a historical cost basis. US FDI in natural resources is comprised of wood products (0.27 percent of US total FDI), petroleum and coal products (0.88 percent), nonmetallic mineral products (0.53 percent), agriculture, forestry, fishing, and hunting (0.09 percent), and mining (5.52 percent). Source: Bureau of Economic Analysis.

TABLE 4.5

Value of Foreign-Owned U.S. Long-Term Securities and Share of Total Outstanding, by Asset Class (billions of dollars)

Type of security	Dec. 1989	Dec. 1994	Mar. 2000	June 2002	June 2003	June 2004	June 2005	June 2006
Equity								
Total outstanding	4,638	7,767	24,703	17,904	17,941	20,779	22,041	23,750
Foreign-owned	275	398	1,709	1,395	1,564	1,930	2,144	2,430
Percentage foreign-owned	5.9	5.1	6.9	7.8	8.7	9.3	9.7	10.2
Marketable U.S. Treasury								
Total outstanding	1,515	2,392	2,508	2,230	2,451	2,809	3,093	3,321
Foreign-owned	333	464	884	908	1,116	1,426	1,599	1,727
Percentage foreign-owned	22.0	19.4	35.2	40.7	45.5	50.8	51.7	52.0
U.S. government agency								
Total outstanding	1,167	1,982	3,575	4,830	5,199	5,527	5,591	5,874
Foreign-owned	48	107	261	492	586	619	791	984
Percentage foreign-owned	4.1	5.4	7.3	10.2	11.3	11.2	14.1	16.8
Corporate and othe debt								
Total outstaning	2,599	3,556	5,713	7,205	7,852	8,384	8,858	9,893
Foreign-owned	191	276	703	1,130	1,236	1,455	1,729	2,021
Percentage foreign-owned	7.3	7.8	12.3	15.7	15.7	17.6	19.5	20.4
Total U.S. long-term securities								
Total outstanding	9,904	15,700	36,583	32,169	33,443	37,499	39,583	42,838
Foreign-owned	847	1,244	3,558	3,926	4,503	5,431	6,262	7,162
Percentage foreign-owned	8.6	7.9	9.7	12.2	13.5	14.5	15.8	16.7

Source: Report on Foreign Portfolio Holdings of U.S. Securities, Department of the Treasury, Federal Reserve Bank of New York, May 2007, 5.

Dependence Issue Number 4: International Finance

The final dependence issue concerns international finance. One aspect of U.S. financial dependence that has received attention in recent years is the growing proportion of foreign holdings of U.S. securities. As noted, the share of total U.S. long-term securities (including stocks, corporate debt, and U.S. government debt) held by foreigners has more than tripled over the past 30 years, from 4.8 percent in 1974 to 16.7 percent in 2005. Table 4.5 shows that the percentage of foreign ownership has increased across all asset classes from 1989 to 2006 and is

121

TABLE 4.6

Value of Foreign Holdings of U.S. Securities, by Major Investing Country and Type of Security, June 2006 (in billions of dollars)

Country	Total	Equity	Treasury long-term debt	Treasury short-term debt	Agency long-term debt ABS[1]	Agency long-term debt Other	Corporate long-term debt ABS[a]	Corporate long-term debt Other	Corporate short-term debt
Japan	1,106	195	535	79	85	99	36	72	85
China[b]	810	26	413	8	112	161	22	49	28
United Kingdom	640	300	47	5	18	10	88	161	16
Luxembourg	549	193	52	7	19	19	50	183	32
Cayman Islands	485	178	19	5	31	7	104	116	31
Canada	382	274	17	5	1	4	21	53	13
Belgium	331	21	12	2	1	43	41	208	4
Netherlands	280	158	17	2	14	4	41	37	9
Switzerland	262	145	33	6	4	6	28	37	9
Middle East oil-exporters[c]	243	111	64	30	6	8	5		41
Country unknown	214	< 0.5	< 0.5	< 0.5	< 0.5	< 0.5	1	212	1
Rest of world	2,476	829	518	104	95	238	157	291	346
Total	**7,778**	**2,430**	**1,727**	**253**	**386**	**599**	**594**	**1,427**	**615**
Of which: Holdings of foreign official institutions	2,301	215	1,213	n/a	118	355	30	67	304

Source: Report on Foreign Portfolio Holdings of U.S. Securities, Department of the Treasury, Federal Reserve Bank of New York, May 2007.

[a] Asset-backed securities. Agency ABS are backed primarily by home mortgages; corporate ABS are backed by a wide variety of assets, such as car loans, credit card receivables, home and commercial mortgages, and student loans.

[b] Includes Hong Kong and Macau.

[b] Bahrain, Iran, Iraq, Kuwait, Oman, Qatar, Saudi Arabia, and the United Arab Emirates.

now particularly high with respect to U.S. Treasury securities.[49] Table 4.6 breaks down by investing country the amount of holdings in each asset class.

Will those foreign governments that are major holders of U.S. federal debt use this as leverage to change U.S. security policies? For four reasons, this is not a realistic threat. First, it is apparent that the major foreign holders are accumulating U.S. Treasury securities for concrete economic reasons and not either as a political favor to the U.S. government

[49] Available at http://www.treasury.gov/tic/fpis.shtml.

or as a means of gaining leverage over its security policy. Japan and China have been the two most significant foreign purchasers of U.S. Treasury securities in recent years. The purchasing behavior of Japan during this period has been driven largely by a desire to prevent the yen from appreciating, which would harm Japanese exporters. Currency intervention is also the driving force behind China's behavior: from 1994 to 2005, China maintained a fixed exchange rate relative to the dollar, and its central bank needed to intervene very heavily to prevent the renminbi from appreciating. Even with its new currency policy, China will face a continued need to intervene to prevent the renminbi from appreciating too substantially or too quickly. In addition, Chinese leaders have long believed that maintaining large U.S. reserves is useful to deal with the potential threat of global financial instability.[50]

To be sure, debt acquired for other reasons might still be used for leverage over U.S. security policy. But this raises the second reason why use of this leverage is very unlikely: any attempt to exercise this potential leverage would require bearing substantial economic costs and risks. The key point is that even if the United States refrained from pursuing any form of retaliation, existing Japanese and Chinese economic policies would become harder to pursue.[51] Moreover, the sale of dollar assets by either country "would result in a capital loss on those assets . . . as well as foreign exchange losses when they traded their dollars for other currencies."[52]

Of course, just because there are substantial economic costs and risks associated with selling off U.S. debt does not mean that foreign governments will necessarily be unwilling to bear them. This brings up the third reason why an attempted use of this financial leverage is extremely unlikely: for the major foreign holders of U.S. debt, political

[50] On these points, see, for example, Catherine Mann, "Managing Exchange Rates: Achievement of Global Re-balancing or Evidence of Global Co-dependency: The United States and Its Trading Partners Have Serious Interests in the Status Quo," *Business Economics*, 39 (2004); Michael Mastanduno, "System Maker and Privilege Taker: U.S. Power and the International Political Economy," manuscript, Dartmouth College, 37–38; Michael Dooley, David Fokerts-Landau, and Peter Garber, "The Revived Bretton Woods System: The Effects of Periphery Intervention and Reserve Management on Interest Rates and Exchange Rates in Center Countries," NBER Working Paper No. 10332, March 2004; and "Oriental Mercantilists," *Economist*, September 20, 2003.

[51] See the discussion in Mann, "Managing Exchange Rates"; Dooley, Fokerts-Landau, and Garber, "Revived Bretton Woods System"; and Mastanduno, "System Maker."

[52] Douglas Holtz-Eakin, Director of the Congressional Budget Office, "The Chinese Exchange Rate and U.S. Manufacturing Employment," Committee on Ways and Means, U.S. House of Representatives, October 30, 2003.

incentives also powerfully point against employing this leverage. This is clearest with respect to Japan—the number one holder that alone accounts for almost one-third of all foreign holdings of U.S. Treasury securities—in light of its very close political and security relationships with the United States. The other major holder, China, does not have a similar close diplomatic relationship with the United States. Yet it is clear that China's leadership wants to narrow the economic gap with the most advanced countries and regards strong participation in economic globalization as essential for doing so.[53] Chinese leaders also clearly recognize that the United States is globalization's dominant actor—both politically and economically—and that pursuing provocative policies that would raise the ire of Washington is therefore extremely risky: doing so would very likely undermine China's ability to benefit from economic globalization to fuel its economic rise.[54] So long as China continues to rely heavily on foreign technology and export-led growth to propel its ascent to advanced country status, it will face powerful incentives to not risk any form of economic retaliation from Washington.

Finally, selling off U.S. foreign debt holdings does not appear to have high potential strategic usefulness for China. Although China's share of U.S. Treasury securities is now substantial enough that selling it all off at once could well have a significant negative economic influence on the United States in the short term, this would be a one-shot effect, exhausting all the potential leverage in one go. There are many reasons to expect that the United States will be able to draw on foreign savings at its current rate in the years ahead.[55] What this means is that barring

[53] Johnston, "China Status Quo Power?" 30.

[54] See, for example, Robert Ross, "Beijing as a Conservative Power," *Foreign Affairs* 76 (1997), who notes, "Since the 1980s, the world's major industrial economies have been eager to participate in Chinese modernization. . . . The accompanying technology and capital transfers have played an important role in modernizing Chinese industry and stimulating economic growth. Beijing recognizes that conservative international behavior was the precondition that encouraged the advanced industrial countries to participate in China's economy. They also realize that provocative policies risk ending China's economic success story" (42). See also the analysis in Jennifer M. Lind, "Logrolling for Peace: How Economic Interdependence Overcomes the Dangers of Democratization," paper presented to the International Studies Association Annual Meeting, Honolulu, March 2005.

[55] Four general treatments of this specific question are Richard Cooper, "Is the U.S. Current Account Deficit Sustainable? Will it Be Sustained?" *Brookings Papers on Economic Activity*, 2001:1, 217–26; Catherine Mann, "Perspectives on the U.S. Current Account Deficit and Sustainability," *Journal of Economic Perspectives* 16 (2002); Ronald McKinnon, "Can the World Afford American Tax Cuts and Military Buildup?" *Journal of Policy Modeling* 24 (2002); and Nouriel Roubini and Brad Setser, "Will the Bretton Woods 2 Regime Unravel

the extremely unlikely scenario in which Japan coordinates with China on a sell-off of Treasury securities in order to alter U.S. security policy, the United States might face the prospect of somewhat higher interest rates only in the short term if China were to employ its financial leverage. The U.S. government would be able to continue to finance its debt and, over the medium to long term, might not even need to offer substantially higher interest rates in order to do so.

This is not to suggest that U.S. policymakers should be unconcerned about the country's rising debt, in general, or its rapidly growing foreign debt, in particular. From an economic standpoint, these trends are very troubling.[56] Rather, the point is that there is no reason to conclude that growing U.S. foreign debt creates a powerful leverage tool that other countries will employ to influence U.S. security policy.

There is also a second potential financial dependence mechanism with a link to U.S. security policy that some IR scholars regard as a realistic threat. Robert Pape maintains that "Europe could challenge

---

Soon? The Risk of a Hard Landing in 2005–2006," paper prepared for the Symposium on the Revised Bretton Woods System, San Francisco, February 4, 2005. McKinnon posits that "the American line of credit with the rest of the world is indefinitely long" (386). Similarly, Cooper argues strongly that the United States will be able maintain its status as a preferred destination for foreign savings for the foreseeable future for a number of structural reasons: the United States accounts for more than a quarter of the global economy; its long-term growth prospects are higher than in Europe and Japan and its economy is also less volatile than the developing world; and there is little uncertainty about the prospect of U.S. repayment (see 219–23). In a more recent analysis, Cooper argues that the United States may even be able to draw on foreign savings to a more significant extent in the years ahead, in part because "the large and rapidly growing pool of savings in China and India have hardly been tapped, bottled up by exchange controls. Investment opportunities in the US economy would be highly attractive to many newly wealthy Chinese and Indians." Richard Cooper, "US Deficit: It Is Not Only Sustainable, It Is Logical," October 31, 2004, available at http://www.ucd.ie/economic/staff/bwalsh/Cooper%20on%20deficit .doc (consulted September 19, 2007). Mann is somewhat more guarded in her optimism: she concludes that "the global investment community seems willing and able to hold sufficient U.S. assets in its portfolios to finance these deficits for now. But global investors will not expand the share of their foreign portfolios that is U.S. assets forever" (149). In contrast, Roubini and Setser are pessimistic about the ability of the United States to draw upon foreign savings at very high levels: they warn that "if the US does not take policy steps to reduce its need for external financing before it exhausts the world's central banks['] willingness to keep adding to their dollar reserves . . . the risk of a hard landing for the US and global economy will grow" (5).

[56] Regarding foreign debt, Barry Eichengreen underscores that the potential does exist for a "grim scenario" if the underlying assessment of U.S. growth prospects were to change: "If new information suggests that the U.S. productivity miracle is a mirage—or simply that it is quantitatively less impressive than suggested by earlier estimates—foreigners may conclude that with slower U.S. growth, the country's external indebtedness is on an unsustainable path. If so, the abrupt termination of foreign finance may

the position of the dollar as the world's reserve currency by, most notably, using euros to purchase its oil. . . . This would substantially reduce demand for dollars, reduce the dollar share of all world reserves to the U.S. share of world GNP, and so largely eliminate seignorage benefits to the United States. This would be painful."[57] Pape's argument might appear pertinent and dire in light of the fact that some leaders—notably Venezuelan president Hugo Chávez and Iranian president Mahmoud Ahmadinejad—have publicly advocated a general switch in the structure of the global oil market to euro pricing.[58]

In fact, Pape's scenario is highly improbable. For one thing, there is little reason to think that a switch to euro oil pricing could occur in the policy-relevant future. In this regard, OPEC's overall stance is most crucial.[59] Over the years, "OPEC has many times said that it would continue pricing oil sales in dollars only."[60] The general aversion of

---

precipitate a sharp recession in the United States." "Global Imbalances: The Blind Men and the Elephant," *Brookings Issues in Economy Policy* 1 (2006): 12.

[57] Robert Pape, "Soft Balancing: How the World Will Respond to US Preventive War on Iraq," University of Chicago, January 20, 2003, available at http://www.opctj.org/articles/robert-a-pape-university-of-chicago-02–21–2003–004443.html (consulted September 17, 2007). See also the related discussion in Pape, "Soft Balancing against the United States," 42.

[58] Moreover, a few oil exporters, most notably Iran and Venezuela, have also recently taken the concrete step of asking their clients to pay for oil in euros (these transactions are, however, still based on dollar pricing that is established in the dominant international oil exchanges, notably the New York Mercantile Exchange in New York City and the International Petroleum Exchange in London). As of March 2007, 57 percent of Iran's income from oil exports was in euros. Hojjatollah Ghanimifard (international affairs director of state-owned National Iranian Oil Company) outlines the current Iranian policy as follows: "We have asked our clients that whenever they are ready to exchange the dollar into any other currency, including the euro, we would be welcoming that. In Europe, almost—I can say—all have accepted, in Asian markets some. . . . Pricing as you know is based on the quotations that we get from the international market and when the international market quotes anything for crude or for the products all of them are for the US dollar." "Iran Gets 60 Pct of Oil Income in Non-USD," Reuters, March 22, 2007, http://www.reuters.com/article/newsOne/idUSBLA24804820070322 (consulted September 19, 2007).

[59] Of the 14 countries exporting more than one million barrels per day, 10 are members of OPEC. Energy Information Administration, http://www.eia.doe.gov/emeu/cabs/nonopec.html (consulted October 17, 2007).

[60] Anna Baraulina, "Russian Leaders Argue Over Euro," *Gazeta*, October 10, 2003. In a March 2006 interview, Edmund Daukoru (the president of OPEC) stressed that even the large fall in the value of the dollar had not produced any movement away from OPEC's long-standing practice of pricing oil in dollars: as he noted, "The dollar has lost 30%. If that's not a trigger, I don't know what would be;" Alexander Kaptik, "OPEC to Stick with Dollar Pricing," *Wall Street Journal*, March 3, 2006. In June 2006, Iran and Vene-

OPEC to switch away from pricing oil only in dollars is grounded in concrete economic factors.[61] The various economic advantages of the dollar for OPEC would be less consequential if there were not downsides associated with pricing oil in multiple currencies. Yet from a transactions cost standpoint, continuing to price oil exclusively in dollars has a number of advantages.[62] For these and other reasons, it thus appears that "OPEC is unlikely to bring about or even try to shift markets to euro-priced oil."[63]

The more important point is that even if a switch to euro oil pricing eventually did occur, the practice of pricing oil in dollars is a very minor contributor to the status of the dollar as the international reserve currency. Global trade flows—of which oil is obviously just one element—are a tiny portion of global financial flows: the average daily

---

zuela did propose putting the sale of oil in euros on OPEC's agenda; this proposal was, however, rejected by all of OPEC's other members; "OPEC United Against Venezuelan Rhetoric," *Financial Times*, June 2, 2006, 7; and "Venezuela's Offer on Oil Sale in Euros Not on OPEC Agenda—Minister," *Financial Times Information*, June 4, 2006.

[61] Because EU financial markets remain less deep than those of the United States, the euro does not offer a range of "financial instruments comparable to those of the dollar." Oystein Noreng, "Oil, the Euro, and the Dollar," *Journal of Energy and Development* 30 (2004): 74. In addition, the "relatively fragmented regulatory system and ambiguous decision making power over financial and exchange rate matters" that exist within the EU also lead to some uncertainty among investors about the euro, which causes it to compare unfavorably to the dollar as a store of value. Kathleen McNamara, "A Rivalry in the Making? The Euro and International Monetary Power," in *The Future of the Dollar*, ed. Jonathan Kirschner and Eric Helleiner, forthcoming. It is also significant that "the United States is OPEC's largest customer and the world's largest exporter and largest importer. It is therefore easier, both for OPEC and its customers, to deal with the United States than anyone else. In addition, the United States is the largest supplier of goods OPEC nations need, or think they need—namely, agricultural products and military material." George P. Brockaway, "Why the Trade Deficits Won't Go Away," *Journal of Post-Keynesian Economics* 23 (2001): 665.

[62] More specifically, Looney underscores that "if a euro price were introduced for one or more of the benchmarks, price-setting would be even more complex. . . . This would burden buyers and sellers alike. It would make the real price of oil less transparent . . . and could make the market less liquid as capital was split between two currencies. In addition, payments systems would need to be overhauled." Robert Looney, "Petroeuros: A Threat to U.S. Interests in the Gulf?" *Middle East Policy* 11 (2004): 34. The same overall assessment is outlined in Jonathan Haughton, "Should OPEC Use Dollars in Pricing Oil?" *Journal of Energy and Development* 14 (1989); and Ronald Cooper, "Changes in Exchange Rates and Oil Prices for Saudi Arabia and Other OPEC Members," *Journal of Energy and Development* 20 (1996): 122. Similarly, George Brockaway underscores that pricing oil only in dollars "has the great advantage of shielding OPEC from the irrational frenzy of the international money markets" ("Trade Deficits," 665).

[63] Looney, "Petroeuros," 36.

turnover in foreign exchange markets is now $3.2 trillion *per day*, while the value of world exports is just under $12 trillion *per year*.[64] Significantly, many of the core contributing factors to the dollar's status as the reserve currency have the weight of path dependency behind them. The dollar's role as the reserve currency is intimately related to the United States' long-standing position as the largest military and economic power in the system.[65] The dollar's status as the reserve currency is also a product of the deep, well-developed nature of U.S. capital and money markets:

> Countries, or more precisely cities within countries, become financial centers when their markets in financial assets are deep, liquid, and stable. Status as a financial center, once acquired, thus tends to sustain itself. When a country succeeds in attracting a critical mass of transactions in the relevant securities, other investors bring their business there to take advantage of the liquidity and depth of the market. Incumbency is an advantage, and the United States is the leading incumbent financial center.[66]

Furthermore, "network externalities" make use of the dollar very attractive: the dollar has long been widely held (around two-thirds of foreign exchange reserves are now held in dollars) and widely used,[67] and "the more often a currency is used in international transactions, the lower the costs associated with using that currency and hence the more attractive is the currency for conducting international exchanges."[68]

---

[64] Bank for International Settlements, Triennial Central Bank Survey of Foreign Exchange Markets and Derivatives Market Activity in April 2007, September 2007, 1, http://www.bis.org/triennial.htm (consulted November 7, 2007). The dollar value of world merchandise exports was US$11.76 trillion in 2006. http://www.wto.org/english/news_e/pres07_e/pr472_e.htm (consulted October 19, 2007). The total value of world exports of fuels in 2005 was US$1.4 trillion. http://www.wto.org/english/res_e/statis_e/its2006_e/its06_toc_e.htm (consulted November 7, 2007).

[65] For a useful overview, see McNamara, "A Rivalry in the Making?"

[66] Barry Eichengreen, "The Euro as a Reserve Currency," *Journal of Japanese and International Economies* 12 (1998): 500.

[67] Statistics on the international use of the euro and the dollar are reviewed in Menzie Chinn and Jeffrey Frankel, "Will the Euro Eventually Surpass the Dollar as Leading International Reserve Currency," NBER Working Paper No. 11510, July 2005. From this analysis, they ultimately conclude (13) that "the euro is the number two international currency, ahead of the yen, and has rapidly gained acceptance, but is still far behind the dollar, which appears comfortably in the number one slot."

[68] Patricia Pollard, "The Creation of the Euro and the Role of the Dollar in International Markets," *Federal Reserve Bank of St. Louis Review*, September–October 2001, 34.

In short, history matters: "the intrinsic characteristics of a currency are of less importance than the path-dependent historical equilibrium. There is a strong inertial bias in favor of using whatever currency has been the international currency of the past."[69] The significance of path dependency explains why the last reserve currency transition (from the British pound to the U.S. dollar) took decades to eventuate and only occurred after a set of massive political and economic disruptions:

> By 1919 the USA had surpassed the UK in terms of overall productive capacity, aggregate trade flows and as a net international creditor. In addition to the growing relative strength of the US economy, economic historians have argued that the creation of a Federal Reserve System in December 1913 and the subsequent development of New York as the world's financial centre provided another strong impetus for the rise of the US dollar's role as a major international currency. However, it was only after the shock of the two world wars and the resulting devastation of other European economies, as well as the gross mismanagement of the British economy that the USA took over the role of the world's reserve currency, thus breaking the de facto 'sterling standard.'[70]

In the end, as Menzie Chinn and Jeffrey Frankel underscore, "under any plausible scenario, the dollar will remain far ahead of the euro and other potential challengers for many years."[71]

ECONOMIC INTERDEPENDENCE BROADLY CONCEIVED

Thus far, we have examined the predominant argument for constraints based in economic interdependence, which concerns how global changes in trade, finance, and production make states more reliant on other states and thereby influence the likelihood and significance of

[69] Chinn and Frankel, "Will Euro Surpass Dollar," 16.

[70] Ramkishen Rajan and Jose Kiran, "Will the Greenback Remain the World's Reserve Currency?" *Intereconomics*, May–June 2006, 124. See also Maury Obstfeld, Jay Shambaugh, and Alan Taylor, "Monetary Sovereignty, Exchange Rates, and Capital Controls: The Trilemma in the Interwar Period," *IMF Staff Papers* 51 (2004).

[71] Chinn and Frankel, "Will Euro Surpass Dollar," 20. As they emphasize, the prospects of the euro someday replacing or rivaling the dollar as the reserve currency ultimately depends on two factors unrelated to U.S. security policy: "(1) do the United Kingdom and enough other EU members join euroland so that it becomes larger than the US economy, and (2) does US macroeconomic policy eventually undermine confidence in the value of the dollar, in the form of inflation and depreciation" (1).

economic statecraft strategies. Yet economic interdependence could potentially limit U.S. security policy more indirectly—that is, a constraint could emerge regardless of any choice by other states to employ economic statecraft. As noted previously, some scholars do conceptualize economic interdependence in a very general way, in which case asking whether it constrains U.S. security policy is exactly the same as asking, "Does the global economy constrain U.S. security policy?" In this section, we will accordingly look beyond economic statecraft strategies and examine a series of additional mechanisms by which economic globalization can potentially constrain U.S. security policy.

There are three pathways by which the global economy can influence interstate security relations: by changing incentives, capabilities, and the nature of the actors.[72] The arguments about economic statecraft strategies that were examined in the previous sections center on the significance of incentives, and this section will accordingly examine the other two pathways. We begin by analyzing whether economic globalization can restrict U.S. security policy by shifting capabilities—specifically, the long-term foundation for military power and weapons capabilities. We will then examine whether economic globalization is likely to lead to any constraints on U.S. security policy imposed by nonstate actors.

Economic Interdependence, Capabilities, and U.S. Security Policy

Can the global economy foster shifts in capabilities that limit U.S. security policy? At the most general level, it is possible that economic globalization could erode the underlying foundation of unipolarity. The specific issue here is whether the acceleration of economic globalization can allow China quickly to catch up with the United States and thereby produce a global power transition.[73] To some observers, the current situation seems redolent of the scenario Robert Gilpin outlined over three decades ago in which a liberal hegemon underwrites its

[72] See the discussion in Brooks, *Producing Security*, 5–6.

[73] As chapter 2 established, China is the only country that has the capacity to match U.S. aggregate GDP within the next few decades. On the significance of power transitions, see, for example, Gilpin, *War and Change*; A.F.K. Organski and Jacek Kugler, *The War Ledger* (Chicago: University of Chicago Press, 1980); and Ronald Tammen, Jacek Kugler, Douglas Lemke, and Carole Alsharabati, *Power Transitions: Strategies for the 21st Century* (New York: Chatham House, 2000).

own demise by sponsoring the very global economic practices that disproportionately favor its great-power rivals.[74] Gilpin portrayed the 1970s in exactly these terms, arguing that economic globalization was undercutting the United States' economic capacity while benefiting other powerful states. He specifically highlighted that the very high level of FDI outflow from the United States at that time, in combination with a very low FDI inflow, would hasten a power transition.

While China's economic growth is indeed assisted by its access to the global economy, the situation radically departs from the one Gilpin described. For one thing, the specific FDI mechanism he highlighted does not apply today. When Gilpin's book was written in 1975, U.S. "outward investment was four-and-a-half times greater than its inward investment." In recent years, in comparison, the U.S. FDI ratio has hovered right around "a perfect balance in terms of outward and inward" FDI.[75]

Of course, China is also aided by inward FDI, likely to a much greater extent than the United States. Yet, the same is true in reverse when we look at other aspects of economic globalization: the United States greatly benefits from globalization in a number of important ways that China either does not or only to a very limited extent. Significantly, many of these specific advantages the United States draws from economic globalization are to a large degree a function of its position in the system, both in terms of the size of its economy and also its status as the "incumbent" leader of the financial system. In particular, the United States profits to a great extent from having the dollar as the world's reserve currency and from its preferred status as a destination for international portfolio investment. With such a wide scope of available opportunities, the U.S. economy has also long attracted far more scientifically trained workers than any other state. By contrast, the renminbi is in no position to become a global reserve currency; just making it convertible will be a major challenge and is unlikely anytime soon.[76] China is also not soon going to rival the United States in any

---

[74] Robert Gilpin, *U.S. Power and the Multinational Corporation: The Political Economy of Foreign Direct Investment* (New York: Basic Books, 1975).

[75] Peter Dicken, *Global Shift: Reshaping the Global Economic Map in the 21st Century,* 4th ed. (New York: Guilford Press, 2003), 59.

[76] As Nicholas Lardy underscores, "The Chinese authorities over the years have repeatedly expressed the goal of moving toward a convertible currency and a more flexible exchange rate regime. There is no debate on the long-term desirability of such a policy. In the short and medium run, however, a convertible currency and a floating exchange rate is not a viable option for China. Chinese households have more than ten trillion

way as a preferred destination for international portfolio investment or for newly mobile scientific and technological talent. Finally, it is also significant that U.S. MNCs have been at the forefront of establishing cooperative partnerships with foreign firms to enhance innovation and they also lead in the geographic dispersal of their production throughout the globe to reap various locational advantages. In contrast, in the years ahead China can at best benefit only slightly from home-based MNCs adopting novel globalization strategies given its current dearth of firms that are large and experienced enough to pursue this course.[77]

Globalization's contribution to China's rise in recent decades should also not be overstated. In contrast to the industrialized great-power challengers Gilpin discussed, China is a developing country whose extremely rapid growth in recent years owes much to factors having nothing to do with economic globalization. In particular, the speed of China's economic ascent since the late 1970s can also be traced to the fact that Chinese leaders put in place the key institutions—land reform, basic property rights—that most economists see as central to economic growth and that it started from an extremely low initial position thanks to decades of Mao-inspired policies that had long blocked the country's economic potential. In sum, China has been able to exploit "the advantages of backwardness" both through basic domestic reforms and through globalization.

Finally, even if China benefits more from enhanced global economic interdependence than the United States, a power transition is simply not in the cards for many decades precisely because the United States now occupies such a dominant power position in the system. The challengers that Gilpin discussed were great powers with advanced economies at a comparable level of development to the hegemon. In those circumstances, aggregate GDP is a far better index of power than in a

---

yuan deposited in savings accounts in the banking system. Very few Chinese savers have had any opportunity to diversify the currency composition of their financial savings. Eliminating capital controls could well lead to a substantial move into foreign-currency denominated financial assets, most likely held outside of Chinese banks. Given the well-known weaknesses of China's major banks, such a move could easily precipitate a domestic banking crisis. As a result, the authorities do not anticipate relaxing capital controls on household savings until they have addressed the solvency problems of the major state-owned banks." Nicholas Lardy, testimony before the House Committee on International Relations, October 21, 2003.

[77] This dearth of outward-oriented MNCs is reflected by the fact that China's outward FDI stock as a share of GDP was, as of 2005, only 2.1 percent, as compared to the world average of 23.9 percent. Source: UNCTAD, *World Investment Report, 2006* (Geneva: United Nations, 2006).

case where the rising state has a very large but comparatively poor population. As chapter 2 established, the power gap between the United States and China is currently immense, especially in military capabilities: no single factor, including globalization, can wipe it away anytime soon.

A LEVELING EFFECT IN CONVENTIONAL WEAPONS?

In the short to medium term, the more realistic way that economic globalization could lead to a shift in capabilities that constrains U.S. security policy is by promoting a "leveling" effect—that is, by allowing other states to secure new military technologies that reduce the magnitude of U.S. military dominance. With respect to conventional military weapons, a number of analysts argue that economic globalization will "lead to the progressive erosion of the military technological advantages of the West, and particularly the United States."[78] In this view, the effect of economic globalization on the United States' aggregate capabilities and its military capabilities run in different directions: globalization augments the overall level of U.S. power through enhanced economic growth while simultaneously undercutting Washington's specific advantage in weaponry in ways that could constrain its security policy.

There are two means by which a leveling effect could occur. First, other countries could purchase weapons systems that rival those fielded by U.S. forces. The effectiveness of this strategy is, however, greatly reduced by three overlapping factors. First, an outgrowth of the advent of unipolarity is that the global arms market has become far more concentrated in the hands of the United States. During the 1990–2005 period, the United States accounted for 42 percent of all arms transfers (see table 4.7).[79] The increased overall importance of NATO arms sales following the end of the Cold War is also significant: in 1989, NATO accounted for 48.9 percent of global arms exports, a figure that increased to 86.3 percent by 1999.[80]

---

[78] Bitzinger, "Globalization of Arms Industry," 191; see also Martin Libicki, "Rethinking War: The Mouse's New Roar," *Foreign Policy* 117 (1999–2000); and Kirshner, "Processes of Globalization," 17.

[79] Congressional Research Service, "Conventional Arms Transfers to Developing Countries, 1996–2003," report prepared by Richard Grimmett, August 2004, 83.

[80] U.S. Department of State, *World Military Expenditures and Arms Transfers (WMEAT) 1999–2000*, 13.

TABLE 4.7.
Total Arms Transfers, 1990–2005 (Trend Indicator Values)

United States	100,701
Russia	49,946
France	20,320
Germany (FRG)	15,440
United Kingdom	13,658
China	5,272
Ukraine	4,662
Netherlands	4,583
Italy	4,319
Sweden	3,971
Israel	2,948
Belarus	1,857
Canada	1,832
Spain	1,548
Switzerland	1,138
Total (world)	241,659

Source: SIPRI Arms Transfers Database.

Notes: Trend Indicator Values represent the volume of arms transfers and not the financial value of the goods transferred. For a full description of this measure, see http://www.sipri.org/contents/armstrad/output_types_TIV.html

Because of the great concentration of the global arms market in the hands of the United States and its NATO allies, whenever the European powers and the United States simultaneously restrict arms sales—as is currently the case regarding many countries, including China and Iran—it will be very difficult to import arms that are capable of rivaling U.S. forces. There is, of course, one significant non-NATO arms supplier that countries can turn to: Russia. However, Russia's arms industry is a legacy of the Soviet military-industrial complex; due to Russia's paltry military R&D budget since the end of the Cold War, many of its weapons systems are no longer on par with those of the U.S. armed forces, and ever fewer will remain competitive in the years ahead.

While European countries and the United States often coordinate on arms sales and are likely to continue to do so, the possibility exists that such coordination will break down in particular circumstances. Yet even if some or all European countries decided not to restrict arms sales to a certain country, it would nevertheless still find it extremely difficult, if not impossible, to obtain systems rivaling those of U.S. forces. Another manifestation of today's unipolar system is the extent of the technological gap between U.S. weapons systems and those of all other states, including in Europe. And even if European countries do have weapons to sell that can rival those of U.S. forces, a massive American advantage would still exist in the ability to effectively use the weapons systems in large part because the United States is far ahead in collecting, processing, and distributing information on the battlefield. The United States is in a class by itself in this regard, owing to its expensive investment in both military training and C4ISR (command, control, communications, computers, intelligence, surveillance, and reconnaissance) capabilities.

These and other factors place a significant limit on the strategy of purchasing weapons systems to reduce the gap with U.S. military forces.[81] Not surprisingly, analysts and policymakers typically stress a different reason why rising economic interdependence can erode the U.S. advantage in weaponry: "globalization has made the technology and resources necessary to develop sophisticated weapons more widely available."[82] Economic globalization certainly does increase the access that countries throughout the world have to the technologies and resources needed for defense production; there is, however, no basis for concluding that this will undercut the current American edge in military technology.

Just having access to components and technology will not be enough for other states to produce and field weaponry capable of rivaling the United States. To produce capable weapons systems, components and technology must be married with sufficient production experience, design skills, and general knowledge of systems integration—areas where other countries fall far short of the United States.[83] The United

---

[81] As Robert Ross notes in his analysis of China, "Power projection cannot be purchased abroad. . . . The necessary managerial expertise is not for sale. Moreover, there are limits to what countries will export to China. Obsolete aircraft carriers from France, for example, may become available, but the hardware for full power projection can only be developed indigenously" ("Beijing as Conservative Power," 38).

[82] Madeleine K. Albright, "Squandering Capital," *Washington Post*, July 20, 2003, B7; see also, for example, Libicki, "Rethinking War," 30.

[83] See, for example, Eugene Gholz, "Systems Integration in the US Defense Industry: Who Does It and Why Is It Important?" in *The Business of Systems Integration*, ed. Andrea Prencipe, Andrew Davies, and Mike Hobday (New York: Oxford University Press, 2003).

States has more of these intangible production resources in part because the immense scope of its economy gives it a greater ability to develop them.[84] U.S. economic size is also significant because it leads to a larger pool of military R&D and production knowledge to draw upon, which makes it much easier to achieve economies of scale in weapons production. Significantly, the economic size of the United States gives it a dramatic advantage in the production of weaponry not just on its own but also in conjunction with economic globalization.[85] The gains to be accrued from pursuing globalization in defense production are a function of how high a state aims in military technology: the more advanced the weapons, the greater the need for a wide range of parts, components, and technologies. In turn, how high a state aims in military technology is largely a reflection of economic size. Finally, even if it were possible for other states to take advantage of globalization to produce weapons systems that could rival those of the United States, a large gap would still exist in terms of their real battlefield effectiveness. And this is largely because the United States is so far ahead in obtaining and processing battlefield information.

ECONOMIC GLOBALIZATION AND WMD PROLIFERATION

What about WMD?[86] Although it is undeniable that the production of such weapons greatly enhances the ability of other states to deter the United States, it is not the case that economic globalization has given other states this capacity. North Korea makes this point clear: it is one of the world's most economically isolated states, and yet it has long had a successful WMD program. The North Korean case not only makes it clear that states do not need to have access to economic globalization to develop WMD, but also that the WMD problem would still exist even if there was no economic globalization to speak of. The nuclear program of autarkic North Korea was able to start due to assistance during the 1960s and 1970s from another autarkic state, the Soviet Union. And during the 1980s and 1990s, the key assistance North Korea received for its nuclear weapons program was from A. Q. Khan,

[84] See the discussion in Richard Samuels, *Rich Nation, Strong Army* (Ithaca, N.Y.: Cornell University Press, 1994); and Brooks, *Producing Security,* 235–37.

[85] For a more detailed discussion of this point, see Brooks, *Producing Security,* 237–38.

[86] In this section, we will only consider how economic globalization influences WMD development by states. Of course, terrorist groups are also a major concern with respect to WMD. Many of the points discussed in this discussion apply equally to terrorists. Moreover, given the various costs and difficulties associated with developing biological weapons and especially nuclear weapons, it is the possibility that terrorists could obtain these weapons from states that looms largest as a concern among analysts and poli-

a man who would have undoubtedly been willing and able to undertake clandestine efforts to aid North Korea no matter how the global economy had been structured at the time.[87]

North Korea is not an isolated example: shutting off economic globalization would not end the WMD proliferation problem, and might not even slow it down to any significant extent. The simple reason why is that the key forms of proliferation assistance come not from private firms, but from foreign governments, individuals, and noncommercial groups (including universities and research institutes). Although much of what is needed to produce chemical weapons is dual-use in nature—and therefore is controlled largely by private firms—this is much less true for biological and especially nuclear weapons. And it is the latter two kinds of weapons, not the former, that truly deserve the label 'weapon of mass destruction.'[88]

That said, economic globalization does potentially make it somewhat easier to develop WMD. However, the core problem to this point has not been something inherent in economic globalization itself, but rather the policy framework that governments in advanced countries have put in place for regulating exports.[89] If governments are concerned about WMD development, they do have the potential to restrain the degree to which economic globalization helps to facilitate such efforts, particularly with respect to nuclear weapons.

Consider the case of Iraq. During the 1980s, dozens of Western companies exported goods to Iraq that were useful for its nuclear program; these companies did so without any real effort by their governments to stop them. For example, "West German companies between 1982 and 1989 supplied about DM 1 billion worth of goods with potential military use, for which the German authorities deliberately

---

cymakers (although chemical weapons are much easier for terrorists to produce on their own, they are also much less destructive than nuclear or biological weapons).

[87] For a useful overview of Khan's assistance to the North Korean nuclear program, see "A. Q. Khan's Network," available at http://www.globalsecurity.org/wmd/world/dprk/khan-dprk.htm (consulted September 19, 2007).

[88] On this point, see for example Gregg Easterbrook, "Term Limits: The Meaningless of WMD," *New Republic*, October 7, 2002, 22; who notes that "chemical weapons are . . . not 'weapons of mass destruction' in any meaningful sense." See also the discussion Richard K. Betts, "The New Threat of Mass Destruction," *Foreign Affairs* 77 (1998): 30–31; and Steve Fetter, "Ballistic Missiles and Weapons of Mass Destruction: What Is the Threat? What Should Be Done?" *International Security* 16 (1991): 23.

[89] There has so far been a dearth of FDI by MNCs in countries that are trying to develop WMD (see the data and analysis in Brooks, *Producing Security*, 230–31). These countries generally lack any features that are attractive to MNCs, such as highly trained workers, significant domestic markets, or a favorable policy and institutional climate for FDI.

waived technology embargo rules."[90] At the same time, it is now clear that the trade restrictions placed on Iraq during the 1990s worked extremely well as a check on the country's nuclear efforts. This is not to say that implementing restrictions on exports relevant to WMD development are easy to set up or will be foolproof; what we can conclude from the Iraq case is that the degree to which economic globalization contributes to WMD development in the years ahead can be influenced by policymakers to a significant extent. In this way, though, economic interdependence does appear to operate as a weak conditional constraint on U.S. security policy: the problem of WMD proliferation will likely be enhanced to some extent if appropriate export regulations are not implemented.

Economic globalization can also influence the decisions made by states that seek to develop WMD. The most prominent example in this regard is Libya: Mu'ammar Gadhafi decided to give up his WMD programs in large part to end U.S. and UN sanctions that reduced Libya's access to needed oil extraction technology from Western, and especially American, firms.[91] This does not mean that the desire to participate in economic globalization is so powerful that other WMD-seeking states, most notably North Korea and Iran, will follow in Libya's footsteps. Economic globalization is clearly only one factor among the many that influence the security policies of all countries. That being said, the lure of increased access to the global economy is one of the few sources of leverage the United States and its allies have in negotiations over the Iranian and North Korean WMD programs. The more general point is that to the extent that economic globalization influences the preferences of Iran and North Korea at all, it will be to reduce, not increase, their motivation to challenge the United States.

It should also not be forgotten that economic globalization now enhances the ability of the United States to counter the WMD threat. This

[90] "A Country That Turned a Blind Eye," *Financial Times*, March 25, 1991.

[91] As Martin Indyk reports, Gadhafi offered to give up his WMD programs in large part because "Libya was facing a deepening economic crisis produced by disastrous economic policies and mismanagement of its oil revenues. United Nations and US sanctions that prevented Libya importing oilfield technology made it impossible for Mr. Gadaffi to expand oil production. The only way out was to seek rapprochement with Washington." "The Iraq War Did Not Force Gaddafi's Hand," *Financial Times*, March 9, 2004, 21. Dirk Vandewalle similarly emphasizes that Libya's "concern over the economic and political toll of sanctions, and the need for international investment in the country's deteriorating oil infrastructure and in developing new oil fields slowly moved Libya to act on

basic point is often overlooked by analysts and policymakers alike: only the WMD downsides associated with economic globalization are highlighted, not the upsides. Yet many of the tools for dealing with the WMD threat are partly the products of globalization. Regarding WMD proliferation, the reality is that economic globalization is a double-edged sword for the United States.[92]

Economic Interdependence, Nonstate Actors, and U.S. Security Policy

The final question that needs to be considered is whether rising levels of economic interdependence could lead to shifts in the nature of the actors that limit U.S. security policy. States and nonstate actors are both potentially relevant in this regard. Although economic globalization could theoretically increase the motivation of states to pose security challenges to the United States, this is not an argument that gained any currency among scholars. Instead, there is every indication that the relationship actually goes in the other direction: scholars have identified numerous cases in which economic globalization has lowered the motivation of states to challenge the United States (China and Libya are two such cases that were already noted in the previous discussion).[93] The basic takeaway is that states now generally seek international economic openness,[94] and confronting Washington is likely to be counterproductive for achieving this objective.

---

western demands." "The Origins and Parameters of Libya's Recent Actions," *Arab Reform Bulletin* (Carnegie Endowment for International Peace) 2 (2004): 4.

[92] For a detailed discussion of the points raised in this paragraph, see Kendall Hoyt and Stephen Brooks, "Wielding a Double-Edged Sword: Globalization and Biosecurity," *International Security* 28 (2003–4); and Brooks, *Producing Security*, 240–41.

[93] Another prominent example is the Soviet Union. Gorbachev and other policymakers realized that only by moderating Soviet foreign policy would it be possible to end the Western "economic containment" policies that restricted the Soviet Union's access to Western firms, capital, and technology. The need to end economic isolation not only provided an impetus for "new thinkers" to initiate Soviet foreign policy retrenchment, but also made it much easier to convince hard-line "old thinkers" of the advisability of this foreign policy course. See the analysis in Stephen G. Brooks and William C. Wohlforth, "Power, Globalization, and the End of the Cold War: Reevaluating a Landmark Case for Ideas," *International Security* 25 (2000–2001), esp. 40–41.

[94] States' openness to the global economy does vary, and there are also some autarkic outliers, but the general trend of the past few decades has clearly been toward seeking greater integration into the global economy. For a good general discussion of this trend, see Geoffrey Garrett, "The Causes of Globalization," *Comparative Political Studies* 33 (2000).

More puzzling is whether rising economic interdependence could lead to constraints on U.S. security policy by nonstate actors. Two key nonstate actors need to be discussed in this regard: private firms or investors, and terrorists.

Let us first examine the former, analyzing each of the three elements of economic globalization—trade, finance, and production—and their potential links to U.S. security policies. With respect to trade, any firm that is subject to market pressures simply cannot opt to refrain from exporting to the U.S. market, whether to advance a political objective or for some other reason. This is because the U.S. market is so large, constituting by far the largest source of spending—both consumer and business—in the world.

The story regarding FDI in the United States is very similar. As noted previously, having a presence in the United States is now especially valuable for foreign firms from a competitiveness standpoint. None of the various attractions of the United States as an investment site for foreign firms—including its market size and its high level of R&D spending and rate of innovation—will meaningfully change in response to U.S. security policy.

Only the behavior of financial investors represents an even remotely plausible potential link to U.S. security policy. In a widely discussed account, Thomas Friedman maintains that aggressive states will be punished by international investors: "The only place a country can go to get big checks is the Electronic Herd. . . . Not only will the herd not fund a country's regional war . . .the herd will actually punish a country for fighting a war with its neighbors, by withdrawing the only significant source of growth capital in the world today. As such, countries have no choice but to behave in a way that is attractive to the herd or ignore the herd and pay the price of living without it."[95] A number of prominent scholars have also emphasized this basic line of argument. As Jonathan Kirshner underscores:

> Financial globalization will affect the likelihood of war generally in the international system, by creating a new disincentive for states to risk both militarized crises and war. This is because all states are now more

[95] Thomas Friedman, *The Lexus and the Olive Tree: Understanding Globalization* (New York: Anchor Books, 1999), 257. Friedman defines the "Electronic Herd" to include both MNCs and international financial investors. Brooks, *Producing Security*, 253–357, provides a detailed evaluation of Friedman's argument with respect to FDI, showing that it does not have much empirical support. Brooks also shows that states that have certain characteristics—particularly, a large international market—are especially unlikely to suf-

beholden to the preferences of the "international financial community" which is simply another phrase for the power of "financial globalization"—the consequences of the collective behavior of thousands of individual agents making their best informed guesses about the future value and attractiveness of various paper assets.[96]

Although Kirshner maintains that financial globalization raises "both the costs and opportunity costs" of initiating international conflict for *all* states, his analysis implicitly makes the point that the United States is far and away least affected by this mechanism precisely because of the position it occupies within the system. Specifically, he emphasizes that the United States has a large pull on global capital flows for a number of structural reasons, including the magnitude of the American economy and the size of its financial markets.[97] In the end, he concludes that "despite the fact that even the enormous U.S. economy is now more beholden to the whims of international financial markets, given its deep capital markets, powerful financial institutions, and enormous influence within the International Monetary Fund (IMF), globalized finance enhances the relative power of the U.S. compared to virtually every other state in the world."[98]

ECONOMIC GLOBALIZATION AND THE TERRORIST THREAT

What about the link between economic globalization and the motivations of terrorists? Many analysts posit that contemporary anti-Americanism is at least partly driven by the fact that "disentangling globalization from Americanization is not always easy or obvious," and, more specifically, by the fact that the United States has greatly benefited from the rapid spread of global economic interdependence.[99] And it is specifically among individuals, not states, that analysts are ultimately most concerned about the link between globalization and anti-Americanism.

---

fer a loss of FDI following aggressive foreign policy behavior. Significant in this regard is that the United States is far and away the world's largest economic market.

[96] Kirshner, "Processes of Globalization," 26. See also Rosecrance, *Rise of Trading State*, 133; and Graham Allison, "The Impact of Globalization on National and International Security," in *Governance and a Globalizing World*, ed. Joseph S. Nye and John Donahue (Washington, D.C.: Brookings Institution Press, 2000), 79–80.

[97] See Kirshner, "Processes of Globalization," 27.

[98] Ibid., 11.

[99] Ibid., 12; see also, for example, Hoffmann, "Clash of Globalizations," 112; and Jean-Francois Revel, "Anti-Globalism = Anti-Americanism," *American Enterprise Online*, June 2004, available at http://www.taemag.com/issues/articleid.18005/article_detail.asp (consulted July 27, 2007).

Many scholars do indeed argue that economic globalization can enhance the motivation of terrorists to strike the United States. For example, Stanley Hoffman emphasizes that today it is possible "for the most deprived or oppressed to compare their fate with that of the free and well-off" and, in turn, that Islamic terrorism is partly fueled by "a resistance to 'unjust' economic globalization. . . . Insofar as globalization enriches some and uproots many, those who are both poor and uprooted may seek revenge and self-esteem in terrorism."[100]

It is possible that economic globalization does enhance the motivations of terrorists to some minimal extent. There is, however, no basis for concluding that rising economic interdependence is a primary, or even a significant, contributor to the severity of the terrorist threat facing the United States. Although the acceleration of economic globalization in recent decades certainly has coincided with the growing threat of international terrorism, it is a mistake to infer causation from correlation. Noteworthy is that there is no evidence that economic concerns themselves act as a motivator for terrorists.[101] Instead, it is political grievances that appear to be the central driver.[102] Looking more specifically at economic globalization itself, a recent Pew survey of opinion leaders provides the best available snapshot of whether it is strongly linked to terrorism.[103] When asked whether economic globalization is a cause of terrorism, this study found that respondents throughout the world "viewed it as a minor factor at best."[104] In the Islamic world specifically, 79 percent of those surveyed said that globalization was not much of a cause or only a minor cause of terrorism.[105]

---

[100] Hoffmann, "Clash of Globalizations," 112. Audrey Kurth Cronin similarly maintains that "the current wave of international terrorism . . . is a reaction to globalization"; Cronin, "Behind the Curve," 30. See also, for example, Michael Mazarr, "Saved from Ourselves?" *Washington Quarterly* 25 (2002): 223–24; Kirshner, "Processes of Globalization," 12, 14; and Michael Mousseau, "Market Civilization and Its Clash with Terror," *International Security* 27 (2002–3).

[101] The most systematic treatment of this issue is Alan B. Krueger and Jitka Maleckova, "Education, Poverty, Political Violence and Terrorism: Is There a Causal Connection," NBER Working Paper No. 9074, July 2002.

[102] See, for example, the discussion in Peter L. Bergen, *Holy War Inc.* (New York: Simon and Schuster, 2002).

[103] Pew Global Attitudes Project, "America Admired, Yet Its New Vulnerability Seen as Good Thing," December 19, 2001.

[104] Ibid., "Introduction and Summary."

[105] 83 percent of those surveyed from Islamic countries also said that they thought the growing power of U.S. MNCs was not much of a cause or only a minor cause of why people in their countries resented the United States. In turn, 90 percent of those surveyed

These survey results resonate with the fact that most of the Islamic world is actually very isolated from economic globalization.[106]

It should also be noted that economic globalization does increase U.S. vulnerability to terror to some degree—most notably by providing more targets to strike, by making the border monitoring problem more difficult, and by facilitating transfers of money among terrorist groups. However, the problem of targets, border monitoring, and tracking terrorist finance would be very significant even if there was no economic globalization to speak of.[107] Compensating strategies also exist that can mitigate a number of the specific vulnerabilities associated with globalization;[108] the key problem in this regard has been a general lack of

---

from Islamic countries said they thought the spread of American culture, through movies, television, and pop music was either not much of a reason or only a minor reason why people in their countries disliked the United States. According to this Pew analysis, resentment of the United States in the Islamic world is instead driven by other factors, most notably U.S. support for Israel, resentment of U.S. power in the world, and the fact that U.S. policies may have contributed to the growing gap between rich and poor. Although these findings indicate that it is not economic interdependence per se that leads to resentment, the general policy environment in which globalization is embedded may play a significant role. Specifically, those international economic policies that the United States is associated with that are seen as contributing to a growing gap between rich and poor may drive resentment.

[106] For a useful discussion of this point, see Brink Lindsey, "Why Globalization Didn't Create 9/11," *New Republic*, November 12, 2001, 12–13. Lindsey underscores, "With a few notable exceptions—Turkey, Malaysia, Indonesia, some of the Gulf States—most Muslim countries have kept international economic integration at bay. Highly restrictive barriers to trade and investment choke off the international flows of goods, services, and capital. . . . Globalization is a messy, disruptive process, but it can't explain Islamic extremism because it hasn't touched most of the Islamic world."

[107] There are clearly innumerable attractive targets for terrorists to strike that are completely unrelated to globalization. The high volume of imported goods and parts across borders associated with globalization does make it easier for terrorists to move assets into the United States, but the huge levels of smuggling of both people and illegal goods makes it clear that terrorists need not exploit official economic transactions in order to do so. Finally, the globalization of financial markets does make it easier for terrorists to shift capital across borders, but the most pressing money transfer problem comes from the informal, ancient *hawala* system—which for centuries has provided an effective means of surreptitiously moving money across borders in the Middle East and South Asia and now accounts for an estimated $200 billion in annual transfers. For a useful overview of the *hawala* system, see John Sfakianakis, "Antiquated Laundering Ways Prevail," Al-Ahram Weekly Online, April 4, 2002, weekly.ahram.org.eg/2002/580/ec1.htm (consulted September 19, 2007).

[108] As Stephen Flynn underscores, there are numerous available procedures and technologies for reducing the severity of the border monitoring problem; see Flynn, "America the Vulnerable," *Foreign Affairs* 81 (2002); and Flynn, "Beyond Border Control," *Foreign Affairs* 79 (2000).

willingness on the part of U.S. policymakers to pursue these compensating strategies.[109] In this way, economic interdependence does function as a weak conditional constraint on U.S. security policy: the threat of terrorism will be enhanced if appropriate policies are not undertaken to reduce the vulnerabilities associated with economic globalization. Since so little effort has been devoted toward implementing these compensating strategies, it is difficult to assess how expensive they are and thus how significant this constraint is.

When assessing the link between terrorism and economic interdependence, it is also important to bear in mind that economic globalization makes it possible to reduce the terrorist threat in a variety of ways.[110] Economic globalization provides two key benefits in this regard, each of which relates to issues emphasized in the previous section. First, just as many of the most effective tools for dealing with the WMD threat are partly the products of globalization, the same is true with respect to capabilities for dealing with the terrorist threat. A prominent example in this regard is vaccines—a critical resource for dealing with the bioterrorist threat:

> The need to pursue partnerships to maintain high rates of innovation for vaccine development has grown rapidly in recent years. . . . International biotechnology companies now play an important role in U.S. biodefense vaccine research. Of the top-six Class A biological threat agents identified by the HHS (anthrax, Botulinum toxin, plague, smallpox, tularemia, and viral hemorrhagic fevers such as Ebola), vaccines for all but one (Botulinum toxin) are being developed in cooperation with international biotechnology companies.[111]

---

[109] Port security is a prominent example in this regard: "The Coast Guard has estimated that the inspectors, scanning equipment and other measures needed to secure the ports would cost $5.4 billion over the next 10 years. But the U.S. port security grant program has allocated less than $600 million since 2002, far less than is needed, and only a small fraction of what is being spent on airport security." "Missing Security Funds Leave America's Ports Vulnerable," *New York Times*, March 1, 2005.

[110] This double-edged quality of globalization is all too often overlooked by analysts and policymakers when they examine the terrorist threat now facing the United States; see, for example, Hoffmann, "Clash of Globalizations"; Cronin, "Behind the Curve"; and Richard Betts, "The Soft Underbelly of American Primacy: Tactical Advantages of Terror," *Political Science Quarterly* 117 (2002): 30.

[111] Hoyt and Brooks, "Wielding a Double-Edged Sword," 136. It should be noted that the importance of pursuing globalization regarding vaccines and other aspects of defense-related production does potentially reduce U.S. freedom of action to some degree: to do so effectively will sometimes require harmonizing U.S. regulations, perhaps within the context of an international institution, with those of other countries that form im-

Second, recall that the United States is globalization's key actor, both politically and economically, and that most states now strongly seek to benefit from the global economy. As a result, Washington often has significant potential leverage to encourage other states to take actions against terrorist groups operating within their borders or in neighboring countries. Consider Pakistan, which is arguably the most important "front line" country in the battle against global terrorism today. That economic globalization gave the Bush administration enhanced leverage concerning the role Pakistan would play in the war on terror shows up clearly in discussions that occurred in the immediate aftermath of 9/11. During his negotiations with the United States in fall 2001, President Musharraf made four key economic requests: (1) improved access of Pakistan's textiles—which constitute around 60 percent of the country's total exports—to the U.S. market; (2) a reduction in Pakistan's massive foreign debt, which amounts to 47.5 percent of Pakistan's GDP and for which debt service payments constitute 35 percent of the country's exports; (3) an increase in the amount of developmental assistance loans; and (4) the elimination of the economic sanctions that were put in place after Pakistan's 1998 nuclear test. After one such negotiating session in October 2001, Secretary of State Colin Powell told the Pakistani leader: "General, I've got it right here across my forehead, two words: 'debt relief.' Say no more."[112] In response to Musharraf's requests, the Bush administration promptly revoked the 1998 nuclear sanctions and also arranged for an immediate infusion of $600 million in developmental assistance. It is also announced in late October 2001 that it would move to reschedule the $3 billion Pakistan owes the United States while urging its allies to do the same. At least in the short term, the Bush administration's economic incentives helped to promote cooperation from Pakistan and thereby created an environment less favorable for terrorists both within Pakistan and also in neighboring Afghanistan.

There are many other countries besides Pakistan over which economic globalization gives U.S. policymakers potential leverage for furthering its counterterrorism strategy. In the end, the key question is whether the United States will use economic globalization to its best

---

portant parts of the defense supplier pool that the United States draws upon (see the discussion of this point with respect to vaccines in Hoyt and Brooks, "Wielding a Double-Edged Sword," 138–47).

[112] *New York Times*, November 13, 2001, B4.

advantage in the war on terror. Unfortunately, there are many discouraging signs in this regard; this is true concerning the effort to harness economic globalization's full potential for developing capabilities to counteract WMD[113] and also with respect to the use of globalization-related leverage for influencing the antiterrorism policies of other states.[114] The larger point, however, is that Washington does have significant potential to make use of economic globalization to further its counterterrorism strategy. This, in combination with the fact that rising economic interdependence does not appear to be a significant motivator for terrorist activity, means that globalization is, if anything, a net benefit to the United States in the war on terror.

CONCLUSION

It is clear that the United States has become much more dependent on economic globalization in recent years. There is also substance to the general liberal proposition that rising levels of economic interdependence will lead states to be more constrained in the conduct of their security policy. However, this chapter shows that the predominant liberal argument about constraints derived from economic interdependence does not apply with respect to U.S. security policy and that the key reason is because its economy stands so large on the world stage. As we have shown, enhanced U.S. dependence on non-U.S. companies for aspects of military production as well as increased overall U.S. dependence on maintaining linkages with foreign countries that are important export markets, suppliers of financial capital, and bases of FDI

[113] For example, U.S. policymakers put in place a regulatory framework that constrains the effective pursuit of globalization in the development of new biodefense capabilities; see the analysis in Hoyt and Brooks, "Wielding a Double-Edged Sword," 138–43.

[114] For example, the Bush administration backed away from its initial successful effort of using economic incentives to secure Pakistan's cooperation in the fight against terrorism: "The United States is continuing to make large payments of roughly $1 billion a year to Pakistan for what it calls reimbursements to the country's military for conducting counterterrorism efforts along the border with Afghanistan, even though Pakistan's president decided eight months ago to slash patrols through the area where Al Qaeda and Taliban fighters are most active. . . . So far, Pakistan has received more than $5.6 billion under the program over five years. . . . Some American military officials in the region have recommended that the money be tied to Pakistan's performance in pursuing Al Qaeda and keeping the Taliban from gaining a haven from which to attack the government in Afghanistan . . . but Bush administration officials say no such plan is being considered." David Sanger and David Rohde, "U.S. Pays Pakistan to Fight Terror, but Patrols Ebb," *New York Times*, May 20, 2007, A1.

do not translate into greater leverage for other states over U.S. security policy principally due to the great importance of the U.S. economy for the welfare of foreign firms and other states.

While IR scholars typically focus on how enhanced economic dependence changes exposure to economic statecraft strategies, economic globalization can also potentially constrain U.S. security policy in other, more indirect ways via shifts in capabilities and actors' preferences. Yet our analysis also shows that rising economic interdependence is, for a variety of reasons, unlikely to produce significant changes in capabilities and actors' preferences that limit U.S. security policy. While there is basis for concluding that economic globalization can somewhat contribute to a few indirect restrictions of this kind on U.S. security policy, they are conditional in nature: if appropriate policies are implemented, they will be greatly attenuated. Moreover, when gauging the significance of these conditional constraints, it must not be forgotten that, because of the U.S. position in the system as globalization's key actor, enhanced global economic interdependence simultaneously enables the use of American power to further its security objectives in a variety of ways.

Institutionalism and the Constraint of Reputation

IN THIS CHAPTER, we will examine the key argument about the restraining influence of today's institutional order that emerges from institutionalist theory (or neoliberal institutionalism, as it is sometimes called).[1] Institutionalist theory has a wide scope and has produced many important insights on the general role that institutions play in world politics.[2] In recent years, the theory's proponents have not spent much time specifically examining the power of a dominant hegemonic state and how it interacts with the institutional order.[3] It is nevertheless possible to apply the general logic of the theory to the U.S. case, and some of the theory's proponents have recently taken this route. What emerges from this exercise is the institutionalist argument on constraints: first,

---

[1] The seminal text that forms the basis for much of the institutionalist literature is Robert Keohane, *After Hegemony: Cooperation and Discord in the World Political Economy* (Princeton: Princeton University Press, 1984). For a brief overview of institutionalist theory, see Robert Keohane and Lisa Martin, "The Promise of Institutionalist Theory," *International Security* 20 (1995).

[2] See Lisa Martin and Beth A. Simmons, "International Organizations and Institutions," in *Handbook of International Relations*, ed. Walter Carlsnaes, Thomas Risse, and Beth A. Simmons (New York: Sage, 2002); and Lisa Martin and Beth A. Simmons, "Theories and Empirical Studies of International Institutions," *International Organization* 52 (1998).

[3] The rise of American primacy happened to coincide with a general waning of interest among institutionalist scholars in the role of hegemonic power; see David Lake, "Leadership, Hegemony, and the International Economy: Naked Emperor or Tattered Monarch with Potential?" *International Studies Quarterly* 37 (1993): 460. More generally, much recent institutionalist work has tended to bracket issues pertaining to power; see, for example, Voeten, "Outside Options," 845, who notes, "Institutionalists believe that power asymmetries are important, but their consequences are rarely explicitly modeled." As the organizers of a prominent team of scholars seeking to move the institutionalist research program forward stress, the analytical framework that guided their collective research "did not emphasize power" because "the formal literature does not offer compelling results"; see Barbara Koremenos, Charles Lipson, and Duncan Snidal, "Rational Design: Looking Back to Move Forward," *International Organization* 55 (2001): 1067; see also the discussion in John Duffield, "The Limits of Rational Design," *International Organization* 57 (2003): 417–18; and Barbara Koremenos and Duncan Snidal, "Moving Forward, One Step at a Time," *International Organization* 57 (2003): 437.

that the institutional status quo provides many benefits to the United States, and, second, that any American effort to revise or insulate itself from the current institutional order is dangerous because it will undermine America's "multilateral reputation" and lead to reduced levels of cooperation in those institutions that the United States strongly favors.

According to the logic of institutionalist theory, therefore, the U.S. faces a strong conditional constraint: the institutional order will be imperiled if the United States does not take the necessary steps to maintain a favorable multilateral reputation. Although this general line of argument is intriguing, it ultimately rests on fragile foundations. In the analysis that follows, we begin by delineating the basic logic for the institutionalist view of constraints. We then show that it is based on a particular conception of reputation that lacks theoretical or empirical justification, at least as applied to the U.S. case. Our ultimate conclusion is that the reputational constraint that emerges from institutionalist scholarship is inoperative with respect to U.S. security policy.

Before proceeding, a brief discussion of terminology is necessary. Although institutionalists describe America as having a multilateral reputation, it should be recognized that using the term *multilateralism* in this context is somewhat misleading. When analyzing America's approach to the institutional order, Beeson and Higgot are correct that "the key distinction is not between multilateralism and unilateralism"; instead, the fundamental issue concerns the general "commitment to institutionalism by the U.S."[4] Even those American policymakers most disposed to "go it alone" do not favor anything close to a complete withdrawal from multilateral institutions and also prefer to have more allies than fewer. When analysts argue that the United States shifted away from multilateralism during the Bush administration, they do not mean that it moved to abandon all institutions and never wanted allies; instead, what they mean is that America did not feel as bound as it did previously to follow the institutional rules of the game when it was inconvenient to do so. In this respect, when institutionalists refer to the U.S. reputation for multilateralism, it is America's general commitment to comply with international institutions that they ultimately have in mind.

<hr />

[4] Mark Beeson and Richard Higgot, "Hegemony, Institutionalism, and Foreign Policy: Theory and Practice in Comparative Historical Perspective," paper presented at the 2003 Conference of the British International Studies Association.

The Institutionalist Argument on Constraints

The starting point for the institutionalist argument on constraints is that international institutions offer marked efficiency gains for states. However, institutions are not just enabling devices; participating in them can sometimes be costly. Although institutionalists recognize that states will be tempted to avoid these costs, the logic of their theory indicates that no state can do so without placing the benefits of institutionalization at risk.

Institutions and Efficiency Gains

Institutionalist theory argues that cooperation within international institutions leads to dramatic efficiency gains. The theory builds on the observation that global problems beyond the control of individual countries cannot be managed in the absence of institutional structures that establish standards for state action and monitor compliance.[5] For all of the many issues that require repeated dealings with many partners over many years, institutionalist theory provides a powerful set of arguments concerning why cooperation through international institutions is far more efficient for the parties involved, including a country as powerful as the United States. The institutionalist argument for why institutions are efficient becomes even stronger to the extent that effective cooperation on an issue requires binding rules where state compliance must be monitored.[6]

The theory also identifies ways by which multilateral institutions can make cooperation more efficient even on matters that the United States could conceivably resolve on its own or by using ad hoc bilateral arrangements or loose coalitions. For example, having an institution in place to facilitate cooperation on one issue makes it easier, and more likely, that the participating states will be able to achieve cooperation rapidly on a related issue.[7] Consider the intelligence sharing network within NATO, which was originally designed to gather information on the threat from the Soviet Union: once in place, it could later be quickly adapted to deal with new unforeseen issues, such as the threat from

---

[5] See, for example, Robert Keohane, *Power and Governance in a Partially Globalized World* (London: Routledge: 2002), chap. 13.

[6] The best general treatment of these various arguments is Keohane, *After Hegemony.*

[7] On this "transaction costs" mechanism, see ibid.

terrorism. The key point, institutionalists stress, is not that the NATO countries would have been unable to coordinate intelligence efforts on terrorism in the absence of their institutionalized alliance, but that deep, effective cooperation was more likely to be achieved quickly and efficiently because of an already existing institution.

Institutionalist theory makes a very compelling case that the United States derives significant efficiency gains from the web of international institutions in the world today, much of which was created at the behest of U.S. policymakers in the decades following World War II.[8] And since the level of interdependence is rising, many analysts stress that the list of global problems that America cannot resolve on its own will only continue to grow, thereby enhancing the need for, and benefits of, institutionalized cooperation over the long run.[9]

Institutions and Costs

Efficiency gains represent only one side of the equation: institutionalization also has potential downsides for the United States. Those American analysts and policymakers who are critical of international institutions center their attention on the global security order. Their general view is that this security order is simply incapable of effectively dealing with the main threats now facing the United States. More specifically, many argue that this security order actually undercuts the effective use of U.S. power in security affairs. One prominent argument they advance in this regard is that international institutions can impede the conduct of U.S. military operations. There are clearly many benefits of cooperation in military operations: common war plans, specialization of military tasks, sharing of burdens and risks, economies of scale, common equipment and interchangeable parts, and so on. But critics argue that those benefits have declined with the dramatic increase in U.S. military power, which devalues the substantive contributions other states can make and renders joint operations involving military units from the United States and many of its allies

---

[8] See G. John Ikenberry, *After Victory: Institutions, Strategic Restraint, and the Rebuilding of Order after Major Wars* (Princeton: Princeton University Press, 2001).

[9] See, e.g., Stewart Patrick, "Multilateralism and Its Discontents: The Causes and Consequences of U.S. Ambivalence," in *Multilateralism and U.S. Foreign Policy: Ambivalent Engagement*, ed. Stewart Patrick and Shepard Forman (Boulder, Colo.: Lynne Rienner, 2002); Nye, *Paradox of American Power*; and Ikenberry, "American Multilateralism in Decline?"

151

difficult or even impossible. And this new "interoperability" problem is in addition to the well-known costs of slow decision-making, loss of secrecy, cumbersome systems of command and control, and circumscribed freedom of action. Those advancing this argument cite the 1999 war in Kosovo as the key exemplar supporting the conclusion that coordination costs are now very large relative to the benefits of cooperation in security issues: because the United States had to coordinate with NATO, they argue, the operational effectiveness of this mission was greatly compromised.[10] The legacy of Kosovo is a key reason U.S. policymakers decided to spurn virtually all offers of military assistance from NATO countries during the 2001 war in Afghanistan.[11]

How would institutionalists respond to this criticism? This branch of scholarship does tend to emphasize the benefits of the institutional order and does not focus as much on the costs associated with it.[12] Nevertheless, institutionalists certainly recognize that the institutional order is far from being unambiguously positive for the United States. At the same time, although those policymakers and analysts who are critical of the institutional order focus on the costs that it imposes on the United States, they would undoubtedly agree that it also has upsides for America. In some respects, the two sides in this debate are talking past each other: those who stress the large gains of institutions for the United States frequently highlight economic matters and not security issues, while those who emphasize costs do the opposite.[13] The

[10] See, for example, Charles Krauthammer, "Bush Blows Away Multilateralist Blather," *Houston Chronicle*, December 13, 2001. Academic analysts share this assessment. In his detailed analysis of the Kosovo operation, Sean Kay underscores that "[c]ontrary to neoliberal expectations, NATO's institutional structure raised the transaction costs of security provision. . . . As the war progressed, states found the best way to lower transaction costs of security outcomes was to skirt NATO's rules and procedures." "NATO, the Kosovo War, and Neoliberal Theory," *Contemporary Security Policy* 25 (2004): 252–53.

[11] See Kay, "NATO"; and Bob Woodward, *Bush at War* (New York: Simon and Schuster, 2002).

[12] In part, this may be because the overriding focus of institutionalist research has not been on areas where disagreements about the terms of cooperation are of key significance; instead, it has been on areas in which state efforts are directed toward the "enforcement problem"; see the discussion in James Fearon, "Bargaining, Enforcement, and International Cooperation," *International Organization* 52 (1998): 270.

[13] Institutionalist scholarship does focus on economic institutions to a greater extent than security institutions; see Beth A. Simmons, "Compliance with International Agreements," *Annual Review of Political Science* 1 (1998): 81. The focus of economic institutions is generally on resolving "dilemmas of common interest"; see Arthur Stein, "Coordination and Collaboration: Regimes in an Anarchic World," in *International Regimes*, ed. Stephen Krasner (Ithaca, N.Y.: Cornell University Press, 1983). Within economic institutions, coordination on mutually beneficial exchange is the typical aim, and the

larger point is that all would undoubtedly agree that the institutional order simultaneously enables and constrains U.S. power and that the extent to which this is the case varies by issue area.

Key in this regard for the United States are the differences between the economic and security realms. In the economic realm, the institutional order certainly does restrict the United States somewhat, but institutionalists are on solid ground in concluding that this is far less significant than the powerful enabling function it serves—in terms of enhancing U.S. growth and promoting other valued objectives, including its security. As we show in chapter 4, because the United States is globalization's key actor, both politically and economically, Washington often has significant leverage that it can use to encourage other states to take actions to promote U.S. security goals.

In comparison to the economic realm, few would question that the balance between constraints and enabling functions is less favorable for the Unites States in the international security order. This is partly a function of the distribution of power: because the magnitude of the U.S. power advantage is so pronounced in the military realm, it has a relatively greater potential to effectively go it alone in this area. It is also partly a function of the order itself: while the economic order has a dense set of deep institutions that are well equipped to deal with the issues that are of key concern, this is less true of the security order. The security order was designed to deal with threats from states, not nonstate actors—which now constitute the security threat of highest salience to the United States.

Perhaps not surprisingly, U.S. actions in these two institutional realms have differed in recent years. Of course, the United States has not been perfectly unilateral or multilateral in either realm; as has

---

enforcement of commonly agreed-upon rules is generally the key cooperation issue. The WTO is a paramount example in this respect. Within the security realm, in contrast, the focus is much less on enforcement of agreed-upon rules; see Charles Lipson, "International Cooperation in Economic and Security Affairs," *World Politics* 37 (1984): 71. This partly reflects the kinds of issues that the security institutions typically deal with: military crises are all unique, making it harder to establish fixed rules for dealing with them; moreover, "the dangers of swift, decisive defection simply do not apply in most international economic issues" as they do in the security realm (Lipson, 75). In the security realm, whether states will cooperate—and the terms that any such cooperation will have—is much more at issue, and it is therefore the bargaining problem, rather than the enforcement problem, which is generally most significant. See the discussion in Fearon, "Bargaining, Enforcement"; and Stephen Krasner, "Global Communications and National Power: Life on the Pareto Frontier," *World Politics* 43 (1991).

always been the case, it has operated somewhere in between.[14] The more important issue concerns the U.S. willingness to pay costs to invest in the respective institutional orders. It is hard to make the case that a dramatic shift occurred in the willingness to pay costs regarding the institutional economic order under the Bush administration as compared to the Clinton administration—or, indeed, that the United States has shifted much in this respect over the past several decades.[15] In contrast, there is every indication the U.S. willingness to pay costs to invest in the institutional order became lower under the Bush administration in the security realm—both in general and also in relative terms when compared with the international economic order. It was in the security realm where President George W. Bush appeared most decisive in reducing the United States' commitment to international institutions in favor of assembling "coalitions of the willing" on an as needed, case-by-case basis.[16]

The Significance of Reputation

While the enabling/constraining ratio of the economic and security realms differ for the United States, institutionalists argue strongly that the United States must now be strongly cooperative in both realms simultaneously.[17] If the United States has a strong interest in complying

[14] As G. John Ikenberry notes, "The United States has been the greatest champion of multilateral institutions in the twentieth century, urging on the world all sorts of new organizational creations, but it has also tended to resist entangling itself in institutional commitments and obligations." "State Power and the Institutional Bargain: America's Ambivalent Economic and Security Multilateralism," in *US Hegemony and International Organizations: The United States and Multilateral Institutions*, ed. Rosemary Foot, S. Neil MacFarlane, and Michael Mastanduno (New York: Oxford University Press, 2003).

[15] Barry Eichengreen and Douglas Irwin emphasize that although analysts "see the Bush presidency as a distinctive epoch in American foreign policy, we argue that there was no Bush Doctrine in foreign economic policy, where we see continuities rather than discontinuities with the past." "International Economic Policy: Was There a Bush Doctrine?" paper prepared for the conference "American Foreign Policy after the Bush Doctrine," University of Virginia, June 7–8, 2007, 1. See also the general analysis of U.S. foreign economic policy by Michael Mastanduno, who emphasizes that "there is a striking consistency in the behavior of the United States across the bipolar and unipolar eras. The role of the United States in the world economy and the nature and pattern of U.S. economic interactions with other major powers are remarkably similar whether we are examining the 1960s, the 1980s, or the 2000s" ("System Maker," 1).

[16] Outlines of the administration's approach to security issues include Donald Rumsfeld, "Transforming the Military," *Foreign Affairs* 81 (2002).

[17] This argument is clearest in Martin, "Multilateral Organizations"; see also, for example, Ikenberry, "American Multilateralism in Decline?"; and Keohane, "Multilateral Coercive Diplomacy."

with international economic institutions but has a relatively lower interest in doing so regarding international security institutions, then why do institutionalists argue that it must simultaneously follow a highly cooperative approach in each realm? The United States must take this route, institutionalists argue, because of the significance of reputation.

To say that reputation plays an important role within institutionalist theory is an understatement.[18] As one analysis correctly notes, reputation "now stands as the linchpin of the dominant neoliberal institutionalist theory of decentralized cooperation."[19] Keohane emphasizes that "the puzzle of compliance is why governments, seeking to promote their own interests, ever comply with the rules of international regimes when they view these rules as in conflict with . . . their 'myopic self-interest.' "[20] Institutionalist theory identifies two key mechanisms for gaining compliance within institutions when doing so is costly for a state's short-term self-interest: credible threats of retaliatory action and reputation costs.[21]

Because retaliation is costly and hard, institutionalists stress its limitations as a compliance mechanism: as Keohane underscores, "[R]etaliation for specific violations is not a reliable way to maintain international regimes. . . . Individual countries find it costly to retaliate. Familiar problems of collective action arise: if a given state's violation of a particular rule does not have a large effect on any one country, retaliation is unlikely to be severe, even if the aggregate effect of the violation is large."[22] The greater the asymmetry of power in favor of a state, the more significant these costs become, and the less credible retaliation is as a compliance mechanism. Out of all states, retaliation is clearly least salient as a constraint on the United States. The United

---

[18] The key role of reputation shows up clearly in Keohane's foundational book, *After Hegemony,* 105–8, 116, 258. See also, for example, Charles Lipson, "Why Are Some International Agreements Informal?" *International Organization* 45 (1991): 508–12; Lisa Martin, "Credibility, Costs, and Institutions: Cooperation on Economic Sanctions," *World Politics* 45 (1993): 418; Martin, "Multilateral Organizations," esp. 365, 370; Beth A. Simmons, "International Law and State Behavior: Commitment and Compliance in International Monetary Affairs," *American Political Science Review* 94 (2000); and Simmons, "Compliance with International Agreements," 81.

[19] George Downs and Michael Jones, "Reputation, Compliance, and International Law," *Journal of Legal Studies* 31 (2002): S95.

[20] Keohane, *After Hegemony,* 99.

[21] See the discussion in ibid., 103–8; and Lipson, "Why Are Agreements Informal?" 511–12.

[22] Keohane, *After Hegemony,* 104–5.

States is so large on the world stage that it will require a great many states acting together in opposition to have a sufficiently strong retaliatory effect. Moreover, precisely because the United States occupies such a dominant position in the system, the value of maintaining a favorable relationship with it is typically very high and, in turn, the United States has more avenues than other states to engage in costly retaliation in response to efforts by other states to influence it.

Especially for the United States, reputation thus emerges as the relevant factor pushing toward compliance within institutionalist theory.[23] The underlying institutionalist argument is straightforward: states that do not comply within institutions "pay a serious price for acting in bad faith and, more generally, for renouncing their commitments. This price comes ... from the decline in national reputation as a reliable partner."[24] For the United States, the general logic of institutionalist theory thus has a clear implication: failure to hew closely to the existing institutional order is costly because it will undermine America's reputation, thereby placing in jeopardy its continued ability to maintain cooperation in areas where it strongly needs and values institutionalization. This theoretical repercussion of institutionalist theory for the United States has been expressed most clearly and directly by Lisa Martin.[25] She maintains that during the Cold War, the United States sought to demonstrate that "although it could maximize its immediate payoffs by rejecting the rules that bound others, it instead would play by the rules. It did so by its commitment to multilateralism throughout the economic and security realms. ... Self-binding therefore describes the U.S. strategy at the heart of the multilateral organizations it created after World War II."[26] Through this pattern of behavior, she argues, the United States "developed a reputation for multilateralism during the Cold War. ... This reputation, in turn, contributed to the success of multilateral organizations."[27]

Institutionalist theory posits that the need to maintain a favorable general reputation for compliance applies to all states that want the

---

[23] The discussion in ibid., 105–6, makes this point clear.

[24] Lipson, "Why Are Agreements Informal?" 511.

[25] Martin, "Multilateral Organizations." While they don't use the term *reputation* specifically, other prominent scholars forward arguments that have the same basic thrust as the one Martin advances; see, for example, Ikenberry, "American Multilateralism in Decline?" and Lake, "Beyond Anarchy."

[26] Martin, "Multilateral Organizations," 365.

[27] Ibid., 370.

gains of institutionalized cooperation. Some scholars suggest that this constraint may be especially significant for the leading state, and that when its relative power rises further—as when U.S. power increased with the Soviet Union's fall—the effect will become more salient still. The critical point is as the United States becomes more powerful, it faces a greater temptation to exempt itself from the rules of the game when inconvenient and it has a greater ability to do so without being punished in the short term.[28] For these and other reasons, Ikenberry emphasizes that "the more that a powerful state is capable of dominating or abandoning weaker states, the more the weaker states will care about constraints on the leading state's policy autonomy."[29] Martin stresses that "operating without the inconveniences of multilateral constraints is a tremendous temptation for the powerful" and consequently that "states with the immense power of the United States face immense strategic challenges. In order to gain the sustained cooperation of others, powerful states need to make commitments to play by the rules themselves. Self-binding is a necessary component of long-term cooperation."[30]

Although it is costly for the United States to maintain a good multilateral reputation, the implication drawn from institutionalist theory is that if it does not do so, then the institutional order will be in grave danger of crumbling.[31] In Martin's assessment, this dangerous scenario is already upon us:

> Reputations can be squandered quickly, and the reputation for multilateralism surely has been. Turning to multilateral organizations only under duress and when it appears convenient demonstrates a lack of commitment, even explicit rejection, of the principles of multilateralism. This in turn leads other states to expect the United States to renege on agreements or operate outside the constraints of multilateral organizations when it is convenient to do so. This hollows out the core of such

---

[28] Ibid., 365, 369.

[29] Ikenberry, "American Multilateralism in Decline?" 535. See also Lake, "Beyond Anarchy," 159.

[30] Martin, "Multilateral Organizations," 369–70.

[31] Ibid. Although Ikenberry does not specifically use the language of reputation in his analysis, he outlines the same basic argument as Martin; as he notes, the key danger is that by "violating core multilateral rules and norms, the credibility of American commitment to the wider array of agreements and norms becomes suspect and the entire multilateral edifice crumbles" ("American Multilateralism in Decline?" 539).

organizations. ... Without self-binding by the hegemon, multilateral organizations become empty shells. ... There is little doubt that the U.S. reputation for self-binding has been largely destroyed and will need to be rebuilt if these organizations are to regain their effectiveness.[32]

Martin argues that the "question now is whether there is any likelihood of a reversal in U.S. policy, moving toward a willingness to invest resources in rebuilding a reputation for self-binding."[33] She notes further that taking this route will be costly: "It will take time and resources to rebuild the U.S. reputation for multilateralism. It will require making concessions and accepting compromises on a wider range of issues on which we might prefer to go it alone or to impose our most-favored solution."[34] Following the theoretical logic of institutionalist theory, taking this course is necessary for the United States even though it may be very costly.[35]

The Argument's Theoretical Weakness

According to the logic of institutionalist theory, the United States thus now faces very significant constraints on its security policy due to the institutional order: the United States must be strongly cooperative across the board to maintain cooperation in those aspects of the order that it favors. As it turns out, the institutionalist argument for why the United States needs to pursue a highly cooperative approach regarding all parts of the institutional order is premised on a particular view of how reputations work. Institutionalist theory rests on the notion that "states carry a general reputation for cooperativeness that determines their attractiveness as a treaty partner both now and in the future. ... A defection in connection with any agreement will impose reputation costs that affect all current and future agreements."[36] Despite the fact that this conception of a general reputation does a huge amount of work within institutionalist theory, the theory's proponents have so far not provided a theoretical justification for this perspective.[37] Rather, they have simply assumed this is how reputation works.

[32] Martin, "Multilateral Organizations," 370.
[33] Ibid., 371.
[34] Ibid., 372.
[35] Ibid., 367, 369, 372.
[36] Downs and Jones, "Reputation, Compliance," S99.
[37] See the discussion of this point, and the citations listed therein, in ibid., S95.

In the most detailed theoretical analysis of the role that reputation plays within international institutions to date, Downs and Jones argue that there is no theoretical basis for viewing states as having a "a single reputation for cooperation that characterizes its expected reliability in connection with every agreement to which it is a party."[38] Downs and Jones maintain that it is more compelling to view states as having multiple, or segmented, reputations: "states develop a number of reputations, often quite different, in connection with different regimes and even with different treaties within the same regime."[39] In other words, there is no reason to think that a state's reputation within the security realm cannot be different from the reputation that it has within the economic realm, or, indeed, that a state cannot have varying reputations within different parts of the security realm. As an illustrative example, Downs and Jones note:

> The United States has one simple reputation for making good on its financial commitments with workers in the UN Office of the Secretary-General and another quite different simple reputation with officials of European states in connection with its financial commitments to NATO. Neither group is much concerned with characterizing the reliability of the United States in meeting its financial commitments in general. Those inside the Office of the Secretary-General are aware of the fact that the United States has paid its NATO bills, and NATO workers know that the United States is behind on its UN dues. However, they design their policies in response to the behavior of the United States in the subset of contexts that is relevant to them.[40]

The essence of the Downs and Jones theoretical argument is that the idea of multiple reputations is more compelling than the institutionalists' general reputation because (a) states have different compliance rates across treaties and it is difficult to believe that it is efficient for other states to simply ignore this fact, (b) states have undoubtedly learned that the rates and timing of defections are weakly correlated across treaties, and (c) in light of points a and b, it would be irrational for a state to readjust its view of a state's cooperativeness across all treaties just in response to a single defection from a particular treaty. To quickly illustrate this basic logic, consider that the United States

---

[38] Ibid., S100.
[39] Ibid., S97.
[40] Ibid., S109.

has one compliance rate vis-à-vis the UN and a different, much better, compliance rate vis-à-vis the WTO. Since the U.S. compliance rate is so different regarding these two institutions and this state of affairs is well known by other governments, Downs and Jones would argue that there is little reason for other governments to conclude that the United States will be less likely to honor its WTO commitments after observing lack of U.S. compliance with the UN. Significantly, Downs and Jones stress that this will be the case even if other states have no knowledge of the underlying interests of the United States (in other words, no knowledge of why the United States is much more compliant with the WTO than the UN).

Downs and Jones make a compelling case for multiple reputations, but the argument can be even stronger theoretically by factoring in two additional considerations. First and most importantly, states have different interests regarding different international institutions. Although Downs and Jones briefly mention this point, they treat it in a peripheral manner: they do recognize that states do not value all institutions equally, but they do not explore what this means in theoretical terms because factoring in interests complicates the mathematics in the formal models they use.[41] Given that our goal is to understand how the constraint of reputation applies specifically to the case of the United States today, it is necessary to consider interests.

It turns out that explicitly considering variation in the value states place on different institutions—and the fact that others know this—dramatically strengthens the argument for multiple reputations. To understand why, consider U.S. interests vis-à-vis the UN as compared to its interests regarding the WTO. For the WTO, it is straightforward for other states to discern that the United States sees it as serving U.S. interests extremely well: the U.S. government clearly values the promotion of international trade very highly, and international coordination is needed to obtain this result. No debate exists within U.S. policymaking circles as to whether the United States can create an open global economy without the WTO. For the UN, on the other hand, it is not difficult for other states to discern that the United States does not see it as serving U.S. interests nearly as well as the WTO. Reflecting this, a substantial debate exists among policymakers as to whether the United States can more effectively address its core security problems without strongly binding itself to the UN. The key point is that if the United

---

[41] See the discussion in ibid., S108.

States doesn't comply with the UN, there is no reason for other states to adjust their understanding of whether it will continue to cooperate in the WTO since they are well aware that (*a*) the United States has a strong interest in furthering the WTO and (*b*) this interest exists independently, and is unaffected by, the interests it has regarding the UN and the approach it takes toward this organization.

Looking beyond the fact that states value different institutions differently, the way in which compliance information is processed and acted upon by state bureaucracies is the second consideration that, once factored in, helps to make the idea of multiple reputations more compelling theoretically. In their analysis, Downs and Jones assume a world in which information about compliance is easily obtained and processed by decision-makers simultaneously across all treaties and regimes. However, even Downs and Jones admit that this is very unrealistic: "The model we have described here is very information intensive. . . . States not only have to keep track of the reliability rates connected with different agreements, but they have to estimate the degree of similarity among them with respect to the values states assign them and the factors that determine variations in their compliance costs. Even if we are correct in believing that states pay attention to these factors, their capacity for making distinctions may not be as refined as efficiency demands."[42]

Ultimately, it is much more likely that many instances of institutional noncompliance may be ignored or not processed by relevant decision-makers. As global interdependence has increased over the past century, the number of international institutions has also greatly increased: from 37 in 1909, to 132 in 1956, to 293 in 1990.[43] An important consequence of this rapid spread of international institutions is that increasingly specialized groups within governments are tasked with dealing with particular institutions, or related sets of them. An example is the Office of the United States Trade Representative (USTR), a group of over 200 people with specialized experience on trade issues who focus largely on trade agreements and other related organizations. The staff of USTR is not tasked with monitoring compliance with international institutions that fall outside its purview. And the USTR is as large as it is in part because trade negotiations have become so

[42] Ibid., S113.
[43] Bruce M. Russett and John R. Oneal, *Triangulating Peace: Democracy, Interdependence, and International Organizations* (New York: Norton, 2001), 160.

161

complicated in recent decades, and thus its staff is unlikely to have much time to closely monitor institutional compliance rates in other issue areas. For these and other reasons, the staff of the USTR is likely to often lack specific knowledge about compliance in other issue areas. The larger conclusion is that to the extent that compliance knowledge is segmented into specific issue areas, then the bounds of reputation are likely to be as well.

The significance of bureaucratic politics also needs to be factored in. Even if members of a specialized agency such as USTR were to obtain information about compliance with international institutions that fall outside its purview, it has a bureaucratic mission that it will in all likelihood focus on irrespective of what is happening in other areas. When, for example, the USTR is tasked with negotiating a new free trade agreement, it will likely focus on completing this assignment unless directed otherwise; to refrain from doing so because of the nature of compliance behavior by states in other issue areas risks the prospect of punishment from U.S. political leaders. And while it is certainly possible that senior U.S. foreign policy makers may decide to direct USTR to proceed differently in trade negotiations in light of the compliance behavior of states in areas not covered by USTR, it is unlikely that such intervention will occur frequently (more on this point below). The larger conclusion is that to the extent that the significance of compliance behavior is bureaucratically divided, reputational effects and any constraints they impose are likely to be as well.

EMPIRICAL PROBLEMS WITH THE INSTITUTIONALIST CONCEPTION OF REPUTATION

The theoretical case for multiple reputations is more compelling than institutionalist theory's standard assumption of a single reputation. The implication is that the negative repercussions of noncompliance are far more bounded than institutionalist scholarship presumes. But if there is strong evidence for a general reputation, its theoretical shortcomings might be discounted. In this section, we reveal that the empirical record is strongly consistent with multiple reputations. There are four relevant patterns of evidence in this regard.

The first pattern of evidence concerns overall compliance rates. As Downs and Jones emphasize, if states have an overall propensity to cooperate and their general reputation greatly influences the prospects for sustaining international cooperation, then we should expect to observe

(1) uniform compliance rates across international institutions and/or (2) high overall compliance rates. In their survey of the literature on compliance with international institutions, they find that neither of these patterns holds. As they stress: "While compliance rates are relatively good in general, they are often considerably lower than one would expect them to be if every defection had important implications for every current and future agreement. . . . It is common for a given state to evidence very different rates of compliance reliability—the building blocks of reputational inference—in connection with different agreements."[44]

Looking beyond compliance rates, a second pattern of evidence concerns linkages across issue areas. Although there are numerous ready examples in which poor compliance levels influence the level of cooperation within specific institutions, there is a dearth of documented cases in which a state's lack of compliance in one area has led to a more general decline in a state's ability to attain cooperation in different areas.[45] For the United States, the key concern in this regard is whether other states engage in linkage across economic institutions and security institutions: the United States clearly wants increased flexibility in the latter area, but it also does not want to undermine the prospects for cooperation in the former area. Surveying the literature on bargaining and international negotiations, Odell finds no empirical support for the notion that states make linkages during negotiations between security issues and economic issues (in the sense of changing their underlying negotiation positions regarding international institutions in one issue area due to the dynamics of cooperation that exist in the other).[46] He stresses this is the case for states across the board.[47] To explain why states refrain from altering their stance in economic negotiations in response to ongoing security dynamics, he emphasizes the significance of interest group pressures: "The proposal to bend trade or financial concessions or threats to security goals is likely to meet at least some opposition from the producers, lenders, and investors who would pay the price, except when commercial moves or opportunities are insignificant economically or when these constituents believe war is imminent."[48]

---

[44] Downs and Jones, "Reputation, Compliance," S96. See the discussion and works cited therein.

[45] Downs and Jones, "Reputation, Compliance," S109.

[46] John Odell, "A Working Paper on Military-Political Conditions and International Economic Negotiations," USC Working Paper, 1997, available at http://www-rcf.usc.edu/~odell/papers.html (consulted September 19, 2007).

[47] Ibid., 7–9.

[48] Ibid., 9.

The first two patterns of evidence are general rather than pertaining to the U.S. case in particular. A third pattern of evidence concerns the consequences of U.S. noncompliance. Following U.S. noncompliance in security institutions, there is a dearth of evidence indicating any general reduction in cooperation with it by other states. As noted previously, in his first term President Bush strongly championed a "coalition of the willing" approach. Cutting across issue areas and individual cases, this seemed to represent a fundamentally new foreign policy approach, which analysts dubbed the "new unilateralism."[49] Yet in response to the actions the Bush administration took toward security institutions at this time—which culminated in the dramatic sidestepping of the UN regarding the 2003 invasion of Iraq—there is no indication that other states reduced cooperation with it in other important institutional settings, such as trade.

For example, there is no evidence that the UN dispute over the Iraq War in 2003 had any influence on the prospects for cooperation within the WTO. In interviews conducted in 2003 with European diplomats, none claimed that the intense disagreement over Iraq between the United States and important members of the EU, especially France and Germany, had any spillover effect in terms of influencing ongoing WTO negotiations. These European diplomats stressed it was not simply the case that an effort by European governments to link the WTO negotiations with U.S. behavior regarding security institutions was lacking, but also that if any such effort had been proposed, its strength would have undoubtedly been undermined by objections from European firms who have a strong interest in the success of the WTO negotiations and with having a positive EU-U.S. economic relationship.[50] This is only one example, but it does correspond with a general pattern in which it is very hard to identify cases in which linkage occurred across international institutions in different issue areas in response to U.S. behavior towards security institutions. Until and unless significant counterexamples can be identified, then we have little empirical basis for concluding that the United States does suffer a reputational penalty in terms of a reduced general ability to gain institutionalized cooperation with other states in response to noncompliance towards security institutions.

[49] For a discussion of why *new unilateralism* is a useful term, see Charles Krauthammer, "The Unipolar Moment Revisited," *National Interest* 70 (2002–3).

[50] These 2003 interviews were conducted by John Odell in Geneva; his recollection of these interviews were relayed in a personal communication on November 30, 2005.

A bigger question is whether the U.S. experience in this regard is typical, or instead whether it faces fewer such linkages across issue areas precisely because it is as powerful as it is. Because the United States is so large on the world stage, reducing cooperation with it generally carries a very high opportunity cost for other states: typically, the United States has much more to offer other states than vice versa. In turn, exactly because the United States has such a substantial global presence and frequently suffers the least if multilateral cooperation fails, it is especially well positioned to itself pursue linkage across different issues with other states. For example, "Yemen found that its entire US aid budget was eliminated three days after it cast a UN vote against the first Gulf War in 1991. An American diplomat reportedly told the country's UN envoy that 'that will be the most expensive 'no' vote you ever cast.' "[51] Another prominent such example is the U.S. decision to exclude New Zealand from the free trade agreement that it established with Australia in 2004. In this case, the Bush administration resisted entreaties at this time from New Zealand to conclude a free trade agreement principally due to disputes between the two countries over security issues—notably, concerning the Iraq War and the 1985 decision to ban nuclear armed and nuclear powered ships from New Zealand's ports.[52]

The bottom line is that other states may be much less likely to pursue linkage across issues when they deal with the United States as compared to when they deal with smaller states who are less well positioned to pursue linkage and whose cooperation is also not as vital to secure. The finding that the United States does not suffer reduced prospects for institutionalized cooperation in other issue areas after lack of compliance regarding security institutions may thus not be generalizable to other states.

Although there is a dearth of evidence of linkage across issue areas in response to U.S. behavior toward security institutions, it is of course possible that the United States could suffer a more circumscribed reputational penalty in terms of a reduced ability to gain institutional cooperation with other states specifically within the security realm itself.

---

[51] Randall Newnham, "Coalition of the Bribed and Bullied? US Economic Linkage and the Iraq War Coalition," paper presented at the Annual Meeting of the Northeastern Political Science Association and the International Studies Association—Northeast, Philadelphia, November 2005, 8–9.

[52] See the discussion in Bruce Vaughn, "New Zealand: Background and Bilateral Relations with the United States," *Congressional Research Service Report*, March 16, 2007;

Yet there is also little evidence of withdrawal of cooperation within security institutions in areas where the United States values strong coordination—such as counterterrorism—by other states in response to the foreign policy approach taken by the Bush administration. In NATO, for example, there is no indication that countries such as France and Germany linked their opposition to the Iraq War to a reduction in cooperation with the United States in areas such as intelligence sharing. Instead, there have been steadily increased efforts within NATO to foster intelligence sharing in recent years, such as the established Terrorist Threat Intelligence Unit.[53]

Of course, one can easily identify situations in which the United States has not been compliant vis-à-vis a security institution and subsequently had difficulty gaining cooperation with other states within that same institution. For example, after the dispute over Iraq at the UN, the United States clearly had difficulty in bringing other key states—notably China and Russia—on board in the effort to impose substantial sanctions on Iran to curtail its nuclear program. Although it cannot be ruled out that these states were less willing to cooperate with the United States in this instance because it is seen as a less reliable cooperation partner due to its past noncompliance in the UN, it seems likely that reputational dynamics are not contributing to this behavior. In the case of China and Russia, their strong commercial ties with Iran are a key factor causing their governments to be very reluctant to take tough measures against it. The Russian and Chinese behavior regarding Iran raises a more general point: when discussing potential cases of linkage, it is costly linkages that are of interest—that is, actions that states would not be doing otherwise. Gaining international cooperation is difficult; if it is not achieved, it could well be because other states do not see an interest in cooperating and not because they do not trust the reliability of other states to cooperate in an effort to reach mutual goals.

The fourth and final pattern of evidence concerns the effects of U.S. noncompliance in the security realm on the formation or revision of security institutions. Even if, as indicated above, other states do not reduce their *current* level of institutional cooperation following

---

Newnham, "Coalition of the Bribed?" 20–21; and Nick Squires, "Splitting Asunder Down Under," *South China Morning Post*, October 15, 2005, 10.

[53] See, for example, Dagmar de Mora-Figueroa, "NATO's Response to Terrorism," *NATO Review*, Autumn 2005. On French-U.S. cooperation, see Meunier, "French Anti-Americanism."

U.S. noncompliance, states may nevertheless be unwilling to pursue *additional* cooperation within new, or revised, international institutions. Significantly, there are strong reasons to expect that the creation, or revision, of an international institution has higher reputational requirements than does maintaining existing patterns of cooperation within an already established institution. The key reason why is that there is no past compliance record to rely upon when making calculations about how other states will act: because the time inconsistency problem is greater, the informational value of a state's reputation is likely enhanced.

Ultimately, the formation or revision of international institutions is thus the easiest test case for the significance of general reputation. In light of the Bush administration's foreign policy approach, we would not expect to find evidence that it was able to create, or revise, security institutions if the institutionalist conception of a general reputation was valid. And yet this is clearly not the case.

With respect to revisions of an existing security institution, consider those that have occurred within the UN. Many significant new forms of UN cooperation have been advanced that were pushed by the Bush administration. Perhaps the most prominent example is UN Security Council Resolution 1540 (which seeks to ensure that states restrict as much as possible nonstate actor involvement in WMD proliferation). As will be stressed in chapter 6, the United States was the principal architect behind its creation and was able to successfully advance this resolution just a little more than a year after the Iraq War began.

Regarding the formation of a new security institution, perhaps the most noteworthy recent example is the Proliferation Security Initiative (PSI). The PSI is an international agreement that grew directly out of the Bush administration's 2002 National Strategy to Combat Weapons of Mass Destruction Proliferation, which outlined a much more activist approach to nonproliferation. The specific goal of the PSI is to provide an enhanced basis for boarding and stopping ships suspected of carrying WMD, their delivery systems, and related materials. More specifically, the PSI aims to impede and stop WMD-related shipments "to and from states and nonstate actors of proliferation concern."[54]

[54] For a description of the interdiction principles for the PSI, see http://www.whitehouse.gov/news/releases/2003/09/20030904–11.html (consulted October 17, 2007). In the PSI, states and nonstate actors of proliferation concern "generally refers to those countries or entities that the PSI participants involved establish should be subject to interdiction activities because they are engaged in proliferation through (1) efforts to de-

The PSI was launched by President Bush on May 31, 2003—just a little more than two months after the U.S.-led war on Iraq began (on March 20, 2003). Significantly, the PSI's principal champion was John Bolton—one of the Bush administration's most outspoken proponents of the position that the United States should not be constrained by international institutions. Despite the leadership role of Bolton and the nearly coincident timing with the dispute at the UN over the Iraq War, both Germany and France signed on as original founding states for the PSI. If nations were best understood as having one general reputation, we would not expect to see this behavior. Nor would we expect to see the level of success that the PSI enjoyed since it was created: over 60 countries voiced support for it and it now provides an enhanced ability to interdict 60 percent of the commercial shipping tonnage on the high seas.[55]

The above examples only reveal that the Bush administration sometimes was able to revise or create security institutions. But how often did it try strenuously to do so? Perhaps it would have liked to revise or create many institutional structures in the security realm, but decided to refrain from putting much effort into doing so because of the constraint of having a poor general reputation. Determining whether this is the case is difficult, but it does seem that out of all recent U.S. administrations that the Bush administration *right from the start* was especially disinclined to invest itself in the creation or revision of international institutions. What is striking is that when the Bush administration did strongly turn its attention in this direction in the security realm, such as regarding PSI and UNSCR 1540, how successful it often was. In light of the particular compliance record that the Bush administration compiled regarding security institutions in the lead-up to these initiatives, such examples alone provide significant evidence against

velop or acquire chemical, biological, or nuclear weapons and associated delivery systems; or (2) transfers (either selling, receiving, or facilitating) of WMD, their delivery systems, or related materials.

[55] According to the U.S. State Department, "The combination of states with which we have boarding agreements and Proliferation Security Initiative partner commitments means that more than 60 percent of the global commercial shipping fleet dead weight tonnage is now subject to rapid action consent procedures for boarding, search, and seizure"; see http://www.state.gov/r/pa/prs/ps/2005/50035.htm (consulted September 19, 2007). This 60 percent figure is obtained by adding together the commercial shipping tonnage of the 18 "core participants" of PSI—which have "formally committed" to PSI and its Statement of Principles—along with that from key shipping countries (such as Panama and Liberia) that have reached bilateral ship-boarding agreements with the United States.

the general reputation view—at least with respect to the United States. If a smaller state with a comparable record of compliance had put forward these initiatives, then the constraint of reputation could well have been a greater drag on the prospects for cooperation. In light of the fact that the United States has so many resources it can bring to bear to advance institutional change, it is reasonable to expect that it will be most likely to avoid the negative consequences of a reputational penalty when it comes to institutional creation.

It is of course also possible that the Bush administration specifically chose to push institution building in areas like PSI and UNSCR 1540 precisely because these were areas where there was substantial agreement among the key states about the mutual benefits of cooperation. Yet both of these efforts specifically grew out of U.S. security initiatives and, moreover, each was clearly shaped by American negotiators to best match up with narrow U.S. self-interests. And even if we were to assume that the narrow U.S. self-interest in these cases happened to match up strongly with the interests of other states (and not that other states shifted their positions so as to match up with that of the United States, which may well have occurred in response to U.S. lobbying) then this would not provide support for the institutionalist conception of a general reputation. Rather, what it would indicate is that even if the United States has recently compiled a spotty compliance record in the security realm, it can nevertheless secure new forms of institutionalized cooperation with other states provided that they see their interests as being compatible with the United States and expect this overlap of interests to endure.

Conclusion

For the United States, as for all states, complying with international institutions can sometimes be costly. Institutionalist theory identifies two mechanisms that can cause states to comply with international institutions even when it is costly for their self-interest: credible threats of retaliatory action and reputational costs. Institutionalists would readily acknowledge that threats of retaliatory action are a particularly weak compliance mechanism for the United States because it occupies such a dominant position within the system. However, the logic of institutionalist theory indicates that even the United States will be restricted by reputational concerns, and, indeed, that it may be especially restricted.

Yet the analysis in this chapter showed that there is no justification for the institutionalist view concerning a general reputation for cooperation. A far more compelling theoretical argument can be made for an alternative view that all states, not just the United States, are better understood as having multiple reputations regarding specific regimes and treaties. In turn, it was shown that the conception of a general reputation that underlies institutionalist theory does not have empirical support. This is especially the case with respect to the United States, which, because it is so powerful, is likely to face fewer linkages across issue areas than other states and is also better able to successfully promote institutional change. Because the institutionalist conception of reputation cannot be applied to the United States, we thus have no basis for accepting the implication drawn from the theory that America must now adopt a highly cooperative policy stance across the board regarding international institutions because to do otherwise will have consequences that put the entire institutional order in danger. In the end, therefore, the reputational constraint that emerges from institutionalist theory is inoperative with respect to U.S. security policy.

Constructivism and the Constraint of Legitimacy

ACCORDING TO THE INCREASINGLY influential constructivist school, constraints on American security policy are bound to operate in a very different manner than is posited by the rationalist theories examined in the previous chapters. The limits and possibilities of the United States' power resources, constructivists contend, depend crucially on collectively held ideas, and these ideas are not reducible to narrow cost-benefit calculations.[1] In particular, the U.S. government's ability to translate its seemingly formidable power resources into favorable outcomes depends crucially on maintaining legitimacy.

The constructivist argument for a constraint based in legitimacy is built on two propositions: losing legitimacy increases the costs of translating capabilities into desired outcomes; and, to avoid such losses, the United States must act in accordance with the formal and informal rules of the current institutional order. In other words, America's preponderant material resources can effectively translate into real political influence only when they are bound by the generally recognized rules that constitute the institutional order. The United States "must pursue its interests in a manner consistent with these norms," Christian Reus-Smit maintains, "or the legitimacy of its leadership will fast erode."[2] As Bruce Cronin explains, "[I]f the hegemon fails to act within the boundaries established by its role, the credibility of the institutions it helped establish weakens. . . . When these organizations are undermined, the legitimacy of the international order is threatened. If this persists over time, the hegemonic order declines."[3]

---

[1] The most prominent overview of constructivism is Wendt, *Social Theory.* See also Ted Hopf, "The Promise of Constructivism in International Relations Theory," *International Security* 23 (1998). We also consider arguments drawn from closely related works from the English school of international relations theory. See, for a general treatment, Barry Buzan, *From International to World Society? English School Theory and the Social Structure of Globalisation* (Cambridge: Cambridge University Press, 2004).

[2] Reus-Smit, *American Power,* 102. Other examples of this argument include Cronin, "The Paradox of Hegemony"; and Lebow, *Tragic Vision of Politics.*

[3] Cronin, "Paradox of Hegemony," 113.

Though advanced in its most sophisticated form by constructivist scholars, and though it flows most directly from their theoretical approach, the argument for legitimacy-related constraints is accepted by analysts and policymakers of all stripes. By the second term of George W. Bush's presidency, many analysts wrote and spoke as if they believed that the administration's experience validated the argument in every sense. Washington broke rules, appeared to lose legitimacy, and suffered a precipitous perceived loss of global standing and voluntary assistance from others. The key question for many observers—including the likes of Zbigniew Brzezinski and Fareed Zakaria—was whether the United States could recapture the legitimacy it appeared to have lost.[4]

In this chapter, we show that the constructivist argument for constraints based in legitimacy is not so much wrong as overstated. We agree that the United States benefits greatly from being seen as legitimate, but conclude that the constraint this creates is not structural or strongly conditional, as constructivists contend. Rather, both theory and evidence suggest that legitimacy constrains U.S. security policy in a weaker and more conditional manner. Building on constructivist premises, we show that there are strong theoretical reasons to expect that the United States is in a position to use its advantageous power position to recover lost legitimacy. Policymakers must heed the legitimacy constraint, but it does them no service to exaggerate its significance.

We begin by setting forth the argument for the constraining effect of legitimacy, showing how it appears especially relevant to the United States today. We then demonstrate its shortcomings. Theoretically, there is little reason to doubt that in abetting the translation of power resources into desired outcomes, legitimacy also imposes real constraints on their use. But scholars often fail to note the equally strong theoretical reasons to expect that power can help build, maintain, and mold legitimacy.[5] Finally, we evaluate the evidence on rule breaking and legitimacy, especially in the 2001–6 period. We find evidence for the contention that changing beliefs about legitimacy help to explain increased costs or unrealized potential gains for the United States in those years. But there is equal if not stronger empirical support for the proposition that the United States is capable of using its preponderance to maintain and shape legitimacy.

---

[4] Zbigniew Brzezinski, *Second Chance: Three Presidents and the Crisis of American Superpower* (New York: Basic Books, 2007); and Zakaria, "How Long Will America Lead?"

[5] In keeping with the discussion in chapter 1, we use the term *power* to denote the resources and capabilities governments can use to pursue their ends.

The Argument for Constraints Based in Legitimacy

The study of legitimacy is as old as social science. Scholars and poli-cymakers alike universally regard it as central to the workings of power in international politics.[6] Among scholars of international rela-tions, constructivists have given the most sustained analytical atten-tion to the question of how legitimacy acts as a systemic constraint on U.S. security policy.

The General Argument

Legitimacy is a set of beliefs about the propriety, acceptability, or natu-ralness of an action, an actor/role, or a political order.[7] These beliefs are influenced—but not determined—by legal rules and moral norms. "To ask whether a particular action is legitimate or not," Ian Clark writes, "is not to ask a question of moral philosophy or jurisprudence. It is to ask a factual question about how it is regarded by the members of international society."[8] An action that is formally illegal or even of dubious morality might still be seen as legitimate; that is, as acceptable, appropriate, or natural—the way things are done. Similarly, the legiti-macy of an international political order is not simply a matter of its constitutionality or justness, but rather hinges on whether its constit-uent members see it as acceptable or better than any possible alterna-tives—the way things must be. Legitimacy is thus not necessarily about normative approval. One may hate war but still think it was the most acceptable response to Slobodan Milošević's actions in Kosovo, despise the United States but think its leadership is natural under the circumstances and all that can be expected today, and decry the inequi-ties of the current order but see no other way to organize things. The

[6] Indeed, many would agree with neoconservative analyst Robert Kagan that the struggle to define and maintain legitimacy may prove to be "as significant in determin-ing the future of the international system and America's place in it as any purely mate-rial measure of power or influence." "America's Crisis of Legitimacy," *Foreign Affairs* 83 (2004): 67. See also Joseph S. Nye, *Soft Power: The Means to Success in World Politics* (New York: Public Affairs, 2004); who views it as a central element of what he calls "soft power."

[7] More precisely, these perceptions and beliefs are the key link in a complex chain implied by the more general concept of legitimacy. The best compact constructivist treat-ment is Ian Hurd, "Legitimacy and Authority in International Politics," *International Or-ganization* 53 (1999). For a comprehensive English school analysis, see Ian Clark, *Legiti-macy in International Society* (New York: Oxford University Press, 2005).

[8] Clark, *Legitimacy in International Society*, 254.

same goes for self-interest. One may believe that an act, actor/role, or order is appropriate and unavoidable even if it is not in one's own immediate self-interest.

Constructivists stress that these perceptions are *external* to the United States. American leaders might assert or claim legitimacy, but such assertions and claims are dead letters unless and until they are accepted by a critical mass of governing elites around the world. While constructivists (and other scholars of legitimacy, for that matter) have a hard time defining precisely when this critical mass is reached, it is clear that the relevant set of perceptions is *general*, applying to some significant portion of international society. It follows that, if legitimacy acts as a constraint on the United States, it is systemic as we have defined the term.

To be a legitimate hegemon, therefore, is to have one's power generally accepted, and even welcomed; to see one's actions at least unopposed and at best actively supported. To be illegitimate is to face a world generally disposed toward opposition, and to have to buy or coerce acceptance of or support for one's actions. Legitimacy is thus the great resource-multiplier. An illegitimate hegemon would have to pour resources into a policy that a legitimate one could implement with ease.

Hence, just like rulers in domestic politics, strong states seek to legitimate their power, and, constructivists stress, in so doing they open themselves up to constraints. If a hegemon appeals to some set of principles to legitimate its power, it is liable to be bound by those principles in the future. Once subordinate actors internalize these principles, they will expect the hegemon to act accordingly. The principles the hegemon fosters to legitimate its power thus amount to a nonmaterial constraint: a petard on which to hoist any hegemon that strays from the legitimate path.

Why It Applies Especially Strongly to the United States

According to constructivists, this general legitimacy-related constraint applies with special force to the United States today. Of key importance is that the institutional order that Washington fostered after World War II is by far history's most elaborate, encompassing an unprecedented range of issues. Constructivists argue that institutions—viewed broadly as persistent and generally accepted sets of rules—both reflect and facilitate actors' socialization to a given international order.[9] While rationalists treat institutions as "congealed preferences" or instrumental solutions to coordination problems, constructivists see them as the embodiment of the taken-for-granted scripts, schema, habits, and routines though which actors interpret the world and so govern what they view as appropriate behavior. Once established, institutions function as important mechanisms for socializing actors to the existing order by fostering their internalization of its precepts.[10] When viewed from this sociological perspective, institutions serve as "the chief legitimizing agents of global politics."[11] That is, to the degree that institutions reflect settled, taken-for-granted social practice, actions taken in accordance with their rules will tend to be perceived as legitimate.[12]

As Michael Barnett and Martha Finnemore stress, moreover, modern rational-legal rules, laws, and institutions have internal dynamics that make them hard for the United States to control.[13] What gives the institutional order its immense capability to legitimate power and socialize other actors, they contend, is precisely the sense of its relative independence from the whims of powerful states. Constructivists stress that the international order is comprised of hundreds of important nonstate actors and organizations with their own agendas that the United States cannot fully control. The result is further diffusion of power away from the system's most powerful state. In short, these powers of socialization make modern international institutions especially potent tools of

[9] On institutions as rules, see Nicholas Onuf, "Institutions, Intentions and International Relations," *Review of International Studies* 18 (2002): 211–28; John Gerard Ruggie, "Multilateralism at Century's End," in Ruggie, *Constructing the World Polity* (London: Routledge, 1997); and Hedley Bull, *The Anarchical Society: A Study of Order in World Politics* (New York: Columbia University Press, 1977). These and other treatments are broadly consistent with Robert Keohane's widely endorsed definition of institutions as "persistent and connected sets of rules (formal and informal) that prescribe behavioral roles, constrain activity, and shape expectations." *International Institutions and State Power: Essays in International Relations* (Boulder, Colo.: Westview, 1989), 3.

[10] Alastair Iain Johnston, in "Treating International Institutions as Social Environments," *International Studies Quarterly* 45 (2001), argues that socialization also takes place in part through processes that do not require internalization: persuasion (convincing actors that their interests align with the hegemon's) and social influence (inculcating pronorm behavior by dispensing social rewards, such as status, and punishments, such as exclusion or shaming). See also Martha Finnemore and Kathryn Sikkink, "International Norm Dynamics and Political Change," *International Organization* 52 (1998).

[11] Cronin, "Paradox of Hegemony," 113, citing Inis Claude.

[12] Hurd, "Legitimacy and Authority"; and Johnston, "International Institutions."

[13] Michael Barnett and Martha Finnemore, *Rules for the World: International Organizations in Global Politics* (Ithaca, N.Y.: Cornell University Press, 2004).

legitimation, but their benefits come at the price of imposing especially strong constraints.

The Strength of the Constraint of Legitimacy

Constructivists thus argue convincingly that U.S. hegemony would be far harder to maintain if other states stopped supporting the current institutional status quo in a habitual, routinized way and began to evaluate the order on the basis of constantly updated cost-benefit calculations. To prevent such a shift, they stress, the United States must earn legitimacy and continue to work to maintain it by acting in accordance with the rules of the order it fostered, even—indeed, especially—when so doing contradicts its own immediate material interests.[14] Thus, all agree that "the notion of societal legitimation is inescapably bound up with the idea of restraint," and that if the United States does not exercise such restraint, it will have to bear legitimacy costs.[15]

Constructivist writings highlight two kinds of costs the United States might incur if it undertakes an action seen as contrary to generally accepted rules: specific and general. Specific costs involve loss of legitimacy for that action, leading to increased costs of pursuing it because others either withdraw support or oppose it, or must be coerced or bribed to support it. General costs involve the corrosion of the legitimacy of the United States' role as a hegemon or of the overall institutional order that it favors, leading to a reduction in rote compliance, voluntary support, or acquiescence, and thus increased costs of hegemony. In the extreme, serial rule violations risk provoking a legitimacy crisis of the order itself that leads other actors generally to opt out of the order or mount a comprehensive alternative.[16]

Constructivists consistently maintain that specific legitimacy costs are to be expected after any notable U.S. rule violation. What is unclear is how strong the links are between losing legitimacy over a given action or even a series of actions in a given issue area and the overall legitimacy of the United States' role and the larger order. Different

---

[14] Reus-Smit, *American Power*; and Reus-Smit, "Unipolarity and Legitimacy," manuscript under review; Lebow, *Tragic Vision of Politics*; and Cronin, "The Paradox of Hegemony."

[15] Clark, *Legitimacy in International Society*, 233.

[16] Christian Reus-Smit, "International Crises of Legitimacy," in "Resolving International Crises of Legitimacy," ed. Reus-Smit and Ian Clark, special issue of *International Politics* 2–3 (2007).

strands of constructivist thinking have contrasting implications for this question. Constructivists often stress that any ramified institutional order is "sticky," that is, more resistant to change than purely rational-actor theories would suggest. Institutional orders are said to be consequential precisely because they become settled and hard to alter. That implies a structural or quasi-structural constraint: systems of rules are not up for renegotiation every time actors' interests change. Yet this also suggests that the current rule-based order is robust, and that the United States would have to experience specific legitimacy costs for some time before general costs kick in. And a few constructivist writings take exception to an overly structural view of rules as external constraints on states, stressing that states' policies and rules are mutually constituted.[17]

The bulk of constructivist analyses resolve these different strands of theory in a manner that adds up to the contention that the constraint based in legitimacy is very powerful. Any major rule violation will likely generate significant specific legitimacy costs; a series of salient violations will raise the specter of more general costs involving the overall institutional order and the United States' role in it. Thus, many constructivists maintain that rule violations such as those perpetrated by the Bush administration did sap U.S. legitimacy, raising the specter of a full-blown legitimacy crisis of the order if the United States were to continue on this course.[18] For them, the practical answer to the ques-

[17] Thus Ian Hurd criticizes constructivist accounts that "overstate the constraining effects of international norms while understating their dynamic nature." "American Revisionism and Crises of Legitimacy," in Reus-Smit and Clark, "Resolving International Crises of Legitimacy," 205. By stressing "the mutually constitutive relations between norms and state practice," Hurd arrives at a far lower assessment of the strength of the legitimacy constraint than most constructivists who have written on the subject. In contrast to Reus-Smit and others, he contends that a legitimacy crisis "is unlikely" (201). Hurd also questions the "overly agentic" view we develop below, but the practical difference between his assessment and ours appears to be subtle. Other writings that take a view similar to Hurd's include Clark's English school treatment (Clark, *Legitimacy in International Society*) and Mlada Bukovansky's *Legitimacy and Power Politics: The American and French Revolutions in International Political Culture* (Princeton: Princeton University Press, 2002), which explicitly integrates realism and constructivism. More generally, recent works do exhibit a trend toward explicitly modeling the interaction between state power and ideas. In *Rethinking the World: Great Power Strategies and International Order* (Ithaca, N.Y.: Cornell University Press, 2006), Jeffrey Legro "presumes the relevance of power in the formation of international order" (40), though he does not focus on international legitimacy.

[18] Thus Reus-Smit, "International Crises of Legitimacy," writes of "the administration's current crisis of legitimacy" (44); Lebow, *Tragic Vision of Politics*, stresses that, notwithstanding its power primacy, "the standing of the United States may be much more

tion of the constraint's strength was "strong enough to have reined in the United States under George W. Bush." They reach this judgment by portraying the constraint of legitimacy as either structural or strongly conditional, in our terminology.

Scholars who argue that it is a structural constraint contend that because equilibrium is itself a foundational norm of international society, reflected in the institutions of the balance of power and multilateralism, unipolarity is structurally illegitimate.[19] In a bipolar system, the argument goes, the legitimacy of the United States and many of its actions were structurally favored by the U.S. role as the key actor upholding international equilibrium. As the unipole, the United States no longer enjoys this presumptive legitimacy, so gaining acceptance for its role and actions is an uphill battle. The mere fact of its massive power renders the United States strongly constrained unless it practices rigorous self-abnegation. As Ian Clark puts it, "The issue is to find a functional substitute for the balance of power *within* the directorial role of the single great power, and this must be in the form of hegemony that respects the equilibrium within international society as a whole. Anything less is doomed to perpetuate a chronic legitimacy crisis at the heart of the contemporary international order."[20]

On balance, however, most constructivist treatments of this issue portray the constraint as strongly conditional: they contend that there is a large range of actions the United States would like to use its power resources for that are forbidden or rendered very costly by legitimacy concerns. As long as the United States hews closely to accepted rules and norms, it is likely to enjoy legitimacy's benefits. To the degree that other actors see the United States as exempting itself from those rules, it will lose legitimacy and face dramatically increased costs.

---

precarious than most realists and members of the national security community recognize," and that "American influence could undergo precipitous decline in the decades ahead" (311). See also Reus-Smit, *American Power*, which was motivated by the "growing disjuncture between America's material resources and its ability to translate those into intended political outcomes" (x); and Reus-Smit, "Unipolarity and Legitimacy" ; and Cronin, "The Paradox of Hegemony."

[19] On the balance of power and multilateralism as core institutions, see Bull, *The Anarchical Society*; and Ruggie, "Multilateralism at Century's End."

[20] Clark, "Setting the Revisionist Agenda," *International Politics* 44 (2007): 334. See also Clark, *Legitimacy in International Society*, chap. 12. For an example, see G. John Ikenberry, "Liberalism and Empire: Logics or Order in the American Unipolar Age," *Review of International Studies* 30 (2004).

The Argument's Theoretical Weakness

This argument clearly commands attention. Among scholars, analysis of the veracity of such an important argument often turns into a debate over analytical assumptions (e.g., the rational-choice "logic of consequences" vs. the constructivist "logic of appropriateness") or methodology (e.g., whether legitimacy can be measured, or how the circular relationship among institutions, identities, and interests could be tested). Such a response would be unhelpful in this case. After all, the argument under discussion here is drawn from formidable research traditions in sociology, law, history, and cognitive and social psychology that have withstood decades of critical attention. It flows logically from widely accepted scholarly treatments of the relationship between power, institutions, and legitimacy in domestic contexts. And it resonates powerfully with the views of many policy analysts and practitioners.[21]

Hence, it is more productive to examine the argument on its own terms, accepting its core premises: that legitimacy exists apart from material power and interest, and that scholars and decision-makers can distinguish legitimacy itself from the effects it is supposed to have. Three considerations—all arising from constructivist or closely related literatures—individually and collectively weaken the argument for constraints based in legitimacy. First, it highlights only one side of the two-way interaction between power resources and legitimacy. Legitimacy can constrain the use of material power, but such power also shapes legitimacy. Constructivist treatments downplay these considerations, which is principally why they generally portray legitimacy as such a strong constraint. Second, the very theoretical scholarship that supports constraints related to legitimacy also predicts that the relationship between breaking rules and legitimacy is complex and contingent, opening up avenues for the use of power unbound by rules or to rewrite rules. Third, constructivist and closely related international legal scholarship points toward numerous strategies by which a unipole can draw on its power to minimize any legitimacy costs associated with making and breaking rules.

---

[21] Examples of this argument in recent policy debates include Robert W. Tucker and David C. Hendrickson, "The Sources of American Legitimacy," *Foreign Affairs* 83 (2004); Robert Kagan, "America's Crisis of Legitimacy"; Francis Fukuyama, *America at the Cross-*

Power and Legitimacy: A Two-Way Street

Constructivist writings recognize that agents can change generally accepted rules. Constructivist scholarship on how rules and norms change, however, focuses on the use of persuasion, argument, framing, and rhetoric by nonstate agents such as NGOs.[22] Most of this research has been at pains to demonstrate the limited explanatory weight of states' material power and so provides scant leverage on the question of whether or how hegemons might use the very same tactics to change settled institutional rules. Scholars of international law, though generally disposed to see law as a constraint on the powerful, have treated this question at greater length.[23]

If the historical record is any guide, the United States has the potential to use its power advantages to revise the order in at least some ways to its benefit without facing legitimacy costs. In his magisterial history of international law, Wilhelm Grewe documents how at the peak of their power Spain, France, and Britain each revised settled international legal rules to suit their interests.[24] For example, Spain fashioned both normative and positive laws to legitimize the conquest of indigenous Americans, France instituted modern legal concepts of state borders to meet its needs as Europe's preeminent land power, and Britain fostered laws on piracy, neutral shipping, and colonialism to suit its interests as a developing maritime empire. Such hegemonic lawmaking took place not just in the kind of grand postwar institutional order-building episodes John Ikenberry studies in his *After Victory*, but also in more normal times when the hegemon conceives a new interest and determines that it might be best served with a new or revised rule or set of rules.[25]

---

roads: Democracy, Power, and the Neoconservative Legacy (New Haven: Yale University Press, 2006); and Brzezinski, *Second Chance.*

[22] See, for example, Finnemore and Sikkink, "International Norm Dynamics"; and Rodger Payne, "Persuasion, Frames and Norm Construction," *European Journal of International Relations* 7 (2001).

[23] See, especially, Gerry Simpson, *Great Powers and Outlaw States* (Cambridge: Cambridge University Press, 2002). For an excellent review of the relationship between international legal scholarship and scholarship on power politics, see Richard H. Steinberg and Jonathan M. Zasloff, "Power and International Law," *American Journal of International Law* 100 (2006): 64–87.

[24] Wilhelm Grewe, *The Epochs of International Law,* translated and revised by Michael Byers (Berlin: Walter de Gruyter, 2000).

[25] Ikenberry, *After Victory.*

Thus, for example, in a decades-long campaign after 1830 involving extensive use of its hard power resources, Britain fostered an entirely new legal regime prohibiting the slave trade.

Grewe shows that dominant states accomplished these feats, in part, through the unsubtle use of power: bribes, coercion, and the allure of lucrative long-term cooperation in exchange for accepting the hegemon's preferred rules. Less obvious but often more important was the way the leading state's bargaining hand was often strengthened by the general perception that it had other, less legalistic options for pursuing its interests that might be even less palatable to other states than accepting its preferred rules. In many cases, while the leading state was sure to be better off with the new rule, it arguably would suffer less than other states in the absence of any rule.[26] Also important, according to Grewe, was agenda-setting power. In each case, the leading state in its heyday affected the development of law indirectly by defining the problems new rules were developed to address.[27] Even when the impetus for new rules appeared to come from weaker states, the end result in each case was a system of rules shaped to address the hegemon's primary concerns.[28]

Constructivism recognizes the importance of agency, but tends to overlook the fact that hegemonic great powers are agents with disproportionate material wherewithal for shaping their social environment. To state that hegemonic order revision is theoretically possible and that it has happened frequently does not tell us how hard it is under current conditions. In making the argument that the United States is powerfully constrained by the need for legitimacy, constructivists contend that there is—especially in the current era—a close link between breaking rules and losing legitimacy, which implies that it is very difficult and costly to alter the current rule-based order. In general, the more direct the relationship between breaking rules and losing legitimacy, the harder it is for a leading state to shape a settled order to its liking, and the stronger the general constructivist argument on legitimacy as a constraint. The more complex and contingent the relationship is, the

[26] This reflects the influence of what Voeten calls "asymmetric outside options" (Voeten, "Outside Options").

[27] Grewe, *Epochs of International Law*.

[28] In the modern era, the legal doctrine of "specially affected states" acknowledges the disproportionate influence of powerful states, formal sovereign equality notwithstanding. See Simpson, *Great Powers*, 52–53.

more space exists for powerful states to use their superior capabilities to create facts on the ground that shape the subsequent development of the institutional order.

Legitimacy and Rule Breaking

How tight is the connection between rule breaking and legitimacy? This matters not only for determining the degree to which a hegemonic power can change rules but also for the more general question of whether a hegemon will face legitimacy costs when it violates a rule without even attempting to revise or replace it. Three factors weaken this link: exceptions to rules; the prevalence of the practice of breaking rules to make rules; and the uneven legitimacy of rules.

EXCEPTIONS

The relationship between rule breaking and legitimacy is highly complex and contingent upon the circumstances under which the hegemon violates a rule.[29] The violation may be a one-shot breach or part of a larger pattern. A violation that appears likely to be an exception to a pattern of compliance is unlikely to generate high general legitimacy costs, and vice versa. Similarly, a rule violation in response to an emergency is unlikely to be seen as an attempt to set a precedent and hence is very unlikely to undermine the legitimacy of the order, especially if the mitigating circumstances are intrinsically persuasive to others.[30]

An example of this logic is the view that the Bush administration blundered not by considering preemptive or even preventive war as an option after 9/11 but rather by aiming to enshrine it as a formal doctrine in its 2002 National Security Strategy. Seasoned foreign policy practitioners including Henry Kissinger, Zbigniew Brzezinski, and Brent Scowcroft argued that this would simply open the door to all sorts of unsavory regimes to claim the same right; that it was unlikely

---

[29] Christine Chinkin, "The State That Acts Alone: Bully, Good Samaritan or Iconoclast?" *European Journal of International Law* 11 (2000); Michael Byers, *Custom, Power, and the Power of Rules* (Cambridge: Cambridge University Press, 1999), chap. 9.

[30] See Michael Byers and Simon Chesterman, "Changing Rules about Rules? Unilateral Humanitarian Interventions and the Future of International Law"; Thomas M. Franck, "Interpretation and Change in the Law of Humanitarian Intervention"; and Jane Stromseth, "Rethinking Humanitarian Intervention: The Case for Incremental Change," all in *Humanitarian Intervention, Ethical, Legal, and Political Dilemmas*, ed. J. L. Holzgrefe and Robert Keohane (Cambridge: Cambridge University Press, 2003).

to be seen by other governments as a legitimate blanket exception to the existing legal norms against preemption; and that it was inferior to the status quo under which rare breaches of the rule do not impose heavy legitimacy costs. As Kissinger put it, "[A] policy that allows for preventive force can sustain the international system only if solitary American enterprises are the rare exception, not the basic rule of American strategy."[31]

If the rule violation comes to be seen as a unique response to a particular crisis, the hegemon can likely bring its resource power to bear in ways that directly violate settled rules without suffering legitimacy costs of any kind. The point is simple but important: there is no theoretical reason to expect an automatic connection between rule breaking and legitimacy costs. This qualification to the constructivist argument is powerfully reinforced by the fact that breaking rules is one way to make new rules.

BREAKING RULES TO MAKE RULES

The tightness of the connection between rule breaking and legitimacy costs is also weakened by the fact that when a hegemon breaks a rule, it could signify an attempt to establish a new rule. Superficially, one might expect such an act to threaten heavy legitimacy costs since it represents a deliberate attempt to undermine part of the existing order that necessarily is not a one-shot violation. This expectation fails to recognize, however, that in many cases, states break rules to make rules. Changing circumstances and state interests sometimes create incentives for new rules. Rules reflect practice, and one way to establish a new rule is to attempt to initiate a new practice. Given the absence of a central legislative body in international relations, the development of rules through this technically illegal manner is far more common among than within states. As legal scholar Thomas Franck puts it, "[I]n the international—as opposed to the national—community, the failure of members of the community to obey a command is still an accepted way to bring about change or reform in the rule or institution from which the command emanates."[32]

---

[31] "American Strategy and Pre-emptive War," *International Herald Tribune*, April 13, 2006.

[32] Thomas M. Franck, *The Power of Legitimacy among Nations* (New York: Oxford University Press, 1990), 151.

When the hegemon breaks a rule in an effort to create a new rule, other states can protest or support the act in word or deed, or they may sit on the sidelines awaiting developments. Whether the violation drains legitimacy or successfully wins legitimacy for a new rule largely depends on the balance between these actions. Without knowing more about the circumstances surrounding the initiation of the new rule as well as the power and interests of the states most concerned with it, it is impossible to determine ex ante what the legitimacy costs are likely to be. As the actor with the most resources to deploy, a hegemon has asymmetric advantages in influencing the outcomes of these complex interactions.

THE UNEVEN LEGITIMACY OF RULES

The strength of the link between rule breaking and legitimacy also depends on the legitimacy of the rule in question. The constructivist argument applies strongly only to legitimate rules—that is, rules relevant actors subjectively believe ought to be obeyed. But the specific causal mechanisms of socialization that are supposed to generate legitimacy are more applicable to some rules than others. Many of the causal mechanisms by which rules acquire legitimacy depend on iteration. Frequency generates clear precedents. As Harold Koh puts it, "[R]epeated compliance gradually becomes habitual compliance."[33] By contrast, things that happen rarely are less likely to be taken for granted. Precedents regarding infrequent occurrences are arguable. As the international legal scholar Michael Byers concludes, "[R]ules based on a limited number of instances of State practice are inherently unstable and relatively vulnerable to change."[34]

Iteration helps foster other properties that, legal scholars argue, enhance the prospects that rules will be regarded as legitimate. Arguably most important, according to Thomas Franck—a prominent theorist of legitimacy in international law—is a rule's determinacy: "that quality

---

[33] Harold Hongju Koh, "Why Do Nations Obey International Law?" *Yale Law Journal* 106 (1997): 2603.

[34] Byers, *Custom, Power*, 159; Detlev F. Vagts, "Hegemonic International Law," *American Journal of International Law* 95 (2001): 854. To be sure, there are exceptions to this argument. Rules concerning rare events may be seen as legitimate if they reflect salient preexisting transnational and transcultural norms, as in the case of the prohibition against genocide. See Margaret Keck and Katherine Sikkink, *Activists beyond Borders: Advocacy Networks in International Politics* (Ithaca, N.Y.: Cornell University, Press, 1998).

of a norm that generates an ascertainable understanding of what it prohibits."[35] A rule's legitimacy also depends on its coherence, which Franck defines as "its connectedness, both internally (among the several parts of the rule) and externally (between one rule and other rules, through shared principles)."[36]

The processes by which lawyers and statesmen are supposed to reach an assessment about the legitimacy of a rule or the relation of a given act to a rule are difficult if not impossible to apply in the case of inconsistent or indeterminate rules and/or rules reflecting infrequent actions.[37] In general, the less coherent and determinate rules are, and the smaller the number of iterations they reflect, the less constraining they are, and the more space there is for the use of superior resource endowments to change them or influence outcomes without heeding them.[38]

The implications for the strength of the constraints imposed by the need for legitimacy as applied to the United States today are profound. If one were looking for a place to demonstrate the relationship between rule breaking and legitimacy, one would hardly choose international security. Though it tends to attract headlines and scholarly attention, the use or threat of force is a relatively rare event in interstate relations. Many of the other realms of activity covered by international legal rules—involving commerce, communications, trade, finance, diplomatic representation, and so on—entail interactions among nearly all states on a daily basis. Because the use of force is so exceedingly infrequent, the rules governing international security are based on many fewer instances of state practice than most other areas. Infrequency also means that cases tend to be incommensurate: each use of force has enough unique aspects to make its status as or relation to precedent arguable. Partly for these reasons, the rules governing the use of force are arguably less determinate and coherent than in the economic sector and other areas.

[35] Thomas M. Franck, "The Power of Legitimacy and the Legitimacy of Power: International Law in an Age of Power Disequilibrium," *American Journal of International Law* 100 (2006): 93.

[36] Franck, *Power of Legitimacy,* 180.

[37] This is true, in varying to degrees, of all the major methodologies for determining the existence of a legal rule. For a review, see Anthony Clark Arend, *Legal Rules and International Society* (New York: Oxford University Press, 1999), chap. 3.

[38] Byers, *Custom, Power*; Vagts, "Hegemonic International Law"; Jose E. Alvarez, "Hegemonic International Law Revisited," *American Journal of International Law* 97 (2003).

One way to gauge the significance of this point is to think of cases in which the use of force was widely seen as clearly lawful before the fact. If legitimacy inheres in rules, then the rules must be clear enough to be able to specify in advance that some action is clearly consistent with the rules and thus will likely be seen as legitimate. While such cases come to mind—the 1991 Gulf War with Iraq is an example—they are few and far between. This is not to say that there are no legitimate rules concerning the use of force or that uses of force cannot lead to lost legitimacy.[39] Rather, the point is that the standard argument about what constitutes legitimacy and how rule breaking can lead to losses of it can be applied much more easily elsewhere. As a general rule, economic institutions are characterized by regularized cooperation on the same kind of issue again and again to a far greater extent than security institutions. Within the security realm, in contrast, the institutional order is more limited in scope and the focus is much less on enforcement of agreed-upon rules. As a result, the taken-for-granted qualities of legitimacy are theoretically far more likely to characterize the economic than the security realm.

Minimizing Legitimacy Costs

The reciprocal interaction between power and legitimacy and complexity of the link between rule breaking and legitimacy undercut the constructivists' argument concerning the constraint of legitimacy at the theoretical level. They do not, however, vitiate it completely. Constructivists have thus far highlighted only those parts of their theoretical architecture that concern the constraining effect of legitimacy on material capabilities while downplaying those parts that illuminate the influence of such power on legitimacy. Our main point here is that when both parts of the theoretical architecture are in view, the constraint of legitimacy remains potentially important, but is weaker and more conditional. Constructivists are right that hegemony without legitimacy is likely to be nasty, brutish, and short; and that the hegemon will have to pay heed to the requisites for legitimacy imposed by the current institutional order. But constructivist and international legal scholarship also suggests that restrictions that result from legitimacy are not

[39] Indeed, Franck argues strenuously to the contrary in *Recourse to Force: State Action against Threats and Armed Attacks* (New York: Cambridge University Press, 2002).

automatic and can be malleable if Washington uses its power strategically in ways that reflect understanding of how the order works.

Nothing in the foregoing analysis suggests that the United States can break rules with no thought about potential legitimacy costs. The risk of such costs is part of doing business as an activist hegemon. But this does not mean that hegemons lack options for minimizing these costs. Constructivist and closely related international legal scholarship outlines a set of mechanisms that sustain legitimate hegemony. Unrecognized in this literature thus far is that these same mechanisms can be employed by the hegemon as strategies to mitigate any widespread legitimacy costs of rule violations.

MINIMIZING THE LEGITIMACY COSTS OF RULE CHANGE

A hegemon's attempt to change rules may lead to legitimacy costs. Yet research by scholars who are sensitive to the role of power in international law suggests many strategies powerful states can adopt to minimize the potential legitimacy costs associated with institutional legal change.[40] Much of this research—by both classic and contemporary legal scholars—reflects the conceptual overlap between prominent theories of the legitimacy of international law and some of the most influential constructivist studies of rules and norms.[41] The mitigating strategies that emerge from this literature all exploit precisely the general mechanisms that constructivists highlight: persuasion, framing, and argument. Legal scholars recognize that these tools are as available to hegemons as they are to the nonstate "norm entrepreneurs," NGOs, and transnational advocacy networks that have thus far featured in constructivists' empirical scholarship. The standard focus on nonstate actors as agents of change has diverted constructivist scholars' attention from the fact that rich and powerful states tend to be particularly well endowed with precisely the intellectual resources that can be useful for changing rules. In his study, for example, Grewe documents in detail how dominant powers used their deep intellectual resources—

---

[40] See Simpson, *Great Powers*; Byers, *Custom, Power*; Vagts, "Hegemonic International Law"; Alvarez, "Hegemonic International Law Revisited."

[41] See, e.g., Franck, *Power of Legitimacy*; Friedrich Kratochwil, *Rules, Norms, and Decisions: On the Conditions of Practical and Legal Reasoning in International Relations and Domestic Affairs* (Cambridge: Cambridge University Press, 1989); Christian Reus-Smit, ed., *The Politics of International Law* (Cambridge: Cambridge University Press, 2004); Arend, *Legal Rules*; and Oona A. Hathaway and Harold Hongju Koh, *Foundations of International Law and Politics* (New York: Foundation Press, 2004).

diplomats, publicists, philosophers, and, not least, international lawyers and legal scholars—to good effect in arguing, persuading, and
strategically framing proposed legal change.

Thus, prominent theories of international law and centuries of state
practice suggest that a hegemon can minimize the potential legitimacy
costs associated with changing accepted rules by using traditional
tools of diplomacy in a way that is sensitive to legal reasoning and the
logics of appropriateness that operate in a given institutional order.
The list of potential legal stratagems is long, and the precise mix that
applies to any specific set of circumstances will always remain a matter
of informed judgment, but four general precepts are most relevant to
the United States today.

1. *Link the new rule to unambiguously legitimate rules.* Standard legal
   reasoning implies that the new rule's probability of success is
   some function of its consistency with the wider pattern of established rules and norms.[42] A hegemon seeking to gain acceptance for a new rule can use its diplomatic and intellectual resources to frame the new rule as a minor amendment to an
   accepted rule and to persuade others of the new rule's strong
   links to well-established precedents. U.S. actions reflect some
   sensitivity to this precept. For example, the U.S. official who
   spearheaded the Proliferation Security Initiative (PSI)—a U.S.-
   sponsored multilateral framework for interdicting WMD at sea,
   in the air, and on land—stressed that it "builds on existing nonproliferation treaties and regimes" and that it is "consistent
   with national and international legal authorities and international law."[43]

2. *Play up reciprocal benefits.* Given that reciprocity is one of the
   basic principles underlying the current institutional order, the
   more states are convinced that they, too, stand to benefit under

---

[42] See, in particular, Arend, *Legal Rules*; Franck, *Power of Legitimacy*; and Kratochwil,
Rules, Norms, and Decisions, chap. 8.

[43] John R. Bolton, "Stopping the Spread of Weapons of Mass Destruction in the Asian-
Pacific Region: The Role of the Proliferation Security Initiative," speech in Tokyo, October 27, 2004. In a similar vein, U.S. officials note that the PSI complements U.S.-Spon-
sored UN Security Council Resolution 1540 on counterproliferation—itself an outgrowth
of Resolution 1373, the major counterterror resolution adopted in the wake of 9/11. See
"UN Security Council Resolution 1540: The U.S. Perspective," Andrew Semmel, Principal Deputy Assistant Secretary for Nuclear Nonproliferation, remarks at Chatham
House, October 12, 2004. (Both speeches archived at www.state.gov).

the new rule, the less they will be inclined to object to it.[44] The PSI is a prominent case that reflects this dynamic at work: although it is a U.S. initiative that is designed to give the U.S. Navy more operational latitude, the Bush administration constantly referred to it as a "global effort."[45] Reflecting this, the PSI initiative carefully specified de jure rights for other parties, even if de facto the United States is the only state that actually gained new rights. For example, the PSI-related bilateral treaty between the United States and Liberia accords each other the right, on the high seas, to board, search, and detain the cargo of any vessel flying each other's flag that is suspected of trafficking in WMD, even though Liberia has no navy (it does, however, have the second largest shipping registry in the world).[46]

More serious are proposed rules that concede reciprocal rights that others might plausibly want and be able to exercise, if not immediately, then in the future. A classic example is Truman's 1945 unilateral assertion of jurisdiction over the resources of the continental shelf adjacent to U.S. territorial waters. Although it was a clear violation of international law that asserted a completely novel right, other states followed suit so swiftly that it assumed the status of customary law in a scant half-decade—in part because so many coastal states plausibly stood to benefit under the new rule.[47]

3. *Persuade others of the necessity of change and the sagacity of the proposed rule as a response.* A hegemon seeking to revise rules should not limit itself to purely legal arguments. Its persuasive intellectual resources should also be devoted to convincing decision-makers in other key states that changing circumstances require new rules and that the proposed new rule is an appropriate response. In this regard, the Bush administration performed remarkably poorly in seeking to persuade others of the

[44] Byers, *Custom, Power*, chap. 6.

[45] See, for example, *The National Security Strategy of the United States of America*, March 2006, 18, available at http://www.whitehouse.gov/nsc/nss.html (consulted November 7, 2007).

[46] Michael Byers, "Policing the High Seas: The Proliferation Security Initiative," *American Journal of International Law* 98 (2004). Byers's conclusion reflects a classic assessment of "hegemonic international law" at work: "PSI as currently structured is not ideal. But given the very real problem it seeks to address, and the alternative paths that the United States might take, this particular instance of a la carte multilateralism is worthy of support" (545).

[47] Byers, *Custom, Power*, chap. 6.

sagacity of its new preventive war doctrine: consultation was almost nonexistent. One French diplomat recalled that in the old days, high-level U.S. officials would travel to Paris for extensive consultations over any new NATO doctrine, even though it was clear that the change had been approved in Washington and no further substantive alterations were possible. "We found out about the Bush Doctrine by downloading it from the White House website," he noted. "The Doctrine has much to recommend it, but that is not the way to communicate with allies."

4. *Strategically exploit inconsistency.*[48] When framing a new rule, the revisionist hegemon has to think about possible objections by other states and seek to minimize their persuasive legal force. It should seek to ensure to the extent possible that the new rule is consistent with its own practice in other areas and the legal positions it has taken in other contexts. The more the new rule seems to contradict the hegemon's other positions, the more hypocritical and self-serving it will appear, and the less persuasive will be the argument it deploys on behalf of the new rule. At the same time, the hegemon should seek to frame the rule so as to make objections by the most important states seem inconsistent. As we discuss in more detail below, the United States executed this strategy with some success in inculcating new rules to combat terrorism. It fell victim to this same strategy, however, concerning the International Criminal Court. The problem was that the United States has long been among the champions of independent war crimes tribunals for nationals of other countries, and the Bush administration continued this support concerning Serbia, Sierra Leone, Darfur, and other cases. It proved difficult for Washington to reconcile its general support for such tribunals with opposition to the ICC—an inconsistency that the court's supporters did not hesitate to exploit.[49]

[48] Here, we are reversing the standard argument that consistency places constraints on the powerful. See Bukovansky, *Legitimacy and Power Politics*; and Stephen Toope, "Powerful but Unpersuasive? The Role of the United States in the Evolution of Customary International Law," in *United States Hegemony and the Foundations of International Law*, ed. Michael Byers and Georg Nolte (Cambridge: Cambridge University Press, 2003).

[49] David Wippman, "The International Criminal Court," in Reus-Smit, *Politics of International Law*; Scott Turner, "The Dilemma of Double Standards in U.S. Human Rights Policy," *Peace and Change* 28 (2003).

These four strategies apply regardless of whether the hegemon seeks to alter rules by convening a formal multilateral convention or by violating existing rules with an eye toward establishing new customary law through practice. In either case the hegemon does not have to persuade every state. For any given rule, there will be a set of particularly influential actors whose decisions will sway many others. The legitimacy risks of any rule-changing attempt will hinge in part on the skill with which the hegemon is able to separate these key actors from the rest and then deploy the appropriate strategies to secure their support or acquiescence.

MITIGATING THE LEGITIMACY COSTS OF BREAKING RULES

What about minimizing the legitimacy costs of rule violations unrelated to rule change? Again, constructivism has not generally focused on strategies that a powerful state can use to mitigate the legitimacy costs of breaking rules, but its underlying theoretical arguments suggest three key compensating mechanisms.

1. *Public goods provision.* The legitimacy of the hegemon's leadership inheres in part in mutual benefit. Subordinate actors are more apt to reconcile themselves to their status when the hegemon is seen to be providing goods for all.[50] When a hegemon breaks a rule, it reminds others of the real inequalities that rules sometimes mask. Successful public goods provision, by contrast, reminds others of the benefits of hegemonic leadership. It follows that if an act of rule breaking eventually comes to be seen as having produced a public good, then its legitimacy costs might be negligible or nonexistent. Indeed, the more positively the relevant states ultimately evaluate the consequences of unlawful behavior, the smaller the legitimacy costs are likely to be, and vice versa. More generally, even if a breach of the rule-based order is not viewed positively, its effect on the hegemon's legitimacy may be counterbalanced if it undertakes efforts to provide public goods in other areas. The less self-interested the United States seems in general, the less likely it is that specific rule violations will result in general legitimacy costs.

[50] Lebow, *Tragic Vision of Politics,* 314.

191

2. *Persuasion, argument, and framing.* Constructivists stress that what constitutes a public good is itself dependent on shared understandings, so the hegemon needs to work to persuade others of the reality and importance of the public goods it believes it is supplying.[51] More generally, diplomatic tools can also be deployed to frame a breach to minimize its implications for the legitimacy of the institutional order. As noted previously, acting contrary to accepted rules in an emergency is much less likely to entail legitimacy costs. Indeed, many areas of international law already accommodate derogations in times of national emergency. And what constitutes an emergency is a matter of perception. If the United States can plausibly argue that its rule breaking is similarly a response to an unprecedented crisis, and if, instead of advancing novel or tendentious legal justifications, it simply argues for a brief derogation of otherwise valid rules, the legitimacy consequences may be minimal. Indeed, Michael Byers has argued that breaking a rule under such circumstances may well bolster the legitimacy of the rule concerned.[52]

The intervention in Kosovo is a case in point. NATO officials argued that the war to stop human rights abuses on the territory of a sovereign state was legal even though it was not sanctioned by the Security Council, claiming that the refugee crisis created a potential threat to regional peace and security and so NATO had a right to act under Chapter VII of the UN Charter as well as in collective self-defense. Most governments and, indeed, most legal scholars, were skeptical of those arguments.[53] U.S. officials, in contrast, tended to stress that the intervention was a response to an emergency situation. As Secretary of State Madeleine Albright put it, "[T]he alliance has the legitimacy to act to stop a catastrophe."[54] Ultimately, the latter argument appeared to carry the day. After the fact, many legal scholars and other observers came to share Richard Falk's view that the war,

---

[51] Reus-Smit, *American Power*, makes this argument.

[52] Michael Byers, "Preemptive Self Defense: Hegemony, Equality and Strategies of Legal Change," *Journal of Political Philosophy* 11 (2003): 187; and Byers and Chesterman, "Changing Rules about Rules."

[53] Mary Buckley and Sally N. Cummings, eds., *Kosovo: Perceptions of War and Its Aftermath* (London: Continuum, 2002); see also Byers and Chesterman, "Changing Rules about Rules."

[54] Quoted in Clark, *Legitimacy in International Society*, 213.

"while technically illegal, was politically and morally legitimate."[55] Once the intervention succeeded in ousting the Serbian army from Kosovo, the UN granted it post-facto legality by authorizing NATO to establish an international security presence in the province.

3. *Reassurance.* A third strategy to compensate for a rule violation is for the hegemon demonstrably to reaffirm other salient rules or norms associated with the order. Both constructivists and international legal scholars stress interdependence between different parts of the institutional order. The order is constraining, in their view, because violations in one area might incur legitimacy costs that affect other areas. By the same token, demonstrable and visible increases in the hegemon's fealty to some aspect of the larger order might compensate for transgressions in others. For example, to compensate for a perceived rule violation, the United States might recommit strongly to the norm of consultation with allies. The key issue here is not whether Washington ultimately gets to decide what to do; rather it is whether it is willing to take the time and effort to inform others, especially its allies, and listen to and discuss their concerns.

While these mitigating strategies are available to all international actors, large and powerful states have the most opportunities to deploy them. Size, wealth, and power open up more and more salient opportunities for mitigating legitimacy costs associated with rule violations by enabling public good provision and facilitating large diplomatic corps and other intellectual assets for international persuasion. Although constructivists argue that having power resources does not necessarily lead to persuasion, there is nothing in constructivist scholarship to suggest that they do not have the potential to help a great deal.

Evaluating the Argument for the Constraint of Legitimacy

Legitimacy emerges from this analysis as a highly contingent and malleable constraint on U.S. security policy. Is the evidence more consistent with this portrayal or with the stronger conditional or structural

---

[55] Richard Falk, *The Great Terror War* (New York: Olive Branch Press, 2003), xvi.

constraint featured in many constructivist writings? The Bush administration is a good case for addressing this question. The scholars primarily responsible for developing the argument concerning constraints related to legitimacy contend that they were strongly in play during the Bush years, and the perception that U.S. rule-breaking had generated significant legitimacy costs spread well beyond the academy.[56] Moreover, despite occasional deference to the mitigating strategies spelled out here, the hallmark of U.S. foreign policy under Bush was a systematic devaluation of persuasion, argument, indeed diplomacy itself. Instead of persuasion, officials frequently used "a language and diplomatic style that seemed calculated to offend the world."[57] And its efforts at public goods provision were repeatedly undermined by seemingly contradictory behavior, such as steel tariffs imposed in 2002 or the attempt in 2003 single-handedly to block an agreement to allow poor countries to purchase generic medicines to fight diseases such as AIDS, malaria, and tuberculosis.

If the constructivist argument that the constraining effect of legitimacy is strongly conditional or structural is right, we would therefore expect to find two patterns of evidence: that particular U.S. actions contrary to existing rules come to be seen as illegitimate and consequently encounter increased costs because others either withdraw support or must be bribed or coerced to support the action (what we term specific legitimacy costs); and that serial U.S. rule violations undermine the legitimacy of its role in the international system and the overall institutional order it supports, leading to a more widespread propensity to opt out of or undermine the order (general legitimacy costs).

The Iraq War and global public opinion have figured prominently in writings on legitimacy. The Iraq case would at first appear to be indisputable support for the proposition that rule breaking by the hegemon leads to specific legitimacy-related costs, while trends in world public opinion after 2003 would seem to be equally unimpeachable regarding general legitimacy costs. As we show below, the evidence is actually much more mixed regarding each. The general pattern of evidence that is most probative concerning the strength of constraints based in legitimacy, however, has received the least attention: whether U.S. rule violations led other states to opt out of the order or move

[56] See, e.g., Reus-Smit, *American Power*; Lebow, *Tragic Vision of Politics*; and Brzezinski, *Second Chance*.

[57] Fareed Zakaria, "The Arrogant Empire," *Newsweek*, March 24, 2003.

toward setting up an alternative. On this question, we find that the evidence is much more definitive and that it disconfirms the constructivist argument.

Iraq

The U.S. experience in Iraq greatly spurred the constructivist argument concerning legitimacy-related constraints. On the surface, it appeared as though the United States acted contrary to existing rules and consequently ended up saddled with heavy military, financial, and political burdens. Iraq would thus seem to be the easiest case to date in favor of the notion that the United States will necessarily pay specific legitimacy costs following a rule violation.[58] However, the evidence even on this case is far from providing definitive support of the constructivist view for two reasons.

First, other U.S. actions with a similarly questionable status vis-à-vis existing rules on the use of force are not generally seen as having encountered significant specific legitimacy costs. Analysts question the legitimacy of the invasion of Iraq primarily because it lacked both an unambiguous justification in international law and specific authorization by the UN Security Council. But this was also true of many other U.S. uses of force, including the Kosovo intervention. The legal justifications U.S. and NATO officials offered (that Serbian reprisals against Kosovars represented a threat to international peace and security, that intervention was consistent with previous UN Security Council resolutions on Kosovo, and that the war was consistent with emerging international norms of humanitarian intervention) were initially no less controversial than those offered by U.S. and U.K. officials on Iraq. And, just as in the Iraq case, governments that opposed the war refused to assist in its prosecution. Indeed, in sending a military contingent to Pristina, Russia actually took more active and dramatic measures than any major power did in the Iraq case.[59] Yet many observers ultimately

[58] Reus-Smit, "Unipolarity and Legitimacy," under review.

[59] Russian officials played a crucial role in persuading Yugoslav president Slobodan Milošević to end the war and apparently had expected to police their own sector of Kosovo, independent of NATO. When this role was denied, anger in Moscow mounted. When NATO peacekeepers prepared to enter Kosovo on June 12, 1999, they discovered that a contingent of 200 Russian paratroopers, stationed in Bosnia, had rapidly redeployed to the Pristina airport. This set up a tense confrontation that was only settled when Russian forces were given a sector in Kosovo, yet not formally subject to NATO command.

came to see the Kosovo action as legitimate, and neither constructivists nor other analysts cite it as an example of the restrictions imposed by the need for legitimacy.

Consider also the invasion of Afghanistan. The United States could have tried to justify it in terms of settled international law, and also could have sought a UN Security Council resolution specifically authorizing it. But it chose to do neither. Instead of using any of the many applicable rules of international law to justify the invasion, the administration chose instead to act under an expanded definition of self-defense that encompassed attacks on countries that harbor terrorists, a new rule long favored by the United States.[60] Instead of requesting a UN Security Council resolution specifically authorizing the invasion, it reached for something far bolder: Resolution 1373, which endorsed the new general rule legalizing the use of force against states that harbor terrorists, and transformed a raft of U.S.-sponsored antiterrorism measures into formal international commitments legally binding on all member states.

To some observers, this represented an effort to revise accepted customary international law in a manner that advantages the United States, which has the military capacity to attack nearly anywhere, and potentially disadvantages weaker states that lack such capabilities and could find themselves accused of harboring terrorists and subject to lawful invasion by the powerful.[61] Yet, the invasion was widely seen as legitimate, and the United States did not experience significant compliance or cooperation problems in carrying it out. What is more, the new rules promulgated in 9/11's wake appeared well on the way to garnering legitimacy. As Ian Johnstone notes, the rapid success of 1373 suggests "that the U.S. tradition of using the UN to shape the normative climate in which it pursues its interests continued right up to 2002, and that much of the rest of the world was prepared to be carried along."[62] Gerry Simpson agrees: "In the end, the United States articulated an expansive doctrine of self-defence and this doctrine was accepted by a number of states within the system and the majority of international lawyers."[63]

[60] The discussion in this paragraph draws on Byers, "Preemptive Self Defense"; Byers, "Terrorism, the Use of Force and International Law after 11 September," *International and Comparative Law Quarterly* 51 (2002); and Simpson, *Great Powers*, chap. 11.

[61] See, e.g., Vagts, "Hegemonic International Law."

[62] Ian Johnstone, "US-UN Relations after Iraq: The End of the World (Order) as We Know It?" *European Journal of International Law* 15 (2004): 814.

[63] Simpson, *Great Powers*, 324.

In Kosovo, Afghanistan, and Iraq, the United States operated far from the standard recipe generally said to be necessary for securing legitimacy: clearly conforming to settled international law and/or obtaining UN Security Council authorization. Of course, these cases are all quite dissimilar in other respects than their conformity to international rules, which raises the second major problem with using the Iraq invasion to demonstrate the constraint of legitimacy: so many other aspects of the case besides its inconsistency with existing rules are so obviously corrosive of legitimacy. Consider some of the factors that influence the legitimacy of an action that we delineated previously: Is the action by the hegemon seen as providing a public good? Is the action regarded as a response to an emergency? Does the hegemon simultaneously enhance the provision of alternative public goods and reaffirm other salient rules associated with the order? If the action is associated with the promulgation of a new rule, are there perceived reciprocal benefits and thus reason to expect others to support the new rule? In undertaking the action, does the hegemon pursue extensive persuasion?

Regarding Iraq, the answer to all of these questions is no. Unlike the war in Afghanistan, the war in Iraq came to be seen by many as producing not a public good but a major public bad. Contrary to Kosovo, it was harder to make a compelling case that Iraq was an emergency that needed to be dealt with on the precise timetable preferred by the Bush administration. As it was moving toward war with Iraq, the United States was not seen to be providing alternative public goods and reaffirming other salient rules; if anything, it was doing the reverse, such as imposing illegal steel tariffs in 2002. As compared to the war in Afghanistan, the Bush administration sought to promulgate a much more dramatic rule change—the Bush Doctrine of preventive war—that was perceived to be more threatening to other actors' security interests, appeared to offer fewer reciprocal benefits, and had already encountered opposition from other governments.

These moves away from the rule-based order were also not matched by enhanced levels of consultation; indeed, the opposite occurred. Although it engaged in some efforts at consultation and persuasion with allies concerning the decision for the Iraq War, this was done for the most part not through direct personal interactions: the level of international travel by senior Bush administration officials during its first term to consult with key allies was at an unprecedented low compared to the experience of previous U.S. administrations from the preceding few decades.[64] And regarding the rule change the Bush administration was propounding at this time, consultation was, as noted previously, almost nonexistent.

Bush officials evidently gambled that success in Iraq would breed its own legitimacy. The bet was that if coalition forces quickly crushed Saddam, were met by cheering crowds, discovered massive WMD programs and ties to terrorist organizations, and facilitated a smooth transfer to a democratizing government, the invasion would be seen as a collective good, the proposed rule change would garner support, and the international community would line up to help the new Iraq.

Only the first of these hoped-for outcomes occurred, and so there is no way to know whether U.S. policy in Iraq ever could have been seen as legitimate even if everything had worked out just as the Bush team had hoped. During the brief period when the action appeared to have been at least marginally successful, some observers did detect signs that it might be on the way toward garnering trappings of legitimacy. On June 8, 2004, the UN Security Council unanimously passed Resolution 1546, which endorsed U.S. arrangements regarding a transfer of authority to an interim government and subsequent elections. As Ian Clark observes:

> From the division and acrimony of early 2003, the Security Council had re-emerged into the bright sunlight of unanimous agreement. Reports widely commented on the significance of this resolution bestowing "international legitimacy" on the arrangements for Iraq. . . . Included amongst these, the Security Council charged the "multinational force" with the responsibility to "take all necessary measures to contribute to the maintenance of security and stability in Iraq." There was some similarity here with the aftermath of Kosovo. . . . It is safe to say that, by scrutiny of the norms of legality, morality, and constitutionality, one would have been unable to demonstrate the reason for this shift in international society's attitude.[65]

Neither Clark's analysis nor ours suggests that the United States faced no specific legitimacy costs. Rather, our point is that the Iraq case

[64] Zakaria, "The Arrogant Empire"; and Glenn Kessler, "Powell Flies in the Face of Tradition: The Secretary of State Is Least Traveled in 30 Years," *Washington Post*, July 14, 2004, A1.

[65] Clark, *Legitimacy in International Society,* 255. For more analysis along these lines, see Carlos L. Yordán, "Why Did the U.N. Security Council Support the Anglo American Project to Transform Postwar Iraq? The Evolution of Hegemonic International Law in the Shadow of the American Hegemon," *Journal of International Law and International Relations* 3 (2007).

is actually not very instructive regarding the overall connections between U.S. power, rule breaking, and legitimacy. What makes them now seem straightforward and obvious to so many constructivists and other analysts is not insight from scholarship but hindsight concerning the invasion of Iraq. The baleful consequences of this action may well have undermined its legitimacy and dried up potential wellsprings of international support for it. But this tells us little about the prospective specific legitimacy costs of other acts contrary to existing rules that do not have so many overlapping factors all pointing in the direction of reduced legitimacy.

Public Opinion

If the Iraq case is inconclusive, international public opinion would seem to present much more compelling evidence for the strength of the argument for constraints related to legitimacy. Polls track a marked increase in unfavorable views of the United States and its policies after the election of George W. Bush in 2001, with several surveys capturing an especially significant increase after the buildup to the Iraq War in early 2003.[66] Many analysts have interpreted these poll results in a manner consistent with the argument concerning the constraining effects of legitimacy.[67] This evidence is important in its own right, and adds credence to the constructivist view. For two reasons, however, it must be considered suggestive rather than conclusive.

First, the polling evidence generally does not directly bear on the constructivist argument for legitimacy-related constraints. Researchers are confident that views that can reasonably be coded as unfavorable toward the United States increased globally in the 2000s, but the reasons for this shift remain a matter of speculation. Andrew Kohut and Bruce Stokes of the Pew Research Center for the People and the Press focus on growing cultural differences and the unpopularity of U.S. foreign policy decisions under Bush, among a number of other hypotheses.[68] A major collaborative study edited by Peter Katzenstein and Robert Keohane highlights three possible explanations—power imbalances, backlash against globalization, and conflicting identities—but

---

[66] The most ambitious global polling project to date is the Pew Global Attitudes Project, Pew Research Center for the People and the Press, Washington, DC, available at www.people-press.org.

[67] See, for example, Fukuyama, *America at the Crossroads*; Walt, *Taming American Power*; Pape, "Soft Balancing against the United States"; Brzezinski, *Second Chance*.

[68] Kohut and Stokes, *America against the World*.

finds that "anti-Americanism is not well explained by any of them."[69] All researchers agree that the phenomenon is multidimensional and unlikely to succumb to any single explanation. The key point is that extant survey research has not examined systematically the specific causal connections highlighted by the constructivist argument on constraints. Beliefs that appear to reflect anti-Americanism, policy differences, cultural gaps, deep-seated bias, and even resentment against overweening power are all conceptually distinct from beliefs about legitimacy. The question of the degree to which U.S. actions widely seen as violations of accepted rules and norms actually prompted foreign publics not just to criticize those specific policies but to question the wider legitimacy of the United States and the role it plays as the sole superpower remains open.

Second, even if we were to accept the poll results as reflecting a loss of legitimacy in the eyes of foreign publics, this would represent only the first of many steps on the road toward the general legitimacy costs the constructivist argument predicts. To translate into lost legitimacy of the U.S. global role or the overall institutional order, the public mood must endure. Yet, as a widely-cited Pew report notes, "[T]he United States has been down the 'ugly American' road before, saddled with a bad image abroad and unable to draw much in the way of international support, even from close allies."[70] The fact that previous waves of negativity about the United States receded underscores the volatility of public views. And the fact that anti-American sentiment varies dramatically not just over time but across space raises the question of whether the core finding of research on the effect of U.S. public opinion we discussed in chapter 1—that it varies according to a complex series of case-specific factors—also applies to foreign public opinion. Indeed, this is one of Keohane and Katzenstein's major conclusions: "Instead of a single anti-Americanism we find a variety of anti-Americanisms. Negative views of the United States wax and wane with political events, in different rhythms, in different parts of the world, in countries with very different kinds of politics."[71] In sum, until foreign public opinion shifts translate into more tangible evidence of lost legitimacy, the possibility remains that they will be reversed before they generate the general legitimacy costs the constructivist argument warns about.

---

[69] Katzenstein and Keohane, *Anti-Americanisms in World Politics*, 309.

[70] Pew, *Trends 2005*, 113.

[71] Katzenstein and Keohane, *Anti-Americanisms in World Politics*, 6.

For even an enduring shift in foreign public opinion to generate strong legitimacy costs, moreover, it has to translate into governmental action. Yet this link has not been established. On the contrary, Keohane and Katzenstein's analysis suggests that "even high levels of anti-Americanism do not translate readily into governmental action."[72] In some cases, public opposition to a specific U.S. policy (whether connected to legitimacy or not) may have affected a government's decision to cooperate with that policy, as in German or Turkish opposition to the war in Iraq, but this did not occur in a great many other cases. Keohane and Katzenstein found little empirical support for a relationship between prior anti-Americanism and a government's decision to support the war in Iraq, join the "coalition of the willing," or sign non-surrender agreements with the United States under Article 98 of the ICC.[73] Just as there is considerable uncertainty over how U.S. public opinion might constrain U.S. foreign policy, as yet there is no reason to conclude that foreign publics' opinion of the United States constrains local governments in any more direct or tractable manner.

Reevaluating the Order

Evidence on international public opinion thus remains suggestive and preliminary on the question of whether the United States confronted general legitimacy costs after its bout of rule breaking under George W. Bush. To address this question, it is necessary to examine general patterns of evidence about the tangible costs to the United States of breaking rules. That is, do we see evidence of reduced compliance or cooperation resulting from legitimacy losses as opposed to other potential causes? Two general patterns of evidence are, at best, mixed on this score.

First, empirical studies find no clear relationship between U.S. rule-breaking, legitimacy, and the continued general propensity of other governments to comply with the overall institutional order. Case studies of U.S. unilateralism—that is, perceived violations of the multilateral principle underlying the current institutional order—reach decidedly mixed results.[74] Sometimes unilateralism appears to impose costs

---

[72] Ibid., 304.

[73] Ibid., 303.

[74] See David M. Malone and Yuen Foong Khong, eds., *Unilateralism and U.S. Foreign Policy: International Perspectives* (Boulder, Colo.: Lynne Rienner, 2003); and Patrick and Forman, *Multilateralism*.

on the United States that may derive from legitimacy problems; in other cases, these acts appear to win support internationally and eventually are accorded symbolic trappings of legitimacy; in yet others, no effect is discernable. Similar results are reported in detailed analyses of the most salient cases of U.S. noncompliance with international law, which, according to several studies, is as likely to result in a "new multilateral agreement and treaties [that] generally tilt towards U.S. policy preferences" as it is to corrode the legitimacy of accepted rules.[75]

The contestation created by the Bush administration's "new unilateralism," on the one hand, and the "new multilateralism" represented by other states' efforts to develop new rules and institutions that appear to constrain the United States, on the other hand, fits the historical pattern of the indirect effect of power on law. Highlighting only the details of the struggle over each new rule or institution may deflect attention from the structural influence of the United States on the overall direction of change. For example, a focus on highly contested issues in the UN, such as the attempt at a second resolution authorizing the invasion of Iraq, fails to note how the institution's whole agenda has shifted to address concerns (e.g., terrorism, proliferation) that the United States particularly cares about. The secretary-general's High-level Panel on Threats, Challenges and Change endorsed a range of U.S.-supported positions on terrorism and proliferation.[76] International legal scholars argue that the United States made measurable headway in inculcating new rules of customary law to legitimate its approach to fighting terrorism and containing "rogue states."[77] For example, UN Security Council Resolution 1373 imposed uniform, mandatory counterterrorist obligations on all member states and established a committee to monitor compliance.

[75] David M. Malone, comments in Byers and Nolte, *United States Hegemony*, 482. Nico Krisch similarly observes that "despite all resistance, international law has given in to United States demands for inequality to a significant degree." "More Equal Than the Rest? Hierarchy, Equality and US Predominance in International Law," in Byers and Nolte, *United States Hegemony*, 156. See also Shirley Scott, "The Impact on International Law of U.S. Noncompliance," in Byers and Nolte, *United States Hegemon*; Peter Tobias-Stoll, "Compliance: Multilateral Achievements and Predominant Powers," in Byers and Nolte, *United States Hegemony*; Detlev F. Vagts, "The United States and Its Treaties: Observance and Breach," *American Journal of International Law* 95 (2001): 332; and Alvarez, "Hegemonic International Law Revisited."

[76] *A More Secure World: Our Shared Responsibility* (United Nations, 2005).

[77] See, e.g., W. Michael Reisman and Andrea Armstrong, "The Past and Future of the Claim of Preemptive Self-Defense," *American Journal of International Law* 100 (2006); Byers, "Preemptive Self-Defense"; Alvarez, "Hegemonic International Law Revisited"; and Johnstone, "US-UN Relations after Iraq."

That said, there is also evidence of resistance to U.S. attempts to re-write rules or exempt itself from rules. Arguably the most salient example of this is the International Criminal Court (ICC). During the negotiations on the Rome Convention in the late 1990s, the United States explicitly sought to preserve great-power control over ICC jurisdiction. U.S. representatives argued that the United States needed protection from a more independent ICC in order to continue to provide the public good of global military intervention. When this logic failed to persuade the majority, U.S. officials shifted to purely legal arguments, but, as noted, these foundered on the inconsistency created by Washington's strong support of war crimes tribunals for others. The Rome Convention rejected the U.S. view in favor of the majority position granting the ICC judicial panel authority to refer cases to the court's jurisdiction.[78] By 2007, 130 states had signed the treaty and over 100 were full-fledged parties to it.

President Clinton signed the treaty, but declined to submit it to the Senate for ratification. The Bush administration "unsigned" it in order legally to be able to take action to undermine it. The United States then persuaded over 75 countries to enter into agreements under which they undertake not to send any U.S. citizen to the ICC without the United States' consent; importantly, these agreements do not obligate the United States to investigate or prosecute any American accused of involvement in war crimes. This clearly undermines the ICC, especially given that about half the states that have signed these special agreements with the United States are also parties to the Rome Statute.[79] At the same time, the EU and other ICC supporters pressured governments not to sign special agreements with the United States, and some 45 have refused to do so—about half losing U.S. military assistance as a result. In April 2005, the United States chose not to veto a UN Security Council resolution referring the situation in Darfur, Sudan, to the ICC. To many observers, this suggests that inconsistency may yet undermine U.S. opposition to the court.[80] If the U.S. campaign to thwart the court fails, and there is no compromise solution that

[78] See David J. Scheffer, "The United States and the International Criminal Court," *American Journal of International Law* 93 (1999).

[79] See, e.g., "Risks for the Integrity of the Statute of the International Criminal Court," European Parliamentary Assembly, 2002, Session. Res. 1300, at http://assembly.coe.int.

[80] See, e.g., Philippe Sands, *Lawless World: America and the Making and Breaking of Global Rules from FDR's Atlantic Charter to George W. Bush's Illegal War* (New York: Viking, 2005).

meets some American concerns, the result will be a small but noticeable constraint: U.S. citizens involved in what might be construed as war crimes and who are not investigated and prosecuted by the U.S. legal system may have to watch where they travel.

The upshot as of 2007 was something of a stalemate on the ICC, demonstrating the limits of both the United States' capability to quash a new legal institution it doesn't like and the Europeans' ability to legitimize such an institution without the United States' participation. Similar stalemates characterize other high-profile arguments over other new international legal instruments, such as the Kyoto Protocol on Climate Change and the Ottawa Landmine Convention. Exactly as constructivists suggest, these outcomes lend credence to the argument that power does not translate unproblematically into legitimacy. What the larger pattern of evidence on rule breaking shows, however, is that this is only one part of the story; the other part involves rule breaking with few, if any, general legitimacy costs, and the frequent use of go-it-alone power to revise or create rules.

AN EROSION OF THE ORDER?

The second general evidence pattern concerns whether fallout from the unpopular U.S. actions on ICC, Kyoto and Ottawa, Iraq, and many other issues has led to an erosion of the legitimacy of the larger institutional order. Constructivist theory identifies a number of reasons why institutional orders are resistant to change, so strong and sustained action is presumably necessary to precipitate a legitimacy crisis that might undermine the workings of the current order. While aspects of this order remain controversial among sections of the public and elite both in the United States and abroad, there is little evidence of a trend toward others opting out of the order or setting up alternatives.

Recall also that the legitimacy argument works better in the economic than in the security realm. It is also in the economic realm that the United States arguably has the most to lose. Yet it is hard to make the empirical case that U.S. rule violations have undermined the institutional order in the economic realm. Complex rules on trade and investment have underwritten economic globalization. The United States generally favors these rules, has written and promulgated many of them, and the big story of the 1990s and 2000s is their growing scope and ramified nature—in a word, their growing legitimacy. On trade, the WTO represents a major strengthening of the GATT rules that the United States pushed for (by, in part, violating the old rules to create pressure for the upgrade). As of 2007, it had 149 members, and the only major economy remaining outside was Russia's. And notwithstanding President Putin's stated preference for an "alternative" WTO, Russian policy focused on accession.[81] To be sure, constructivists are right that the WTO, like other rational-legal institutions, gets its legitimacy in part from the appearance of independence from the major powers.[82] Critical analysts repeatedly demonstrate, however, that the organization's core agenda remains powerfully influenced by the interests of the United States.[83]

Regarding international finance, the balance between the constraining and enabling properties of rules and institutions is even more favorable to the United States, and there is little evidence of general legitimacy costs. The United States retains a privileged position of influence within the International Monetary Fund and the World Bank. An example of how the scope of these institutions can expand under the radar screen of most legitimacy scholarship is the International Center for Settlement of Investment Disputes (ICSID)—the major dispute settlement mechanism for investment treaties. Part of the World Bank group of institutions, it was established in 1966, and by 1991 it had considered only 26 disputes. With the dramatic growth in investment treaties in the 1990s, however, the ICSID came into its own. Between 1998 and 2004, over 121 disputes were registered with the Center.[84] This increase reflects the rapidly growing scope of international investment law. And these new rules and treaties overwhelmingly serve to protect investors' rights, in which the United States has a powerful interest given how much it invests overseas.

Looking beyond the economic realm, the evidence simply does not provide a basis for concluding that serial U.S. rule-breaking imposed general legitimacy costs sufficient to erode the existing order. On the contrary, it suggests a complex and malleable relationship between

[81] After Putin's comment, senior Russian officials continued to speak of Russian membership as a matter of when, not whether. For background, see Stephen Hanson, Philip Hanson, Juliet Johnson, Stephen Wegren, and Peter Rutland, *Russia and the WTO: A Progress Report* (Seattle: National Bureau of Asian Research, March 2007).

[82] Barnett and Finnemore, *Rules for the World*.

[83] See, e.g., Joseph Stiglitz and Andrew Charlton, *Fair Trade for All: How Trade Can Promote Development* (New York: Oxford University Press, 2005).

[84] For data: http://www.worldbank.org/icsid/index.html.

rule breaking, legitimacy, and compliance with the existing order that opens up numerous opportunities for the United States to use its power to change rules and limit the legitimacy costs of breaking rules. The evidence also suggests that just as rules do not automatically constrain power, power does not always smoothly translate into legitimacy. As our review of the ICC issue showed, the United States is not omnipotent, and its policies can run afoul of the problems of hypocrisy and inconsistency that constructivists and legal scholars identify. Indeed, neither the theory nor the evidence presented in this chapter can rule out the possibility that the United States might have enjoyed much more compliance, and had much more success promulgating its favored rules and quashing undesired rule change, had it not been such a rule breaker or had it pursued compensating strategies more energetically.

Conclusion

Constructivist scholarship suggests that the United States' need for international legitimacy produces a strong constraint on its security policy, either structurally induced by the contradiction between unipolar power and the international system's constitutive norms of equilibrium or one that is strongly conditional upon U.S. actions seen to violate core rules. As we showed, however, there are no grounds for the constructivists' argument that rule breaking always leads to lost legitimacy, nor for the contention that constraints derived from the need for legitimacy necessarily rise in tandem with U.S. power. On the contrary, advantages in power capabilities expand the range and scope of various strategies the United States can use to build legitimacy and mold institutions to its purposes. Ultimately, our analysis shows that the constraint of legitimacy is weakly conditional, not strongly conditional or structural, as many constructivists now posit.

The result is a very different picture of legitimacy and American primacy. History's leading states have used power resources to shape rules to suit their interest—and not just in the aftermath of major upheavals, as established by John Ikenberry and others, but also in situations more analogous to the one the United States seems to face today. Indeed, even the Bush administration—saddled with globally unpopular policies and maladroit diplomacy—endeavored on occasion to deploy strategies of hegemonic rule revision with some modest success.

At the same time, we come away from a critical examination of legitimacy with the conviction that though it is hard to examine empirically, it is of crucial importance. Hegemonic powers want and need rules and the legitimation they bring, which is why they devote resources to shaping them. And, as the Bush experience also amply demonstrates, raw power is hardly sufficient for hegemonic rule change. Indeed, by pointing toward strategies a hegemon can use to mold legitimacy and shape rules, constructivist scholarship may make an important contribution to debates on American grand strategy.

A New Agenda

SCHOLARS HAVE SPENT decades developing theories of how the international environment influences the security behavior of states. The idea that systemic constraints on the United States' security policy rise with its relative power was a reasonable initial inference from this previous base of research. Missing thus far has been a rigorous analysis to determine whether this relationship actually holds. Having presented such an analysis, we find that it does not: as the concentration of power increases beyond a certain threshold, systemic constraints on the leading state's security policy become largely inoperative. Although the decades-long quest for theories of systemic constraints may have paid dividends in previous eras, we do not find grounds to conclude that they will do so for unipolarity.

Two major implications emerge for future research. First, the misplaced focus on theories of systemic constraints has diverted scholars' attention from other kinds of hindrances that have greater potential relevance in today's unipolar system. Second, the mistaken belief in the salience of systemic constraints has generally led analysts to overestimate the costs of a concerted effort to revise the international system to better advance U.S. security interests. As a result, the current debate overlooks an important potential grand strategy: using American hegemany to reshape international institutions, standards of legitimacy, and economic globalization.

NEW DIRECTIONS FOR INTERNATIONAL RELATIONS SCHOLARSHIP

Restrictions on U.S. security policy surely exist; the problem is that they are not the systemic phenomena featured in international relations theory. It takes only a quick look at contemporary discussions of U.S. security policy to identify a number of other salient constraints ripe for sustained analysis. Among the policy challenges that dominated the agenda after 9/11 and the Iraq War, the following five potential constraints stand out as having particular relevance to U.S. security policy.

Nuclear weapons proliferation. Both conceptual and empirical work on nuclear deterrence theory waned after 1991. Yet, as Patrick Morgan argues in his important reconsideration of deterrence after the Cold War, traditional deterrence theory is ill suited to the contemporary challenges presented by unipolarity and nuclear proliferation.[1] To be sure, scholars and analysts are very certain—as certain as they can be about anything in international politics—that states with secure second-strike nuclear capabilities can be relatively sanguine about their basic territorial security. In sufficient numbers and with sufficiently dispersed deployments and robust control systems, nuclear arsenals will almost certainly render incredible any U.S. threat to invade and occupy. But very few states have such robust arsenals, and no one regards a barrier to the invasion and occupation of states like Russia and China as relevant to U.S. security policy.[2] The farther we get from arsenals of that size and kind, and the more we move away from core territorial security and invasion to other uses or threats of force, the less certain we can be about the limits nuclear weapons impose on U.S. security policy. Do robust second-strike nuclear capabilities constrain U.S. actions that do not bear on other states' core territorial security? What is the constraining effect of small, nonsurvivable nuclear arsenals, and/or arsenals with little or no capacity to strike the United States? These are the relevant questions, yet they have hardly figured in research and theorizing by IR scholars.

Insurgency. The U.S. experience in Iraq highlighted the popular post-Vietnam argument that the ease of insurgency constrains the use of military force to shape the behavior or political destinies of other societies. The implication of this argument is that the United States not only will be averse to intervene, but other states will be aware of this aversion—thereby greatly diminishing the strategic utility of U.S. threats of force. Surprisingly, the core propositions underlying this argument have not been the subject of systematic IR research and theorizing.[3]

---

[1] Patrick Morgan, *Deterrence Now* (Cambridge: Cambridge University Press, 2003).

[2] Lieber and Press ("The End of MAD?") draw attention to the fact that U.S. nuclear superiority may even undermine the classic second-strike criterion between the United States and both Russia and China.

[3] Benjamin Valentino and Paul Huth present the outlines of a research project to address the questions noted herein: "To Have and to Hold: Foreign Occupations, Insurgency, and Consolidating Peace in the Aftermath of Interstate Wars since 1900," manuscript, Dartmouth College, 2006. Although there is a vast literature on counterinsurgency tactics, most studies focus on particular cases. Those studies with a broader empirical

Scholars do not know what explains the timing of insurgency—why some develop rapidly, as in Iraq, while others take as many as 15 years to get under way, as in the case of Israel's occupation of the West Bank. They lack leverage on the question of severity—why some remain marginal, festering for years or decades without seriously challenging the intervening power, and others become all-consuming threats. As yet they have not engaged in a research-driven debate over the causes of the constraint: the degree to which it is the result of the rise of nationalism, the increased availability of lethal weapons, new domestic or international norms against harsh counterinsurgency tactics, or other factors. As a result, they do not know the degree to which the likelihood, timing, or intensity of insurgency varies on the basis of actions taken by the occupying power or locally specific factors, and, if so, which factors.

Imperial overstretch. Paul Kennedy coined the term *imperial overstretch* to describe the fate of past leading states whose "global interests and obligations" became "far too large for the country to be able to defend them all simultaneously."[4] Mounting budget deficits, increased foreign indebtedness, and armed forces stretched thin in Iraq led many analysts to warn that the United States was in danger of following suit.[5] But these first two strains are chiefly the result of domestic choices to cut taxes while increasing spending, while the latter can largely be traced to the priority placed on the Pentagon's force modernization plan over a significant increase in the size of the army.

---

focus generally lack strong theoretical underpinnings, concentrating instead on lessons learned concerning particular policies that were employed; see, for example, Walter Laqueur, *Guerilla: A History and Critical Study* (Boston: Little, Brown, 1976); John Nagl, *Learning to Eat Soup with a Knife: Counterinsurgency Lessons from Malaya and Vietnam* (Chicago: University of Chicago Press, 2005); and D. Michael Shafer, *Deadly Paradigms: The Failure of Counterinsurgency Policy* (Princeton: Princeton University Press, 1988).

[4] Paul Kennedy, "The (Relative) Decline of America," *Atlantic Monthly,* August 1987. Though he did not use the term, Kennedy provided a more fulsome definition in his magisterial *Rise and Fall of the Great Powers* (New York: Random House, 1987): "it has been a common dilemma facing previous 'number one' countries that even as their relative economic strength is ebbing, the growing foreign challenges to their position have compelled them to allocate more and more of their resources into the military sector, which in turn squeezes out productive investment and, over time, leads to the downward spiral of slower growth, heavier taxes, deepening domestic splits over spending priorities, and a weakening capacity to bear the burdens of defense" (533).

[5] See, for example, Ash, "Stagger On"; Jack Snyder, "Imperial Temptation," *National Interest,* Spring 2003; and Layne, *The Peace of Illusions.*

Analysts who argue that the United States now suffers, or soon will suffer, from imperial overstretch invariably fail to distinguish between latent power (the level of resources that could be mobilized from society) and actual power (the level of resources a government actually chooses to mobilize).[6] In his original formulation of imperial overstretch, Kennedy had in mind a situation in which a state's actual *and* latent capabilities cannot cope with its existing foreign policy commitments. To date, there is virtually no research on whether the United States faces this prospect. Part of the problem is that because the Bush administration made no attempt to ask the public for greater sacrifice, there is no observable evidence of whether it would be possible to extract more resources for advancing U.S. foreign policy interests. The Cold War experience indicates that the U.S. public is capable of supporting, over long periods, significantly higher spending on foreign policy than current levels.[7] Yet this does not necessarily mean that the U.S. public would be willing to support a dramatic increase in foreign policy spending now if policymakers called for it.

The larger issue is that though IR scholars use the term, they have not theorized or researched imperial overstretch as a constraint independent of counterbalancing. In the historical cases highlighted by Kennedy and others, leading states suffered from imperial overstretch in significant part because they faced counterbalancing that demanded more resources than they were able to extract domestically. As chapters 2 and 3 showed, the United States does not face a counterbalancing constraint. This raises a key question of whether there are limits to the U.S. polity's capacity to generate power in the absence of the threat posed by a geopolitical peer rival. Lacking a focused research effort, scholars can now only answer with speculation.

Terrorism. Analysts have long debated the causes of terrorism and the nature of its relationship to U.S. security policy. Some scholars argue that terrorism is highly contingent on specific U.S. foreign policy

[6] See the discussions of this distinction in Mearsheimer, *Tragedy of Great Power Politics*, chap. 3; and Klaus Knorr, *The Power of Nations: The Political Economy of International Relations* (New York: Basic Books, 1975), chap. 1.

[7] The United States currently spends only around 4 percent of its GDP on the military, as compared to an average of 7.5 percent during entire the Cold War and 10 percent during the 1950–70 period. And it spends around 0.1 percent of its GDP on development and humanitarian aid (around 0.6 percent of federal budget outlays), but such spending reached 0.6 percent of GDP (3.1 percent of federal budget outlays) in 1962; figures are from Richard N. Gardner, "The One Percent Solution," *Foreign Affairs* 79 (2000): 8.

actions; others see it is a broader limit on overall U.S. policy toward the Middle East; while yet others portray it more as a response to conditions independent of U.S. security policy, such as globalization, the spread of Western culture, or the specific historical experience of certain societies. Only after 9/11 did IR scholars in significant numbers begin to produce analyses that usefully supplement the work of scholars in other disciplines who seek to answer these questions.[8] IR scholars may be even better positioned to offer research-based assessments of the strength of the terrorist constraint.[9] These assessments hinge not just on estimates of the capabilities of terrorist organizations, but also and more importantly on questions of mass psychology, public opinion, and the sensitivity of modern polities and economies to periodic disruption from even comparatively small-scale attacks.

Oil dependency. Imports now account for around 60 percent of total U.S. oil consumption, and most U.S. policymakers and analysts perceive this dependency on foreign oil supplies to be an important restriction on U.S. security policy. The United States is hostage to any potential reduction in supplies from the Persian Gulf, many stress, and needs to maintain a substantial American military presence in the region in order to forestall this from happening. Yet the strength and scope of the oil constraint depends in part on the feasibility and cost of energy alternatives as well as the vulnerability of the U.S. and world economies to sharp increases in oil prices—both matters of debate among economists and energy analysts.[10] They also depend on answers to questions on which IR scholars might have leverage: Does political instability and war in oil-rich regions—notably the Persian Gulf—really pose a major threat to global oil supplies? What kind of political incentives could prompt a leader of an oil-exporting state to cut off its only meaningful source of revenue? And what size, and type,

---

[8] A notable example is Robert Pape, *Dying to Win: The Logic of Suicide Terror* (New York: Random House, 2005).

[9] See the discussion in John Mueller, "Six Rather Unusual Propositions about Terrorism," *Terrorism and Political Violence* 14 (2005), and the sources cited therein.

[10] Some studies find support for the view that oil price shocks have strong negative effects on the U.S. economy; see, for example, Steven Davis and John Haltiwanger, "Sectoral Job Creation and Destruction Responses to Oil Price Changes and Other Shocks," *Journal of Monetary Economics* 48 (2001). Other recent studies have strongly challenged the validity of this assessment for the post-1970s period; see, for example, Mark Hooker, "Are Oil Shocks Inflationary? Asymmetric and Nonlinear Specifications versus Changes in Regime," *Journal of Money, Credit, and Banking* 34 (2002); and Michael LeBlanc and Menzie Chinn, "Do High Oil Prices Presage Inflation? The Evidence from G-5 Countries," *Business Economics* 39 (2004).

of a military presence in the Persian Gulf is required in order to advance U.S. interests in secure oil supplies? With rare exceptions, IR scholars have not addressed these questions.[11]

In sum, IR scholars' research agenda needs to be readjusted. Decades ago, scholarship veered away from examining the kind of issues just discussed in favor of more "systematic" studies. We do not deny that this orientation yielded dividends. Balance-of-power theory is useful for analyzing historical international systems, and its irrelevance today helps us understand how the current unipolar system differs from its predecessors. Liberal theories of economic interdependence remain vital for understanding globalization and a variety of important security issues. Core insights from constructivist and institutionalist theory concerning the effects of institutions and rules are central for explaining how the current international order functions. These theories remain useful; they simply are not terribly instructive on the constraints on U.S. security policy. To speak knowledgably about that issue, IR scholars will need to refocus research on the more policy-relevant agenda these five potential constraints suggest.

Many IR scholars may find it self-evident that these five constraints are strong, and they might well be right. If so, then a new scholarly conventional wisdom would emerge in light of our analysis: under unipolarity, these five constraints have taken on a new salience even as the systemic constraints featured in IR theory have receded in importance. If this is the case, then it would have profound implications for the study of international relations and U.S. foreign policy. Yet the six preceding chapters stand as a clear cautionary tale against a rush to judgment. Before we accept such a new conventional wisdom, these remaining potential constraints require a much closer examination.

---

[11] The chief exception is Eugene Gholz and Daryl Press, "Protecting 'The Prize': Oil and the U.S. National Interest," manuscript, Dartmouth College, 2004, who question the conventional wisdom. They conclude that a large U.S. military presence in the Persian Gulf is not needed for the purpose of advancing U.S. oil interests because supply disruptions in the Middle East "tend to trigger a set of predictable adjustments by the world's oil producers, quickly restoring supply to worldwide consumers and generally mitigating the disruption-induced spikes in oil prices" (3). Also relevant is the contentious scholarly debate on the independent effectiveness of U.S. airpower, which has not yet been directed specifically to the question of what forces are needed to protect U.S. oil interests in the Persian Gulf; see, for example, Robert Pape, "The True Worth of Air Power," *Foreign Affairs* 83 (2004); Andrew L. Stigler, "A Clear Victory for Air Power: NATO's Empty Threat to Invade Kosovo," *International Security* 27 (2003); and Daryl Press, "The Myth of Airpower in the Persian Gulf War and the Future of Warfare," *International Security* 26 (2001).

A NEW ALTERNATIVE FOR U.S. FOREIGN POLICY

It is clear that the portfolio of security challenges facing the United States has been transformed since the Cold War ended. In significant part for reasons we spelled out in chapters 2 and 3, the fundamental security challenge the current order was designed to address—a sustained geopolitical challenge by a great-power peer rival—is not in the cards for the relevant future. As noted, other security problems have grown in significance: terrorism, nuclear weapons proliferation, and ethnic and civil conflict. At the same time, many "nontraditional" security issues have also increased in salience during this period, including the augmented threat of infectious disease; the increasing destruction of the global environment; and enhanced flows of illegal migrants between the poorest and the richest states. Facing an environment in which systemic constraints are inoperative or weak, one is hard-pressed to argue plausibly that there are no activist policies that would make it easier for the United States to address this transformed security agenda, and thus that conservatism is necessarily the best route.

To many, a status quo orientation appeared vindicated by the Bush administration's experience: Bush administration officials saw the United States as being in a position to effectively use military power to change aspects of the system, and the results of this strategy are unlikely to be seen by future historians in a positive light. Thus for Jervis, as for most IR scholars, "The odd fact [is] that the United States, with all its power and stake in the system, is behaving more like a revolutionary state than one committed to preserving the arrangements that seem to have suited it so well."[12] This reflects an implicit assumption that the Bush administration's travails internationally are indicative of the fate of any activist foreign policy the United States might pursue. Analysts routinely contrast the Bush policy with a conservative, status quo approach and invariably conclude the latter is preferable to the former, as if these are the only two options.[13]

But the Bush administration's foreign policy hardly exhausts all the possible alternatives to a status quo approach. In his seminal book on

[12] Jervis, "Remaking of Unipolar World," 7. Similarly John Ikenberry has repeatedly argued that the current system serves U.S. interests extremely well and that it should therefore seek to "perpetuate the existing international order" ("The Rise of China," 34).

[13] Some prominent treatments of this kind include G. John Ikenberry, "America's Imperial Temptation," *Foreign Affairs* 81 (2002); Pape, "Soft Balancing against the United States"; Lisa Martin, "Multilateral Organizations"; Keohane, "Multilateral Coercive Diplomacy"; Lebow, *Tragic Vision of Politics*; and Reus-Smit, *American Power*.

how system change occurs in world politics, Robert Gilpin considered leading state strategies concerning change not just in the territorial status quo, but also in the structure of the global economy and the rules and standards of legitimacy that frame international interactions.[14] In developing his overall argument that the leading state will pursue system change if the expected gains exceed the expected costs, Gilpin makes clear that seeking changes in the nonterritorial element of the system exists as a strategy that the leading state can pursue as an alternative to relying on military force to pursue territorial aggrandizement.

The Bush administration's experience tells us little about the feasibility of this alternative approach to systemic activism for the simple reason that the Bush team did not take it seriously. Indeed, neoconservatives were positively averse to the use of U.S. power to reshape international institutions and standards of legitimacy to further U.S. security goals: they denigrated institutions as hindering, not enabling, U.S. power, and they had a profoundly traditional view of political legitimacy as uniquely the product of the people's will as expressed through domestic democratic institutions rather than as a general feature of the international environment.[15] That being said, the Bush administration did not completely ignore this alternative form of systemic activism: through its proposed preventive war doctrine and other efforts to obtain exemptions for the United States from existing and emerging global rules, it did attempt to revise the system in some ways via this approach. And, as we showed, even with its signature knack for choosing precisely the mix of policies and attitudes least likely to persuade others, the Bush team actually did propel some potentially useful alterations to the existing order, particularly regarding counterterrorism.

With its emphasis on the use of military power and disdain for diplomacy, however, the Bush administration helped give the pursuit of systemic activism—indeed, the assertion of U.S. power generally—a bad name. Against the backdrop of the scholarly conventional wisdom about systemic constraints rising with U.S. power, this undermined the notion that another systemic activist approach might exist as an alternative to maintaining the status quo. Such an alternative might not only run into less resistance, but also might promise much higher potential returns for U.S. security policy and for the world more generally than sticking to the status quo.

[14] Gilpin, *War and Change*, 23–24.

[15] Michael C. Williams, "What Is the National Interest? The Neoconservative Challenge in IR Theory," *European Journal of International Relations* 11 (2005).

What would such an alternative strategy look like? Nothing in the preceding chapters undermines the scholarly conventional wisdom about the benefits to the United States of legitimizing its hegemony, institutionalizing its preferred solutions to problems, and furthering the globalization of economic activity. Our core contribution is to show that these benefits do not come at the price of strong constraints on the use of power, as scholars now assume. The implication is that U.S. policymakers would be wise to consider deploying the power resources at their disposal to reshape legitimacy standards, international institutions, and economic globalization.

Scholars may have much to contribute to the national conversation on how best to do this. Unfortunately, the debate over U.S. foreign policy is greatly circumscribed by the fact that the very scholars who most recognize the significance of globalization, institutions, and legitimacy have also generally been most skeptical of the notion that the United States can take advantage of its global position to reshape the international system without suffering serious negative consequences. It is difficult avoid the conclusion that an important reason for this general reluctance to consider U.S. systemic activism is that so many scholars accept the conventional wisdom that the United States is tightly bound by systemic constraints. The current scholarly understanding portrays the international environment as configured to create strong disincentives for the United States to use its power in an assertive manner to reshape elements of the international system in its long-term interests. It encourages the view that globalization, institutions, and legitimacy are not variables that the United States can manipulate strategically, but are instead more or less exogenous features of the system that constrain U.S. power.

Fortunately, there is some indication that the long-standing reluctance of IR scholars to consider systemic activism by the United States is breaking down. A few scholars have recently outlined detailed proposals of how the United States can seek to make fundamental changes to the international system in order to better advance American interests. The most prominent and comprehensive proposal of this kind thus far is the final report of the Princeton Project on National Security (PPNS).[16] The report's authors, John Ikenberry and Anne-Marie Slaughter, emphasize that "the system of international institutions that the

[16] G. John Ikenberry and Anne-Marie Slaughter, *Forging a World of Liberty under Law: U.S. National Security in the 21st Century: Final Paper of the Princeton Project on National*

United States and its allies built after World War II and steadily expanded over the course of the Cold War is broken. . . . America can no longer rely on the legacy institutions of the Cold War; radical surgery is required."[17] To make the international system more capable of furthering U.S. security interests, they both propose major revisions to existing security organizations such as the UN and the Nuclear Non-Proliferation Treaty as well as the creation of new institutional structures—most notably, the creation of a "Concert of Democracies." They stress that if the United Nations cannot be quickly reformed to better deal with contemporary security challenges, this Concert of Democracies could well emerge as an alternative, competing forum for the authorization of military force.[18]

In forwarding their various policy recommendations, Ikenberry and Slaughter simply assume that America does, in fact, have an opportunity to recast the international system.[19] Yet if this assumption is not valid, then it is difficult to see why many additional scholars would think it worthwhile to take the time to offer and debate proposals about how the United States should pursue system change, nor why many policymakers would listen seriously to any such ideas. Ikenberry and Slaughter also do not say anything specific about how the United States can and should use its power to advance the institutional changes they outline. Their reticence on this issue may further limit policymakers' motivation to act on their recommendations.

Our book provides the necessary analysis for concluding that the United States does, in fact, have an opportunity to revise the system—and, moreover, that this opportunity will long endure. Our examination shows that the United States can push hard and even unilaterally for revisions to the international system without sparking counterbalancing, risking the erosion of its ability to cooperate within international institutions, jeopardizing the gains of globalization, or undermining the overall legitimacy of its role. Portions of our analysis, especially our study of legitimacy, also concretely lay out some of the

---

Security, Woodrow Wilson School of Public and International Affairs at Princeton University, September 2006, available at http://www.wws.princeton.edu/ppns/report.html (consulted September 19, 2007). It should be noted that this represents a shift from Ikenberry's writings in the early 2000s, which strongly emphasized the great value the United States should place on the institutional status quo.

[17] Ibid., 7.
[18] Ibid., 25–26.
[19] See ibid., 58.

costs and benefits associated with different strategies the United States can pursue to change the system.

It is important to recognize that the constraints reviewed earlier in this chapter that currently dominate the debate on policy do not appear to bear strongly on systemic activism. There is no indication that nuclear weapons, terrorism, insurgency, and oil dependency stand in the way of the assertive use of U.S. power to reshape the international system. On the contrary, systemic activism may well be the best available means of reducing their salience. Thus, even if domestic resistance limits the resources available for an effort to revise the system, the overall restrictions on such a policy are far lower than currently presumed.

In his classic study *The Twenty Years' Crisis*, E. H. Carr argued that scholars tragically overestimated the potential to remake the post-1918 international system because their theories ignored or misunderstood the role of power in international politics.[20] Realistic theories with a clear-eyed appraisal of the rapidly shifting multipolar power configuration of the day, he argued, would have allowed them to see their hopes of remaking the order for the pipe dreams that they were, confounded by the implacable constraints of an international system primed for violent conflict. The preceding chapters yield the opposite conclusion. Because their theories ignore or misunderstand the implications of the unipolar distribution of power, scholars have generally underestimated the U.S. potential to remake the post-1991 international system. More realistic theories with a clear-eyed appraisal of the workings of a unipolar system would lead them to see the systemic constraints they believe stand in the way of such a policy for what they are: artifacts of the scholarship of previous eras.

Of course, this is not to say that some of the ideas for remaking the interwar order that Carr branded as utopian have magically become realistic. Nor can we yet claim to know precisely what kinds of systemic activism would work best to advance U.S. security interests. Rather, the point is that all indications are that the United States has a "twenty years opportunity" to reshape key elements of the system to better serve such interests. IR scholars are in a very good position to advance the discussion of how the United States can best seize it, and we hope they will make a strong contribution in this regard. Regardless, IR scholars should expect U.S. policymakers to be tempted to pursue systemic activism in the years ahead.

---

[20] Edward Hallet Carr, *The Twenty Years' Crisis, 1919–1939: An Introduction to the Study of International Relations* (New York: Harper and Row, 1946).

INDEX

Page numbers in italics refer to tables or figures in the text.

Afghanistan: Soviets in, 58; U.S. invasion of, 58, 74, 89, 152, 196–97
aging populations, 34n25, 41
Ahmadinejad, Mahmoud, 126
Albright, Madeleine, 192
Alexander, Gerard, 66, 95
alliances. *See* external balancing
anti-Americanism, 141, 200–201
Argentina, *115, 119*
arms sales and transfers, 75–77, 133–36
Ash, Timothy Garton. *See* Garton Ash, Timothy
Australia: as export market, *107*; foreign direct investment and, *113*, 114n37, *115, 119*, 120
Austria, *30, 115*

Bahrain, *115*
balance-of-power theory, 7–8, 19, 22–59, 213; absence of counterbalancing and, 48–58; argument for, 24–27; capabilities distribution and, 27–35; comparative case studies and, 40–45, 51–58; overview, 22–24; unipolarity and, 35–48
balance-of-threat theory, 19–20, 60–97; argument for, 64–67; comparative case studies and, 63, 72–95; criteria for testing the argument for, 67–71; overview, 60–64; perceptions of intentions and, 61, 65–66; systemic difference and, 95–97; unipolarity and, 62, 65–66, 71–95
Baldwin, David, 98, 102
Balkans conflict, 59. *See also* Kosovo intervention
bargaining. *See* policy disputes and bargaining
Barnett, Michael, 175
Beeson, Mark, 149
Belarus, *134*

Belgium: as export market, *107*; foreign direct investment and, *115, 119*; securities holdings of, *122*
Berinsky, Adam, 5n10
Bermuda, *115, 119*
bioterrorist threats, 144
Blair, Tony, 93–94
Blix, Hans, 93
Bolton, John, 168
border monitoring problems, 143
Brazil, *107, 115, 119*
Bretton Woods system, 65
Brezhnev, Leonid, 55–56
Brockaway, George, 127n62
Brooks, Stephen G., 105, 140n95
Brzezinski, Zbigniew, 57, 172, 182
Bush, George W. (administration): economic interdependence and, 145, 146n114; imperial overstretch and, 210–11; International Criminal Court and, 190, 203; international system change and, 214–15; legitimacy constraint and, 172, 177–78, 182–83, 189–90, 194, 198, 202–3, 206–7; premptive/preventive war and, 182–83, 189–90, 197; reputational constraint and, 154, 165, 167–69; "soft balancing" constraint and, 61, 81; unilateralism of, 61, 164, 202. *See also* Iraq War
Byers, Michael, 184, 189n46, 192

Canada: arms transfers and, *134*; as export market, 106, *107*, 108; foreign direct investment and, 112–13, *113–15, 119*, 120; securities holdings of, *122*
Carr, E. H., 218
Carter, Jimmy (administration), 57
Cayman Islands, *115, 122*
Central Asian states, 56, 73–74. *See also individual states*

Cha, Victor, 104n20
Chamberlain, Joseph, 1n3
change. *See* international system change
Chávez, Hugo, 126
Chechen separatist movement, 74
Cheney, Dick, 85
China: arms transfers and, 134, *134*; potential for counterbalancing by, 13, 40–45; currency policy of, 123, 131; defense spending by, 23, *29*, *41*, 43–44; economy of, *32*, 40–42; foreign direct investment and, 111, *115*, *118*, 131; Iranian nuclear efforts and, 166; material capabilities of, *30*, 130–33; securities holdings of, *122*; Sino-Russian strategic partnership and, 43, 63, 72–77; "soft balancing" by, 63, 72–77; technological power of, *33*; as U.S. export market, *107*
Chinn, Menzie, 129
Chirac, Jacques, 88, 89–94
Clark, Ian, 173, 178, 198
Clinton, Bill (administration), 154, 203
Cold War: counterbalancing in, 54–58; reputational constraint in, 156
collective action problems, 36, 108, 155
collective goods theory, 35–37
command of the commons, 28–29, 43
Concert of Democracies, 217
constraints, systemic, 2–3; conventional wisdom on, 3, 4, 5–10, 215–16; definition of, 3–4; power of, 13–15. *See also* *specific types (e.g.,* counterbalancing constraint)
constructivism, 9, 20, 171–207, 213; applicability to U.S., 174–76; argument for legitimacy in, 173–93; evaluating the legitimacy argument of, 193–206; general argument for legitimacy in, 173–74; overview, 171–72; discussion of power in, 180–82, 205; rule breaking in, 171, 182–86; theoretical strength/weakness of legitimacy in, 176–78, 179
Cooper, Richard, 102, 124n55
Cooper, Robert, 82
Costa Rica, *115*

counterbalancing constraint, 19, 22–59; absence of, 48–58; argument for, 24–27; capabilities distribution and, 27–35; comparative case studies and, 40–45, 51–58; external balancing and, 25, 35–37; imperial overstretch and, 211; inoperability of, 27, 35; internal balancing and, 24, 35, 37–38; opportunity costs and, 35, 38–40, 50, 54; overview, 22–24; unipolarity and, 35–48
Cronin, Audrey Kurth, 142n100
Cronin, Bruce, 171
currency policy, 123, 126–29, 131

Daukoru, Edmund, 126n60
debt, foreign. *See* finance, international
defense spending. *See* material capabilities
Denmark, *115*
Downs, George, 159–63

economic interdependence, 9–10, 98–147, 213; argument for, 102–6; as broadly conceived, 129–46; capabilities distribution and, 130–39; conventional weapons, leveling effect in, of, 133–36; defense production and, 108–17; dependence issues in, 106–29; export markets and, 98, 101, 106–8, 140; foreign direct investment and, 108–20, *112–15*, *119*, 140; international finance and, 98, 101, *121–22*, 121–29, 140–41, 143; legitimacy constraint and, 204–5; nonstate actors and, 102, 139–46; opportunity cost and, 99, 120; overview, 98–102; terrorist threats and, 136n86, 141–46; weak conditionality of constraint from, 20, 138, 144, 147; WMD proliferation and, 136–39, 146
economic interest, protection of, 68, 70; comparative case studies in, 77–80, 87–88; statecraft strategies used in, 103–4
economic sanctions, 99–100, 112
Eichengreen, Barry, 125n56, 154n15
empire, 1, 11, 12
Erdogan, Tayyip, 86

European Security and Defense Policy (ESDP), 80–83, 90
European Union, 13, 90; International Criminal Court and, 203–4; international finance and, 126–27; material capabilities of, 28, 31–32; security/defense policy of, 63, 80–83
euro oil pricing, 126–27
Everts, Phillip, 5n8
export markets, U.S., 98, 101, 106–8, 107, 140
external balancing, 7, 24–25, 35–37, 47

Falk, Richard, 192–93
FDI. See foreign direct investment, U.S.
Feaver, Peter, 5n9
finance, international: economic interdependence and, 98, 101, 121–22, 121–29; institutionalism and, 152–54; legitimacy constraint and, 205; private firms/investors and, 140–41; terrorism and, 143
Finland, 115
Finnemore, Martha, 175
foreign direct investment (FDI), U.S.: 131–32, 137n89; inward, 101, 108–17, 112–15, 140; outward, 98, 101, 119, 118–20
Foucault, Michel, 11n29
France: arms transfers and, 134; counterbalancing by, 51–52; defense spending by, 28, 29; economy of, 32; as U.S. export market, 107; foreign direct investment and, 112, 113–15, 114n37, 119; international system change and, 180; Iraq War and, 63, 83–84, 89–95, 96, 164, 166; material capabilities of, 30, 31; "soft balancing" by, 63–65, 83–84, 89–95, 96; technological power of, 33
Franck, Thomas, 183, 184–85
Frankel, Jeffrey, 129
Friedman, Thomas, 140

Gadhafi, Mu'ammar, 138
Garton Ash, Timothy, 1n3
Gelpi, Christopher, 5n9

geography, 39, 61, 66
Germany: arms transfers and, 134; counterbalancing by, 53; defense spending by, 28, 29; economy of, 32; as U.S. export market, 107; foreign direct investment and, 113–15, 114n37, 118, 119; Iraq War and, 63, 84–87, 95, 164, 166; material capabilities of, 30; "soft balancing" by, 65, 84–87, 95; technological power of, 33
Ghanimifard, Hojjatollah, 126n58
Gholz, Eugene, 105n21, 213n
Giddens, Anthony, 104n20
Gilpin, Robert, 16, 130–32, 215
globalization. See economic interdependence
Gnesotto, Nicole, 81
Goldstein, Avery, 44–45
Good-Neighborliness, Friendship, and Cooperation Treaty (Russia-China, 2001), 73
Gorbachev, Mikhail, 139n93
Great Britain: arms transfers and, 134; counterbalancing and, 51–54; defense spending by, 28, 29; economy of, 32; as U.S. export market, 107; foreign direct investment and, 111–13, 113–15, 118–20, 119; international system change and, 180–81; material capabilities of, 29, 30, 31, 41; securities holdings of, 122; technological power of, 33
Greece, 115
Grewe, Wilhelm, 180–81, 187–88
Gries, Peter, 44n47
Guéhenno, Jean-Marie, 104n20
Gulf War. See Persian Gulf War

Haas, Mark, 34n25
Hagelin, Björn, 28n15
Hapsburg Empire, 30
hegemony, definition of, 22
Higgot, Richard, 149
Hoffman, Stanley, 18, 142
Hong Kong, 107, 115, 119
Howorth, Jolyon, 31, 82–83
Hurd, Ian, 177n17

IAEA (International Atomic Energy Agency), 79–80
ICC. *See* International Criminal Court
ICSID (International Center for Settlement of Investment Disputes), 205
Ikenberry, G. John, 1n1, 17, 154n14, 157, 180, 216–17
IMF. *See* International Monetary Fund
imperial overstretch, 210–11
IMU (Islamic Movement of Uzbekistan), 74
India, 13, 40–41, 76, *107, 115*
Indonesia, *119*
Indyk, Martin, 138n91
institutionalism, 8–9, 20, 148–70, 213; argument on reputation in, 150–58; efficiency gains in, 150–51; empirical problems and, 162–70; international finance and, 152–54; new, 37; opportunity costs of, 151–54, 165; overview, 148–49; retaliatory actions and, 155–56; theoretical weakness of reputational argument in, 158–62
insurgency, 209–10
intentions, perceptions of, 61, 65–66
internal balancing, 7, 24, 35, 37–38
International Atomic Energy Agency (IAEA), 79–80
International Center for Settlement of Investment Disputes (ICSID), 205
International Criminal Court (ICC), 190, 203–4, 206
International Monetary Fund (IMF), 141, 205
international relations theory (IR), 2; new scholarship directions for, 208–13; power and polarity in, 11–13; problems of, 4–5, 10. *See also specific theories*
international system change, U.S. foreign policy and, 17–18, 21, 214–218; legitimacy and, 180–82, 183–84
interoperability problem, 152
IR. *See* international relations theory
Iran: arms transfers and, 134; nuclear efforts of, 63, 77–80, 138, 166
Iraq, 137–38. *See also* Iraq War (2003–); Persian Gulf War (1990–91)

Iraq War (2003–): counterbalancing constraint and, 27, 59; economic leverage and, 100; imperial overstretch and, 210; insurgency and, 209–10; legitimacy constraint and, 194, 195–99; reputational constraint and, 164; "soft balancing" constraint and, 63, 83–96
Ireland, *115, 119*
Irwin, Douglas, 154n15
Islamic extremism, 73–74, 142
Islamic Movement of Uzbekistan (IMU), 74
Isneria, Pierangelo, 5n8
Israel, *107, 115, 134,* 210
Italy, *107, 115, 119, 134*
Ivanov, Igor, 87

Japan: currency policy of, 123; defense spending by, 28, *29;* economic leverage by, 100n10, 123–24; economy of, *32;* as U.S. export market, 106, *107;* foreign direct investment and, 112, *113–15,* 114, *119;* material capabilities of, *30;* securities holdings of, *122;* technological power of, *33*
Jervis, Robert, 2, 17, 49, 214
Johnston, Alastair Iain, 175n10
Johnstone, Ian, 196
Jones, Michael, 159–63

Kagan, Robert, 173n6
Katzenstein, Peter, 199–201
Kay, Sean, 152n10
Kazakhstan, 75
Keidel, Albert, 42
Kennedy, Paul, 1n1, 27, 29, 31, 35, 210–11
Keohane, Robert, 26n10, 103, 155, 199–201
Khan, A. Q., 79, 136–37
Khrushchev, Nikita, 55
Kirsch, Nico, 202n75
Kirshner, Jonathan, 140–41
Kissinger, Henry, 1n1, 182–83
Koh, Harold, 184
Kohut, Andrew, 199

Kosovo intervention, 59, 93, 152, 192–93, 195
Kupchan, Charles, 81
Kurdish separatist movement, 86
Kyocera Corporation, 100n10
Kyoto Protocol on Climate Change, 204

Lake, David A., 8n21
Landmine Convention, 204
Lardy, Nicholas, 131n76
Layne, Christopher, 25, 27, 47, 53n68, 66n14
Lebow, Ned, 2n5, 177n18
legitimacy constraint, 9, 171–207; applicability to U.S., 174–76; argument for, 173–93; economic interdependence and, 205; evaluating the argument for, 193–206; general argument for, 173–74; institutional order and, 201–6; international finance and, 205; overview, 171–72; power and, 180–82, 205; public goods provision and, 191–92; public opinion and, 199–201; rule breaking and, 171, 182–86; theoretical strength/weakness of, 176–78, 179; unipolarity and, 178; weak conditionality of, 20, 172, 186, 206
Legro, Jeffrey, 177n17
Levy, Jack, 22, 50
liberalism, 9–10, 20, 98–147, 213; argument for constraints in, 102–6; capabilities and, 130–39; economic dependence issues in, 106–29; export markets and, 98, 101, 106–8, 140; foreign direct investment and, 108–20, 112–15, 119, 140; interdependence broadly conceived in, 129–46; international finance and, 98, 101, 121–22, 121–29, 140–41, 143; nonstate actors and, 102, 139–46; overview, 98–102
Liberia, 189
Libya, 138, 139
Lieber, Kier, 66, 95
Lindsey, Brink, 143n106
local and regional security, 39–40, 68, 70; comparative case studies in, 75, 77–80, 83, 90–91, 94
Looney, Robert, 127n62

Lukes, Steven, 11n29
Luxembourg: foreign direct investment and, 113, 115, 118; securities holdings of, 122

McGrew, Tony, 104n20
McKinnon, Ronald, 124n55
Malaysia, 107, 115, 119
Mann, Catherine, 124n55
Martin, Lisa, 156–58
Mastanduno, Michael, 66n16, 154n15
material capabilities: arms sales/transfers and, 75–77, 133–36; defense spending and, 23, 28, 29; distribution of, 27–35, 130–39; economic interdependence and, 133–36; foreign direct investment and, 108–17; power and, 11; research/development spending and, 28, 38; technological power and, 32, 33, 111, 135
Mearsheimer, John, 36
Menon, Anand, 31, 82
Merkel, Angela, 95
Mexico, 106, 107, 108, 115, 119
Middle East, 58, 122
Mikhailov, Viktor, 78
Moran, Theodore, 100n10, 109–11, 114–17
Morgan, Patrick, 209
multilateralism, 18, 71, 149
multipolarity, 71, 91
Musharraf, Pervez, 145

NATO. See North Atlantic Treaty Organization
neoconservatism, 215
neoisolationism, 96
neoliberal institutionalism. See institutionalism
Netherlands: arms transfers and, 134; as export market, 107; foreign direct investment and, 112, 113–15, 119, 120; securities holdings of, 122
new institutionalism, 37
New Zealand, 115, 165
NGOs (nongovernmental organizations), 180

nonexistential security concerns: counter-balancing constraint and, 49–50, 54; "soft balancing" constraint and, 67–69

nongovernmental organizations (NGOs), 180

nonstate actors, 102, 139–46, 153, 187

North Atlantic Treaty Organization (NATO): arms sales and, 133–34; counterbalancing and, 23, 36–37; efficiency gains and, 150–51; intelligence sharing and, 150–51, 166; legitimacy constraint and, 190, 192–93; reputational constraint and, 159, 166

North Korea, 89, 136–38

Norway, 115

nuclear deterrence, 28, 54–58, 209

Nye, Joseph, 103, 104n20

Odell, John, 163, 164n50

Office of the United States Trade Representative (USTR), 161–62

offshore balancing, 15–16

oil dependency, U.S., 101n11, 126–27, 212–13

oil embargo (1973), 58, 100n7

oil exporters, Middle East, 122

OPEC, 126–27

opportunity costs: counterbalancing constraint and, 35, 38–40, 50, 54; economic interdependence and, 99, 120; institutionalism and, 151–54, 165; legitimacy constraint and, 176–77, 186–93, 205; "soft balancing" constraint and, 63, 71

Ottawa Landmine Convention, 204

Pakistan, 115, 145, 146n114

Pape, Robert, 61, 62n9, 65–66, 81, 125–26

Paul, T. V., 60

Persian Gulf War (1990–91), 58, 86, 101n10, 165, 186

polarity, definition of, 12–13

policy disputes and bargaining, 69–70, 89–94, 95–96, 163

population aging. See aging populations

port security, 144n109

Posen, Barry, 28–29, 43

Powell, Colin, 145

power: conceptions of, 11–13, 46–47; legitimacy and, 180–82, 205

Press, Daryl, 105n21, 213

Prikhodko, Sergei, 88

Proliferation Security Initiative (PSI), 167, 188–89

Prussia, 30

PSI. See Proliferation Security Initiative

public opinion, 5–6, 194, 199–201, 211; anti-Americanism, 141, 200–201; domestic politics and, 69–70, 84–87, 91, 94

Putin, Vladimir, 80, 87–88, 205

RATS. See Regional Anti-Terrorism Structure (RATS)

realism, 7–8, 26, 67. See also balance-of-power theory; balance-of-threat theory

Regional Anti-Terrorism Structure (RATS), 74–75

regional security. See local and regional security

Reifler, Jason, 5n9

reputational constraint, 8, 148–70; argument for, 154–58; empirical problems of, 162–70; inoperability of, 149, 170; multiple reputations and, 159–62, 170; opportunity costs and, 165; overview, 148–49; strong conditionality of, 20, 149; theoretical weakness of argument for, 158–62

research and development, military, 28, 38. See also material capabilities

retaliatory actions, 63, 108, 112, 120, 155–56, 169

Reus-Smit, Christian, 9, 171, 177n18

Rice, Condoleezza, 89, 95

Rome Convention, 203

Rosecrance, Richard, 103, 109

Ross, Robert, 124n54, 135n81

Roubini, Nouriel, 124n55

rules and rule breaking, 9, 171, 182–93. See also international system change

Russia: Afghanistan War and, 58; arms transfers and, 134, 134; counterbalancing by, 52–53; defense spending by, 29,

75; economic interdependence and, *115*, 134, 205; economy of, *32*; foreign direct investment and, *115*; Iranian nuclear efforts and, 63, 77–80, 166; Iraq War opposition of, 63, 87–89; Kosovo intervention and, 195; material capabilities of, *30*, 31; military industrial complex decline in, 75–77, 134; Sino-Russian strategic partnership and, 43, 63, 72–77; "soft balancing" by, 63, 72–80, 87–89; technological power of, *33*, 76. *See also* Soviet Union

Sarkozy, Nicholas, 95
Saudi Arabia, *115*
Schröder, Gerhard, 84–85, 90, 95
Schweller, Randall, 26n9, 37–38
SCO. *See* Shanghai Cooperation Organization (SCO)
Scowcroft, Brent, 182
secondary security. *See* nonexistential security concerns
securities. *See* finance, international
security policy, U.S.: definition of, 3; future research needs and, 21, 208–13; international system change and, 17–18, 21, 214–18; new alternative for, 214–18; stakes of analysis for, 15–19, 64
Setser, Brad, 124n55
Shanghai Cooperation Organization (SCO), 72–75
Simpson, Gerry, 196
Singapore, *107*, 114n37, *115*, *119*
Sino-Russian strategic partnership, 43, 63, 72–77
Slaughter, Anne-Marie, 216–17
Snyder, Jack, 10
"soft balancing" constraint, 19–20, 60–97; alternative explanation to, 67–70; argument for, 64–67; bargaining and, 95–96; comparative case studies and, 63, 72–95; criteria for testing the argument for, 69–71; inoperability of, 62, 64, 71; opportunity costs and, 63, 71; overview of, 60–64; strong conditionality of, 61; systemic difference and, 95–97; unipolarity and, 62, 65–66, 71–95

South Africa, *115*
South Korea, *107*, *115*, *119*
Soviet Union: counterbalancing by, 26, 54–58; economic interdependence and, 139; material capabilities of, *30*, 31; North Korean nuclear program and, 136. *See also* Russia
Spain, *30*, *115*, *119*, *134*, 180
states, proliferation of, 39–40, 68
Stein, Arthur, 102n14
Stoiber, Edmund, 85
Stokes, Bruce, 199
strong conditional constraint, 14; legitimacy as, 178, 193–94, 206; reputation as, 20, 149; "soft balancing" as, 61
structural constraints, 14; legitimacy as, 177–78, 193–94, 206
Sumitomo Chemical Company explosion (1992), 116
Sweden: arms transfers and, *134*; foreign direct investment and, 112, *113*, *115*, *119*
Switzerland: arms transfers and, *134*; as export market, *107*; foreign direct investment and, 112, *113*, 114, *115*, *119*; securities holdings of, *122*
system change: U.S. foreign policy and, 17–18, 21, 214–18; legitimacy and, 180–82, 183–84
systemic theory, 6–7

Taiwan, *107*, 114n37, *115*, *119*
technological power, 32, *33*, 111, 135
territorial waters, rights to, 189
terrorism: economic interdependence and, 136n86, 141–46; institutional counters to, 74–75, 188n43, 196, 202; international perspectives on, 88–90; international relations scholarship on, 211–12; rule changes/legitimacy and, 190
Thailand, *115*
Thompson, William, 22, 50
Trade Representative, Office of the United States (USTR), 161–62
Truman, Harry (administration), 189
Turkey, opposition to Iraq War by, 84–87

Uighur separatist movement, 74
Ukraine, *134*
unilateralism, 18–19, 149, 201, 217; of
    Bush Administration, 61, 164, 202
unipolarity: definition of, 12–13; interna-
    tional relations theory and, 4–5, 10
United Nations (UN), 159–61, 164, 167,
    202, 217
United Nations (UN) Security Council,
    87, 90–93, 195; Resolution 1373, 188n43,
    196, 202; Resolution 1441, 87–88, 92;
    Resolution 1540, 167–69, 188n43; Reso-
    lution 1546, 198
United States: defense spending by, 28,
    29; economic primacy of, 31, *32*, 98–99,
    136; export markets and, 98, 101, 106–8,
    107, 140; finance, international, and, 98,
    101, *121–22*, 121–29; foreign direct in-
    vestment and, 98, 108–20, *112–15, 119*;
    material capabilities of, 27–35, *30, 134*;
    technological power of, 32, *33*, 111, 135.
    See also security policy, U.S.
USTR (Office of the United States Trade
    Representative), 161–62
Uzbekistan, 74–75

vaccines, 144
Vandewalle, Dirk, 138n91
Van Ness, Peter, 104n20

Vietnam War, 65
Villepin, Dominique de, 89, 91–92
Virgin Islands, *115*

Wallander, Celeste, 75
Walt, Stephen, 61, 65n13, 66, 81
Waltz, Kenneth N., 7, 12, 25n6, 27n12,
    46–47, 49, 104n20
war, 24, 49, 140–41; cooperation in,
    151–52; premptive/preventive, 182–83,
    189–90, 197; public opinion and,
    5–6, 211
weak conditional constraint, 14, 214;
    economic interdependence as, 20, 138,
    144, 147; legitimacy as, 20, 172, 186, 206
weapons, conventional, 23, 28, 108–17,
    133–36
weapons of mass destruction (WMD),
    136–39, 146, 167–69, 188–89
Westad, Arne, 56n76
WMD. *See* weapons of mass destruction
Wohlforth, William C., 47
World Bank, 205
World Trade Organization (WTO), 100,
    153n, 160–61, 164, 205

Yemen, 165

Zakaria, Fareed, 172